I Have Come a Long Way

I HAVE COME
A LONG WAY

—

JOHN W.
DE GRUCHY

CASCADE *Books* • Eugene, Oregon

I HAVE COME A LONG WAY

Copyright © 2016 NB Publishers. All rights reserved. Except for brief quotations in critical publications or reviews, no part of this book may be reproduced in any manner without prior written permission from the publisher. Write: Permissions, Wipf and Stock Publishers, 199 W. 8th Ave., Suite 3, Eugene, OR 97401.

Originally published by Lux Verbi, an imprint of NB Publishers,
Copyright © 2015 J.W. de Gruchy, Cape Town, South Africa.

Poetry by Isobel de Gruchy is reprinted with the permission of Wipf and Stock Publishers www.wipfandstock.com

A Gratitude Song composed by Gretchen Sleicher. From her website *Songs for the Great Turning*. Used with the kind permission of the composer.

Cascade Books
An Imprint of Wipf and Stock Publishers
199 W. 8th Ave., Suite 3
Eugene, OR 97401

www.wipfandstock.com

PAPERBACK ISBN: 978-1-4982-9311-2
ELECTRONIC (EBOOK) ISBN: 978-1-4987-9312-9

Manufactured in the U.S.A.

CONTENTS

Foreword: Emeritus Archbishop of Cape Town   7
Prologue: Who do I think I am?   11

PART ONE
Where I have come from, 1939-1972   19
1. From whom I have sprung   20
2. The soul of the child I was   28
3. Studying Theology and falling in love   38
4. On a sharp learning curve   51
5. Chicago, Chicago!   56
6. A Confessing Church?   65
7. Thrown in at the deep end   74

PART TWO
Through extraordinary times, 1973-1990   93
8. An aspiring academic   94
9. To leave or to stay?   101
10. Becoming an author   109
11. A church leader of sorts   116
12. Nothing but a heresy   127
13. A moment of truth   138
14. Some kind of expert   145
15. Not only a tourist   152
16. Unforgettable days   159

PART THREE
Embracing the changes, 1990-2003 — 169
17. Transition and travel — 170
18. Saved by hope — 179
19. Proudly South African — 188
20. Restoring justice — 199
21. An aesthetic turn — 209
22. Critical solidarity — 217
23. A new millennium — 223
24. A time for endings — 230

PART FOUR
The Volmoed years, 2003-2015 — 237
25. Life in community — 238
26. A Christian humanist — 244
27. Special moments — 259
28. A road unforeseen — 265
29. Completing the circle — 273

Notes — 283
Acronyms and abbreviations — 287
Index of subjects and places — 288
Index of names — 296

FOREWORD

Emeritus Archbishop of Cape Town
Desmond Mpilo Tutu

The World Council of Churches (WCC) provoked the anger of the vast majority of white Christians in South Africa with its Programme to Combat Racism (PCR). This anger was stoked further by the grants the programme made to what the majority of blacks regarded as liberation movements and the nationalist Afrikaner government and most whites regarded as terrorism. The government wanted the churches to withdraw from membership of the WCC. The prime minister, Mr John Vorster, agreed to meet a delegation of church leaders to discuss this hot topic in August of 1970. To prepare for this crucial meeting, this delegation gathered at St. Peter's Theological College – the Anglican seminary run by the Community of the Resurrection – in Rosettenville, a white suburb to the south of Johannesburg. John de Gruchy, working for the South African Council of Churches (SACC), was the organiser of the gathering. He invited me to give one of the Bible studies, and I think I met him then for the first time. As it happened, the meeting with Mr Vorster never took place. But little did we know back then that John would become such a magnificent scholar with a very impressive international reputation.

When I went to work for the much maligned WCC as an associate director of its Theological Education Fund based in Bromley, Kent, in the UK, I invited John to become a member of its Africa Committee, an invitation I was glad he accepted. He was at ease hobnobbing with rising theologians like himself from South America and Asia, as well as more established figures from the UK, Europe and North America. His stature as a theologian and writer, especially as an authority on Dietrich Bonhoeffer, was growing in quite a spectacular way. In my view, nothing attested to this more than the holding of the Seventh International Bonhoeffer Congress in Cape Town in 1996, thereby proclaiming that South Africa was no longer the world's pariah state following the accession of Nelson Mandela as the first democratically elected president of a free South Africa.

John has held visiting professorships at prestigious universities overseas and given lectures in many of them. At home he was a professor of Christian Studies and held the Robert Selby Taylor Chair at the University of Cape Town. He was sought-after as a lecturer, both in South Africa and in many other parts of the world. His rise was indeed amazing and meteoric. We could not have imagined anything so electrifying when we sat in the garden of St. Peter's College all those many, almost light years ago.

Isobel, his wife, was meanwhile carving out a niche for herself as a writer and publisher of poetry, and as a painter. John's autobiography quotes from this poet at some significant moments in their lives. They are a remarkable couple, these descendants of immigrants from France and Jersey, England, Cornwall and Germany. After a very full life, they intended to enjoy the quieter pace at Volmoed, a community that offers retreats and opportunities for personal growth and renewal.

But their bliss was shattered by the death by drowning of their son Steve, who had been prominent in the anti-apartheid struggle, and who had followed John as a writer, teacher and theologian.

Isobel lost a loving and beloved son. John lost a son and a theological colleague and collaborator, with whom he was planning another joint publication. Isobel turned to her poetry and painting to find solace and healing. Contemplating such a devastating loss, John wrote *Led into Mystery* to try to produce a satisfying theodicy.

I believe John has spent many a long hour churning over and over again: "If only." He is not the man he would have been had Steve been alive. I think he weeps often; it has been a shattering and devastating loss for them, and for us. What he has said about facing such a traumatic experience has helped to help others. And for this we give thanks to God. Many of us also give thanks for John's intellectual brilliance and outstanding scholarship. But most of all, I give thanks for the humility of revealing his vulnerability.

PROLOGUE
Who do I think I am?

Is it vanity to write the story of one's life? Partly, no doubt. But partly not. For it is also the story of millions of people, and they are my countrymen and women.

(Alan Paton)[1]

Isobel and I were waiting for our flight from Cape Town to London. It was January 1993. An Anglican priest and activist friend, Clive McBride, greeted us in the waiting lounge and asked where we were going.

"To Oxford for a sabbatical," we replied, "and to explore family roots in Cornwall and on Jersey Island. And you?"

"I am going to Indonesia for the same reason," he said to our surprise, given his surname.

The changes taking place in South Africa were sending us in opposite directions in search of our ancestral roots. For whereas our grandparents arrived in South Africa as European settlers in the nineteenth century, Clive's maternal forbear was brought here as a slave. As a result, we were classified "white" and he "coloured" under apartheid laws. This made a huge difference to our status and prevented us from knowing much about each other's story. Racial identity either opened doors to privilege or slammed them shut in servitude. Ours meant opportunity and possibility; that is why our grandparents came to South Africa. In doing so, they needed neither visas nor the approval of the people of the land, for the Cape colony was part of their empire. In our recent past, the question "Who do you think you are?" was a challenge to such racial arrogance. Today it also motivates a quest for an identity that might bind us together, prompting self-reflection about what I am doing here.

I cannot understand my story apart from that of the many others I have met on my journey. My life is inseparable from family, friends and fellow travellers to whom I am variously connected. For that reason their names recur in telling my story, though I cannot mention them all. I would also not be who I am if I had not been born and brought up in South Africa in the mid-twentieth century. So in telling my story I have to locate it in the country's narrative as well. But my story also goes well beyond these shores, for it is entwined with many others in faith, action and mutual interests the world over.

Much of my life has been spent in writing, but this book is presumptuous by its very nature and different from anything I have written before. An autobiography is, after all, about the person writing it; a story constructed by the author even if based on fact. The challenge is to tell it with due humility but not false modesty, suitable honesty yet appropriate reserve, and in a way that makes it worth reading. I can only hope I have succeeded.

What has spurred me on in this quixotic task has been the fact that, for the past few years, I have often been asked to speak about my life and have been interviewed for oral history projects and the like. I have also received some unexpected honours. I presume that is because my life and experience is of some interest. But if it is, it is chiefly so because I have lived through interesting times in an interesting country, travelled to many interesting places, and been accompanied along the way by interesting folk.

PROLOGUE

The latter inevitably leads to name dropping. I make no apology for having some well-known friends and excellent mentors, and for rubbing shoulders with celebrated people. In group photographs there is always someone partly hidden in the background or sitting at the feet of others more illustrious. That is often me, but at least I am in the picture, if not the most prominent. So it gives me pleasure to acknowledge all who have been within the frame of my life, and I apologise in advance for inadvertently or out of necessity leaving some out of the narrative.

Looking back, I have often thought about my own role in the struggle against apartheid. Too often, when introduced as a speaker or being awarded some prize, I have been embarrassingly described in terms that exceed what I actually did. In honestly trying to understand who I am, it does not help to believe everything that others say about me – except acknowledging criticism and accepting affirmation where appropriate.

My children might well have asked, "What did you do in the struggle, Dad?"

Their mother provided the words for my reply:

> I added my stitch or two and the tapestry
>   would not be diminished if I had not.
> But I would. And as the work was hung
>   for all to see, I was glad that my few stitches
>   were part of the whole.[2]

I was not a radical activist fighting in the trenches. Compared to those who were banned, detained, tortured, exiled and murdered, most of us should remain silent. Yet I can at least say that, from the 1960s through to the end of apartheid, I added my voice in support of those who were leading the fight. I suppose I was, as has been said of me, "a leading voice in the church struggle against apartheid". But I have no right to claim more, or look back to the past with nostalgic satisfaction. The struggle continues, and a new generation is rightly challenging the adequacy of what some of us tried to do.

Writing an autobiography is a risky undertaking, which requires self-examination filtered through hindsight; much must remain unrecorded and some purposively hidden. It is not only impossible to tell everything; it is also unwise. I owe it to family and friends to respect their privacy, revealing chiefly that which helps document my life as I have come to own it in relation to them. You can be certain that they are somewhere on most pages, even if not always mentioned. This is especially true of Isobel, to whom I have now been married for fifty-five years and whose poetry frequently finds a place in these pages.

Carl Jung described his outer life as "hollow and insubstantial", and tells us he could only understand himself "in the light of inner happenings".[3] But there can be no separation of the inner and outer journey; they belong together, informing and feeding each other. My "soul" is who I am in my body, in relationship to others and the world in which I live with them. My greatest struggle through the years has been to ensure that the inner and outer, the emotional and the cerebral, are creatively meshed. And nothing has more traumatically galvanised me in doing so than Steve's tragic death in 2010 – something that pervades my story as I now tell it. I would have told it differently otherwise, if I had told it at all.

I sometimes wonder how it would have been if, at some critical junctures, I had chosen differently. It is not good to brood over what might have been, though. The truth is I don't regret the choices I made, am grateful for the many doors that opened, and even for some that slammed shut in my face. Not everything that has happened to me, however, has been the result of my choosing. I did not choose grief and deep darkness; that comes uninvited. But what I have done with such experiences has depended on choices I have made.

I have long moved away from academic writing in which the subject is "we", a device that has enabled me to hide behind scholarly pretension. I have written many articles in scholarly journals that have conformed to such conventions, but about fifteen years ago I was encouraged to break with tradition and rid myself of the habit. Despite the dangers of egocentricity, I wrote myself into the text, blending the academic with the personal, enclosing my reflections within the narrative of my life. I began to find my voice especially in *Being Human: Confessions of a Christian Humanist* (2006), and most notably in *Led into Mystery* (2013) in which I owned my grief over the death of Steve.

Those who are interested to know more about what I personally believe as a Christian should read these books in particular. But it was, in part, the reader response to them that encouraged me to tell my story less constrained by the need for peer reviews. This led me to write two semi-autobiographical books during 2014. The first was *A Theological Odyssey: My Life in Writing*, published in conjunction with a conference hosted by Stellenbosch University honouring my seventy-fifth birthday. The second was *Sawdust and Soul: A Conversation about Woodworking and Spirituality*. Co-authored with Bill Everett, a friend of many years, the book tells my story through the lens of my working with wood.

As writing books and essays has been so much a part of my life, I cannot avoid referring to these in passing, so I suggest that those who would like more information should consult *A Theological Odyssey*. My life-long engagement with the legacy of Dietrich Bonhoeffer, the German theologian and martyr, is also a strong thread running through my story, so I cannot refrain from mentioning conferences, lectures and books related to my journey in dialogue with him. The details can be found elsewhere.

Life's complexity refuses to be condensed into the framework that literary convention requires, but its telling needs to be anchored within a manageable timeline. I have divided my story into four chronologically determined sections. In the first part, I trace my ancestry and formative years from my birth in 1939 to my years as a young pastor in Durban, and then to my time as an ecumenical activist working for the South African Council of Churches (SACC). In the second part, I tell the story of how I became an academic at the University of Cape Town, starting in 1973. I conclude this part in 1990 when Mandela was released and South Africa emerged from the dark night of apartheid into a new day of hope and possibility. In the third part, my story is set within the context of a country in transition and a rapidly changing global society, ending with the birth of a new millennium and my formal retirement from the university in 2003. In the fourth part, I recount the last twelve years spent as a member of the Volmoed community and draw a line at the end of my seventy-fifth year.

There is a mixture of ways in which I tell my story. There are the anecdotes of age that have come to mind as I have remembered the past. I have not found the need to search for illustrations; I have more than enough stories of my own residing in what Dante called my "cargo of experience".[4] Then there are what I think of as snapshots: events that I have tried to capture as though I was still operating the Brownie camera I got as a teenager, pointing at and shooting things that were interesting and important in passing.

Insofar as an autobiography – perhaps especially one of an

academic – recounts the history of ideas as they have evolved in the mind, I cannot but share reflections along the way about concerns and issues that have shaped my journey. In order to give each chapter some coherence and direction, I have highlighted these in the title and in a quotation that leads into the text. But the chapters proceed chronologically, giving an account of the passing years and using dates as signposts.

Lapse of memory is undoubtedly a problem in writing one's autobiography at the end of a long journey. Fortunately I have considerable data at my disposal, which I have accumulated over the years and Isobel has kept detailed diaries, photo albums and journals of our travels and family life. With her scientific eye for detail, I have been kept on my toes. We also have comprehensive family archives; in fact, the De Gruchy side has a complete genealogy from the fourteenth to the present century.

It is impossible to thank everyone by name who has helped to write my story over the past seventy-five years, among them many colleagues and students, but I can and must thank those who have helped me bring it together between the two covers of this book. I am most grateful to Rosemary Townsend and Mary Bock whose language and literary skills helped fine-tune what I had written; Susan Jordaan, the commissioning editor at Lux Verbi, who did not hesitate to support the project and guide me through it; and Isobel above all, for coming this long way with me, and making sure that I got the details right in committing the story to print. Archbishop Desmond Tutu readily agreed to write the foreword despite his many commitments, even though he has retired several times. He has been a remarkable friend over many years, and has never declined a request to commend my work. Then there is the Volmoed community, especially Bernhard and Jane Turkstra, Mike and Alyson Guy,

Barry and Molly Wood, Penny Pelders and the amazing maintenance staff led by Andries Hendricks, whose care and support Isobel and I have deeply appreciated during the past twelve years.

Cape Town is very different today from when my grandfather arrived or I grew up. But for Capetonians it is always the same place, if only because Table Mountain majestically towers above it and Table Bay stretches out before it. Much of my story is based somewhere between those slopes and the sea. No matter where I have travelled or lived for a while, this is where I belong. My life has not been parochial, however, and as my story unfolds it will soon become evident that, while I am proudly South African, I am also a global citizen. I have travelled across continents, visited cities from Monrovia to Melbourne, from Beijing to Berlin, and traversed the Atlantic more times than I care to remember. I think I inherited my travelling genes from my paternal grandfather, whose story I will soon tell. But he was glad to make Cape Town his home, and it is on these shores that I know I belong, even if I go in search of my ancestors in distant places. In more ways than one, I have come a long way.

Volmoed
Easter 2015

PART ONE

Where I have come from

1939-1972

*When we have passed a certain age,
the soul of the child we were
and the souls of the dead from whom we have sprung
come to lavish on us
their riches and their spells.*

(Marcel Proust)[1]

1.

From whom I have sprung

The Viking name de Gruchy is already mentioned in a 9th century Norman marriage contract. Two de Gruchys were knights on the First Crusade in 1096, and another was in England in 1100 AD. When the French kings re-conquered Normandy in 1204 the de Gruchys scattered. Jean de Gruchy, the son of Hugh, a royal official, fled to Jersey, a small island off the coast of Normandy. All the de Gruchys who come from Jersey are descendants of Jean who lived at La Chasse in Trinity Parish.

(Walter J. Le Quesne and Guy M. Dixon)[2]

"Grouchy" is an Old Norse word which means "spear-wolf". A ninth-century Viking contract confirms that the first Grouchys settled in Normandy ("men from the North") in what is now France. From there, the crusader knights Nicolas and Guillaume de Grouchy rode off to participate in the Siege of Jerusalem in 1099. My father always wore a gold signet ring with their coat of arms engraved on it. Both my sister and I received such rings on our twenty-first birthdays, as was then the custom in our extended family. I still have the metal stamp used for this purpose.

There is a hamlet in Normandy named Gruchy. It is portrayed in paintings by the impressionist Millet. There is also a De Gruchy chateau nearby, which briefly appeared in the film *The Da Vinci Code*. But by the end of the thirteenth century, long before either the hamlet or chateau existed, our branch of the family had settled in Trinity Parish on Jersey Island, eleven kilometres off the coast of France. There they dropped the "o" in Grouchy to distinguish themselves from their mainland relations.

In the documents of the Jersey Assizes for 1299, we are told that Jean de Barentin was accused of beating Richard, son of the priest De Gruchy. This is the first mention of a small handful of priests in our family tree, which includes many more soldiers and sailors.

In Trinity churchyard there are dozens of De Gruchy tombstones, many bearing the name Jean or John. I am related to them all, even if only distantly. The original Jean was the son of Hugh, a Norman nobleman, who fled to Jersey at the end of the thirteenth century when the Frankish kings invaded the territory. The control of Jersey fluctuated between the French and the English as fortunes in war waxed and waned during the Middle Ages. But by the end of the fourteenth century, Jersey was finally brought under the reign of the English monarch, and remains so to this day. From then on, it has been governed by its own parliament or states and by the councils of the twelve parishes into which it is divided. At the time of the Reformation, the island's allegiance switched from Rome to Canterbury.

My branch of the De Gruchy clan starts with Jean's descendant Robin (c. 1362), who lived at La Chasse on La Profonde Rue in Trinity Parish. The farmhouse still stands, now much enlarged and no longer in the family. It was there, following the custom of their cousins in Normandy, that some of the family dropped the "de". Our branch kept it, but our most illustrious ancestor on the mainland, Marshall Emmanuel de Grouchy, dropped the "de" after the French Revolution, but kept the "o".

My father was the first to introduce me to Emmanuel Grouchy and gave me his portrait, which still hangs in our house. Historians blame him for losing the Battle of Waterloo. The truth is more complex, but if he had not arrived too late on the battlefield to save the day for France, the Cape of Good Hope might not have become a British colony, my grandparents would not have settled there, and I would not exist.

Emmanuel's sister, Sophie, was absent from the family story as told to me. She was a celebrated poet and painter, whose Parisian salon attracted distinguished Enlightenment thinkers. Both siblings miraculously survived the French Revolution and lived long lives.

Emmanuel visited Jersey in 1836, when he acknowledged all the descendants of Jean as his relatives, irrespective of how they spelt their name. My great-grandfather Jean, who was sixteen at the time, must surely have seen the distinguished visitor.

Jean became a farmer and married Caroline de Quetteville in May 1842, and ten years later my grandfather Frederic Abram was born on 27 August 1852. Like all Jersey school children, he spoke French, English and Norman, but his formal education went no further than primary school. At thirteen he bade farewell to his parents and left Jersey to go to sea. There was no future for him in milking Jersey cows, growing Jersey royal potatoes, or building sailing ships at one of the island's harbours, even though there were several shipbuilders with the name De Gruchy.

Records in the Jersey Maritime Museum document my grandfather's early years as a sailor. But the story goes blank around the 1870s when he sailed out of Southampton rather than Jersey's chief port, St. Helier. Sometime during the late 1880s he became the captain of a tea-trading clipper, which regularly sailed around the Cape to China. His days as a seafarer came to a dramatic end in 1883, however, as recounted in our family records:

> His clipper *Velocity* and two other vessels were sunk during a tropical storm ... Frédéric and crew took to lifeboats in the turbulent sea. To add to their plight, after the storm abated they were pursued by Chinese pirates for two days and nights. Fortunately during the third night the pirates went ahead of their lifeboat and de Gruchy, by changing direction, was able to elude them. Frédéric, with 14 sailors aboard, spent a total of nine days short of food and drinking water, before being sighted and rescued by a passing ship bound for New Zealand.[3]

My grandfather continued on the ship when it began its return journey to England, but disembarked in Cape Town. On the Sunday after his arrival, he attended worship at the Metropolitan Methodist Church in Greenmarket Square, where he met Mary Irish, a striking young woman who had recently arrived from England. Within a few weeks they were engaged, and were married in the same church on 18 December 1883.

Mary was born in March 1862 in Climping, Sussex, a hamlet on the Duke of Norfolk's Arundel estate where her grandfather was bailiff. Her mother died when she was young, and there is no reference to her father in the baptismal register of the parish church in Climping; so she was brought up by her grandparents, kept their name, and her paternity was wrapped in secrecy. When she turned twenty-one, she was sent to the Cape Colony in the care of the Garlick family, friends of the Norfolks', and wealthy shop owners in Cape Town. There exists an intriguing story that Mary received a diamond ring, sent to her from England, on each of her birthdays for several years thereafter. While the story cannot be verified, my mother believed it was true. If it was, then my paternal grandmother might well have been an illegitimate daughter of the Duke of Norfolk. For who else in the county could have afforded such a ring, and would have reason to keep the scandal a secret? It would also explain why my grandmother was sent to the colonies in the custody of the Garlicks.

Frederic Abram and Mary had nine children, of which my father, Harold, born in November 1902, was the second youngest. He and his siblings grew up in Cape Town in the Seaman's Home on Dock Road, of which my grandfather was the director. I remember seeing it years later near the grand old Alhambra cinema, but both buildings were demolished when the Foreshore was redeveloped. Some old photographs of the waterfront and the pier in front of the Seaman's Home show young children playing on the beach among the rowing boats. I can imagine my father being one of them.

My grandmother Mary died in 1927, twelve years before I was born, but I was told that I had met my grandfather when I was three. I have very vague memories of that occasion, but I know his bearded face from family photographs. I also remember visiting their graves with my parents in Woltemade Cemetery outside Cape Town once long ago; but I have never returned and wonder whether anyone now knows where they are located. How different their final resting place is to Trinity Parish cemetery on Jersey Island.

My father, Harold, went to the South African College (SACS) Junior and High Schools, as did some of my uncles and male cousins.

After matriculation, Harold studied at the Technical College, and then became a telephone technician working for the government. He became an expert in setting up communications networks, and later pioneered the first telephone connection between South Africa and the United States. I was at the Cape Town telephone exchange on the night the first phone call was made between the two countries. But that was still some years away.

In his early twenties, Harold was transferred to Port Elizabeth where he met my mother, Mabel, the daughter of Herbert and Lily Hurd, both devout Methodists. Herbert came from London, and Lily's parents had come to Port Elizabeth from Hull in Yorkshire. They were married in the St. John's Methodist Church in Havelock Street in November 1896. Within ten years they had seven children, of whom my mother was the third eldest. They lived in Walmer, then a town separate from Port Elizabeth, in a rambling Victorian house I remember well.

By all accounts my grandparents Hurd were down-to-earth, generous people. On occasion they entertained visiting royalty when, during the First World War, Herbert became the mayor of Walmer. He was also the founder of the Methodist Church in Walmer. Much later, one of the high schools in Port Elizabeth was named after him.

Lily, a formidable, small woman who drove an Oldsmobile into her late eighties and sometimes drove the fear of hell into me in doing so, was also a founder of the Women's Christian Temperance Union. I really liked her.

My mother, Mabel, was born in 1900. She often told me that at that time there were no motor cars in Port Elizabeth, the Anglo-Boer War was in its second year, Queen Victoria was on the throne, there was no South Africa, and the Wright brothers had yet to fly the first aeroplane. Mabel had the honour of switching on the electricity when it finally reached Walmer, but she had little schooling or opportunities to develop her innate abilities. Instead she helped bring up her siblings and served as a nurse aid during the great flu epidemic.

When Harold came courting, Mabel's parents insisted that they could not marry until he had sufficient income and a house. So he set to, built a house in Walmer, and made all the furniture for it, too. I still have some of the tools he used for this task.

Harold and Mabel were married in St. John's Methodist Church on 2 August 1928. Four years later my sister, Rozelle, was born. She was named after a small fishing village in Trinity Parish, Jersey.

In 1938 Harold was transferred to Pretoria, where I was born on 18 March 1939. My names, given at birth, were Cedric Walter, but shortly before my baptism they were changed. I only discovered this later when I got married and my parents sent me my birth certificate, accompanied by other documents that registered the change to John Wesley. The reasons for the change are a little unclear, but it seems Cedric Walter was not a name my Hurd grandparents thought I should be burdened with. And so I was baptised John Wesley in the Hatfield Methodist Church in Pretoria on 9 April 1939. Later in life, in order to avoid denominational confusion, I began to refer to myself as John W. de Gruchy – something that our son Steve would poke fun at, especially when George W. Bush was president of the United States.

By the time I was born, my parents were already touching forty and Rozelle was six years old. Her relationship with my parents was firmly established. I was a *laatlammetjie* (late lamb) as the Afrikaans has it – an unexpected arrival, if not a mistake. But I had no intention of taking the backseat. On the contrary, my earliest memory is of me, probably aged three, wandering away from our house in Hatfield and ending up on the railway station nearby, watching the trains go by.

My mother was understandably frantic, but she found me talking happily to a stranger.

In 1942 my father was transferred back to Cape Town. He had not been called up for overseas service in the army, because his communications job was deemed essential for homeland security. So we all caught the train to the Mother City, and it was there that I grew up.

My life would have turned out very differently if we had stayed in Pretoria and I was known as Cedric Walter.

2

The soul of the child I was

> When I was a boy and chirruping ten, a decade after the end of the Second World War, when I was Tarzan and Batman and could sing "Rainbow over the River" like Bobby Breen – in those red-white-and-blue days I remember especially the weekends …
>
> (Richard Rive)[4]

We initially moved into a rented semi-detached house, number thirty-three Bellevue Street, at the top of Kloof Street and within walking distance of the lower cable station on Table Mountain. The house was small but adequate, and had a pocket-sized garden. My father had a tin shanty of a workshop in the backyard where I first learnt some carpentry. He also rented a garage for his 1936 Willys, a half a mile away down the steep hill. That did not make any sense to me, but I guess he had his reasons.

Even after the Second World War we had to live on food rations for some time. I remember the day when real chocolates and fizzy drinks appeared at the corner shop at the bottom of Bellevue Street.

The shop was owned by a Muslim family – "Cape Malays" my parents called them. I can still smell the exotic spices in the large sacks that lined the floor and greeted me as I entered. Bellevue Street was very steep, so it was quite an effort to walk back home, but getting chocolates made it worthwhile.

During 1948 grandpa Hurd came to visit. With his financial help, my parents bought a bigger house – number forty-three in the same street, with a large garden and a garage big enough for the Willys and my father's workshop. Grandpa also bought me my first bicycle, a BSA. It was heavy and without gears, but I manfully rode it around the steep roads in the neighbourhood.

The number four trackless tram's journey from the city centre ended close to our house, and for two pence I could safely get to the Colosseum Bioscope within twenty minutes on a Saturday morning. That weekly ritual, with the bartering of comic books while we queued outside, and the pandemonium that broke out once we were inside watching cowboy movies we would later re-enact, remains a vivid memory.

Another weekly ritual was church. At first we attended the Metropolitan Methodist Church in Greenmarket Square, where my grandfather Abram had met and married my grandmother Mary. We soon moved to the Union Congregational Church in Kloof Street, about a mile and a half from our house, because it was within walking distance. I don't think my parents had any idea about Congregationalism, but its worship and preaching was barely different from that of the Methodists, and they soon felt at home. My mother later became a leader in the Women's Association, and my father a deacon. Rozelle and I sang in the junior choir. I even won medals for singing in the Cape Town Eisteddfod, until my voice embarrassingly broke while singing "Who is Sylvia?". We attended

Sunday school of course, and were confirmed in a perfunctory sort of way. Eventually, Rozelle rebelled and left the church, while I, negotiating those awkward years, stayed put.

Sometimes during church services, I read the large plaques on the sanctuary wall. One told me that the first minister of the congregation, when it was founded in 1820, was John Philip, superintendent of the London Missionary Society (LMS) and a leading figure in the anti-slavery movement. Another told me that his wife, Jane, had pioneered schooling for the children of slaves. Their stories intrigued me long before I learnt their significance, or knew that Congregationalism came to South Africa at the end of the eighteenth century through the work of the LMS. Later I also learnt that Johannes van der Kemp, its first missionary, gained notoriety when he married a Khoi woman and opposed slavery on the Eastern Cape border. Basil Brown, our minister, was neither a Philip nor a Van Der Kemp, but he did on occasion speak out against injustice, and later became the general secretary of the Christian Council of South Africa (forerunner to the SACC). I was fortunate to grow up in what was, for those days, a reasonably liberal church environment.

At the age of five I started school at Tamboerskloof Primary, to which I walked every day in the company of Rozelle. At the end of my first year, then named sub-A, it was decided that I should skip sub-B and proceed to standard one (now grade three). This meant that, for the rest of my school and university life, I was a year younger than virtually everyone else in my class. In retrospect, that was not a good thing, but it did mean that I got going on most things in life earlier than the norm. At the end of standard one, I was awarded a copy of *Aesop's Fables* for not missing a single day of school. I later learnt that Aesop was a Greek slave whose fables still have much to teach us about ourselves. I never won any more prizes for the rest of my school years; certainly none for academic prowess.

Our age difference was too great for Rozelle and me to be playmates; her role was to look after me, organise birthday parties, and sometimes take me to movies with her friends. On one occasion, we saw *The Wizard of Oz;* on another we watched Esther Williams and her water nymphs perform endless manoeuvres in a large pool.

My parents came to Scout functions and church concerts, but I don't recall them watching me play sport or attending a school prize-giving – well, yes, there was no reason for them to do that.

Our family outings included Saturday nights at the cinema, and Sunday drives in the Willys to The Doll's House in Sea Point for an ice cream. The Green Point lighthouse, painted in red and white stripes, stood nearby. I recall the comforting sound of its horn on misty nights, even from as far away as the city bowl.

We also visited my parents' (mostly boring) friends, and the wider circle of our family. All my cousins were older than me, though, so I had no one to play with, and had to use my imagination to amuse myself.

At home there was little intellectual stimulation, few books and little encouragement to read or even study hard. But I read the boys' magazines that arrived from England on the mail ship every Thursday. I collected stamps and developed an interest in photography, and eventually had a darkroom in the cellar.

Though by no means well-off, Rozelle and I never lacked anything, and we were loved. Our mother was always at home, waiting for us after school with food and drink on hand.

The 1936 Willys was a faded blue vehicle with black bumpers and the licence plate CA 6. This indicated that it was registered in Cape

Town, but 6 would normally mean that its owner was some civic dignitary, which was not the case. The car, so crude compared to the posh new American cars of our friends, made a grinding noise going up hills, and became an embarrassment to us children. We asked our dad to park some distance from the school when he came to fetch us. On family outings, though, we happily chugged along a narrow De Waal Drive, past the Old Mill and the University campus, down to Muizenberg for a picnic on the beach. Back then there was no Black River Parkway or Blue Route Parkway, let alone Ou Kaapse Weg over the mountain into Noordhoek Valley.

I once rode my bicycle along the coastal road to Hout Bay and then over Chapman's Peak Drive to Kommetjie. After a few days' camping, I pedalled back in the rain, but gave up when, drenched, I reached the house of an acquaintance in Bakoven. On that occasion, I was glad when the Willys arrived to fetch me for the final haul over the mountain. When it was finally sold, my dad got far more for the licence plate than he did for the vehicle.

My mother persuaded my father to move me to St. George's Grammar School for standard two in 1947. From now on my schooling would always take place in a male environment. Situated next to St. George's Cathedral at that time, the school was an alien environment to me, with daily morning prayer following the Book of Common Prayer.

1947 was memorable, though, because King George VI, Queen Elizabeth and their two princess daughters visited Cape Town. I was one of the many pupils lining the fence of our school along Government Avenue, waving Union Jacks to welcome them. As a Wolf Cub pack leader, I shook hands with Princess Margaret at a Scouting parade, and was struck with awe on a guided tour of the battleship HMS *Vanguard*. Those were what Richard Rive would've called "red-white-and-blue days". My mother was an ardent royalist, and we were all part of the Empire, whether we lived across town in Rive's District Six or in Kloof Nek. I was oblivious of the fact that there were Afrikaners who had a very different opinion.

By the end of the year, my father put his foot down. He feared I might become a choir boy if I stayed at St. George's, so I was moved to SACS Junior at the top of Government Avenue, where Cape Town High School is now located. SACS High was nearby in Orange Street, in the historic buildings that have since become the UCT Hiddingh Hall campus. I walked to school down Hof Street every morning, a distance of three kilometres, carrying a case full of books and sports togs.

At junior school I learnt the basics, did woodworking, played rugby and cricket, flunked boxing and received cuts (corporal punishment) from the headmaster for telling our singing teacher, Miss LaCock, to the raucous amusement of the class, that she had sung a false note. Once a week we watched travelogues provided by various embassies in the city, and I decided that I would one day visit these exotic places around the world. At lunchtime we played marbles or *bok-bok makierie* on the dusty playground, which left us dishevelled and sweaty for the rest of the day.

I was mad about sport. In standard four I was captain of the under-eleven rugby team, and I have the photograph to prove the fact. Saturday after Saturday, I made the train journey to Newlands Rugby Stadium to watch senior club rugby, sitting with other school boys on the touchline in front of the old Railway Stand. In 1948 I went to the Newlands Cricket Ground to watch the test match between the Springboks and the touring MCC or English side – the first after the War. The next year I was at the Newlands Rugby Stadium, watching the Springboks beat the All Blacks from New Zealand fifteen to eight. Sport has remained an integral part of my life.

Living on the slopes of Table Mountain, I spent much time exploring its terrain. On one occasion a friend and I – probably aged eleven, for we had just become Sea Scouts – climbed too far up the mountain face above the cableway station to turn back, and had to be rescued in the late evening. As the years passed, my friends and I thought little of walking for almost two hours over Kloof Nek on a Sunday afternoon, for the pleasure of swimming in the icy water of the world-famous Clifton beach.

Another boyhood memory was being introduced to Prime Minister Jan Smuts, who regularly passed by our house after his Sunday walks on Table Mountain. One evening, not long after, my father and I sat listening to the national election results on that fateful day in 1948, when the National Party came to power on the ticket of its apartheid policy and Smuts was ousted. I was vaguely aware that something ominous was happening.

My father, a follower of Smuts, declared that the results were disastrous. He was no political liberal (nor was Smuts), but he had experienced the influence of the secretive and powerful Afrikaner Broederbond at his work, where he was denied promotion in favour of younger *broeder* colleagues he had taught. He had learnt Dutch at school and could speak Afrikaans reasonably well – he had to, in order to progress at work. But he thought I needed to improve my ability in this regard, so one holiday I was sent to a farm in Citrusdal for this purpose. I recall picking oranges every day and sleeping in a bed with three other boys every night. I am not sure my Afrikaans improved.

My parents were probably more bothered by the rise to power of Afrikaner Nationalism than they were by the new apartheid laws. After all, racial segregation was nothing new, and their heritage was colonial. What *was* new, was the strict racial classification and obsessive racial controls that changed the social fabric and demographic face of Cape Town. When I turned sixteen, I had to register as a "white person". I then received my identity document, which was my passport to privilege. By then I had already witnessed the segregation of our street and the buses, which now had a limited section at the back for those deemed "coloured". I felt embarrassed, as I had always been taught to stand up and let older people, irrespective of who they were, have my seat. As a "coloured" Capetonian wryly observed, "Only roads and telephones were allowed to remain non-racial."[5]

In SACS High, where I started in 1952, I received a classical education, which included Latin, and was selected to play cricket and hockey for the first teams when I was only in standard eight (now grade ten). I was good at table tennis and learnt to play chess, but I was bored to death by religious instruction, which, in my first year, meant reading the Bible in class from beginning to end. We never seemed to get beyond Leviticus and Numbers.

Many of my classmates were Jewish, mainly the children of families from eastern Europe, who had fled pogroms early in the century. There were also boys from St. John's Orphanage, and many more whose families were struggling to make their way after the Second World War. Several of my teachers had served in the army, and we all knew families who had lost someone in combat.

We were all drafted into the cadets, and I joined the band and learnt to play the bagpipes – badly. We attended school in cadet uniform on a Tuesday, when we were on parade for an hour to the sound of bugles, drums and pipes. Once a month, we also had shooting practice with antiquated .22 rifles.

Outside of school, I became a member of the Cape Town Photographic Society, and could amuse myself for hours on end in my darkroom at home. I also went on photographic expeditions, invariably the youngest in the group, and with somewhat primitive equipment compared to that of the others. As a Sea Scout, I spent many Saturday afternoons rowing boats in Cape Town's harbour, Duncan Docks, and learning to tie an endless series of knots.

In 1952 we celebrated the Van Riebeeck Festival – the tercentenary of the establishment of "white" South Africa. In the evenings, I went with friends to watch motorbikes race on a cinder track in the stadium erected for the festival. In the exhibition hall nearby, we gaped at real-life Bushmen on exhibit. The idea that they were "first-nation people" did not vaguely occur to us, or tally with what we were celebrating as a white nation. But the festival was regarded by most English-speakers as an Afrikaner celebration, so no one in our circle was particularly involved.

By the time I was in high school, Rozelle had a life of her own. Family holidays, few and far in between at the best of times, became rarer. Instead I was sent off to spend holidays with cousins old enough to be uncles and aunts, or to innumerable Scout camps. But then, at the invitation of my closest school friend, Rodney Dinan, I went to my first Scripture Union camp and, at age fourteen, I became a "Christian". This happened one evening around a camp fire on the mountain slopes above Rooi Els, looking down on False Bay. I guess peer pressure played a large part in my decision; after all, as captain of both the cricket First XI and the rugby First XV, Rodney was a good role model. Adolescence, in any case, is a peak time for commitments and enthusiasms of all kinds. Or perhaps my Methodist genes had at last caught up with me.

My parents found it all a little odd, as I already was a Christian – or so they told me. I had been baptised, attended Sunday school, had been confirmed, and my name was John Wesley, for God's sake! My father, more so than my mother, was bewildered by this "religious" turn of events. It was beyond his frame of reference, and that of his friends and the wider De Gruchy family – if not the devoutly Methodist Hurd one. But according to some of my close school friends, I had become a real Christian.

Whichever way I now assess what happened, it changed the course of my life. I do not regret that for a moment, but I do regret the extent to which I was then drawn into a legalist, fundamentalist Christianity, which made me feel guilty about youth's peccadilloes, narrowed my perspective on life, and insisted on an understanding of Christian faith and the Bible that became increasingly untenable; though none of this was obvious to me at the time.

I was now part of a new "gang" of teenagers in Cape Town who had made the same commitment, attended rallies organised by Youth for Christ, watched Billy Graham movies, and went to Saturday night house fellowship meetings. I read my Bible every day, aided by Scripture Union notes, and tried to pray. I joined and became a leader in the Student Christian Association (SCA) at school, and, under Rodney Dinan's influence, I briefly attended a Plymouth Brethren assembly where I was re-baptised, much to my parents' consternation. But I soon became disenchanted with the narrowness of it all, so different from my home church, though I wished that the latter was more evangelical.

In any case, I determined to remain a member at Union Congregational Church, even though I had little guidance there in negotiating my adolescent faith. Fortunately I was embraced by others who offered the nurturing I needed, even if the explanations given, reinforced by chapter and verse from a narrow selection of biblical texts, soon proved inadequate. I had walked through a narrow door and embarked on a spiritual journey without knowing where it would take me or what it really meant. I still had a long way to go to find out.

3

Studying Theology and falling in love

> Anyone who thinks or acts, prays or worships, as if there is some ultimate mystery known by many names but often as "God", is a theologian, however rudimentary or sophisticated. But not everyone who does such things or believes in God discovers that doing theology can become a personal odyssey driven by a passion that can become all-consuming.
>
> (From *A Theological Odyssey*)[6]

I matriculated in 1955 at the age of sixteen, a year below average and with average grades, and registered at the University of Cape Town (UCT) for a BA with English and History majors. I was the first in my extended family to go to university. Nobody, except my mother, thought I would succeed – not with my matric results. I must confess that I did not think so either. As there was a possibility that I might go into the ministry, I added Greek to my list of courses, along with Philosophy. My Philosophy professor, Martin Versfeld, was an Afrikaner convert to the Catholic Church and an authority on

Plato and Augustine. To the surprise of everyone, including myself, I received high marks in the subject at the end of the first semester.

I joined the university's Student Christian Association (SCA), which, at that time, was becoming more politically liberal, though it remained conservative evangelical in ethos. On some Sunday afternoons, I would go with other students to District Six, a predominantly "coloured" area not far from the city centre, to teach Sunday school. I recall the trek up Harrington Street to the small semi-detached house in Ayre Street where the class was held.

Little did I know that District Six would soon be flattened by bulldozers and its inhabitants dumped on the Cape Flats – one of the many apartheid crimes that destroyed the lives of communities and families around the Peninsula. Long before that, Africans had been excluded from living within the "white" areas of Cape Town, so there already existed poor black townships on the city's perimeter, which served white interests. Not everyone who lived in Cape Town was a privileged Capetonian enjoying the mountain, the sea and its many other attractions.

At this stage, there were handfuls of "coloured" students on the UCT campus who challenged our prejudices. There was also a lively political debate among sections of the university community. Anti-apartheid student protest action was beginning, and would gather momentum over the next few years.

After teaching Sunday school in District Six on Sunday afternoons, I would sometimes stand on the Grand Parade and listen to anti-apartheid speeches by leaders of the African National Congress (ANC) and the South West Africa People's Organisation (SWAPO). Within a few years, these gatherings became illegal, but I have often wondered whether I heard some of the great liberation leaders speak.

So my political education began at the same time as I was being introduced to Aristotle, Kant and the existentialists, and while I taught Sunday school.

My father was not keen that I should go into the ministry, but my mother thought it a good idea. In the end, they left it up to me to decide. And so, during that first year at UCT, when Basil Brown, pleased by my examination results, asked me if I was serious about the ministry, I confidently answered in the affirmative and was invited to preach at our church one Sunday morning. My sermon, the first of many to come, was on the healing of Naaman the Aramean (2 Kings 5). It is a wonderful story of prophetic insight and the humbling of power, but I doubt whether I understood that at the age of eighteen.

I was subsequently interviewed by another senior minister, Noel Tarrant, a wise and venerable man, who probed my intention with searching questions. I was adamant (perhaps even too self-assured) that this was my calling, and my application was approved by the Congregational Union of South Africa (CUSA). Today that would be impossible: There is now a minimum age requirement and a lengthy process for testing vocations.

By this time, I was aware that CUSA was a predominantly coloured denomination – at least in the Western Cape – even though the majority of congregations that I knew well were all-white. From time to time, ministers from other racial groups preached at our home church, and I would attend meetings or services at theirs, but it was all rather paternalistic. Being a majority black denomination did not mean that the majority was in control. I also discovered that most of the white ministers were expatriate Englishmen who had little knowledge of the church on the other side of the tracks, and no knowledge of Afrikaans and Xhosa – the main languages spoken there. They could just as well have been ministering in Manchester, Birmingham or London. I was, in fact, one of a small handful of South African-born white candidates for the ministry in CUSA.

The ministerial committee decided that I should go the next year to Rhodes University in Grahamstown, about a nine-hundred kilometres to the east of Cape Town, where an ecumenical Faculty of Theology had been established in 1947. This would enable me to finish my BA begun at UCT, and to take some pre-theological subjects before proceeding to the Bachelor of Divinity (BD) – the equivalent of today's Master of Divinity. I was excited by the prospect.

My sister, Rozelle, married Ramon Dempers from Windhoek in January 1957. I was one of the best men at the wedding, and was fitted out for the occasion in a tailor-made suit. At the wedding, I met a young woman who had recently moved from Johannesburg to Windhoek. She told me to look out for her close school friend Isobel Dunstan, who was now studying at Rhodes. The consequences of this conversation would be life changing, but I had little premonition that this was so at the time.

Late that January, along with James Elias – a Presbyterian friend who was also going to Rhodes – I left home and caught the Union Castle mail ship to Port Elizabeth. Rozelle and Ramon happened to be on honeymoon on the same boat. I didn't see anything of them during the trip, but then I was only on board for one day and night. It must have been very sad for my parents to say farewell to both of us at the same time, but my sights were set on what lay ahead. Arriving in Port Elizabeth, we took an overnight train that stopped at virtually every siding along the way for the last hundred kilometres to Grahamstown.

Situated in a hollow in the hills, Grahamstown had something of the charm of an English country town. After all, it began as a

British and largely Methodist and Anglican settler village in the early nineteenth century, soon after the arrival of the 1820 Settlers. These unsuspecting arrivals were sent to the Cape at the end of the Napoleonic Wars to become a buffer between the expanding colony to the south and the Xhosa-speaking peoples to the north-east.

When I arrived, the legacy of that conflict was still apparent in the architecture and social stratification of the city, with the majority of blacks living in poor townships, struggling to find employment in town and at the university. The "coloured" population fared better, but not by a great deal. In contrast, the "white" Settler city boasted many churches, fine boarding schools, an Anglican theological seminary, as well as the university and the regional law courts. Settler Grahamstown was conservative and racist, with pockets of liberalism an exception to the rule.

There were two Congregational Churches in town, both situated on its outskirts as a result of segregation. I preached at one of them several times, but it was a long walk to attend regularly, so I worshipped at the "white" Methodist and Presbyterian Churches, along with my fellow theological students, or "toks" as we were known. In those days, going to church on Sundays was the norm for most people, even students, though that was changing by the time I left. During vacations, it was not always possible to go home, so some of us went to run evangelistic missions at churches in nearby towns, under the banner of the Varsity Trekkers.

In 1957, Rhodes was a small English-speaking university of eight hundred students. Largely segregated like all South African universities, it was twinned with the University of Fort Hare in Alice, where Nelson Mandela had once studied, some 160 kilometres away. Given its modest size and geographical isolation, Rhodes had some remarkably able and progressive professors, whose work was internationally acknowledged.

The theological students' residence was named Livingstone House after the LMS missionary explorer David Livingstone. Although it was reserved for senior students, I was placed there from the outset to make up the Congregational quota and, as always, was the youngest in the residence to begin with. The majority of the seventy or so students in the Faculty of Theology were studying for the Methodist or Presbyterian Churches. There were a few Anglicans (they had their own St. Paul's College across the valley) and only a handful of Congregational students, as the majority were at Fort Hare.

Apart from a few rather pious fellows, the "toks" were a boisterous bunch of men (there were no women in the ministry then), most of them older than the average student. Some had a fair amount of life experience behind them. I recall one had been a London policeman, and another a champion wrestler. Both of them were part of a group of English Methodists sent to South Africa for training before serving in local churches. I will remain silent about the pineapple punch we brewed and sold to other students, but I will say that I learnt to play squash and became reasonably good at it.

I soon settled into the routine of Livingstone House. Our regime was by no means as strict as St. Paul's Anglican College across the valley. But it was obligatory to attend evening prayers each day in the chapel, wearing our black academic gowns, which we were also required to wear in the dining hall. Lectures were given every morning, so most afternoons we were free to study or play sport. On the weekends, there was not much to do in Grahamstown apart from going to church, except going to the two small bioscopes to see outdated movies (but never on a Sunday), playing sport, or courting female students – a major pastime for most of us. Only one student in Livingstone House had a car during the four years I was there, and as there was no public transport in the town, we walked everywhere.

I remember my first week of lectures well, because Isobel Dunstan, about whom I had heard at my sister's wedding, was sitting right behind me in one of my classes. She was in her second year and, out of interest, was doing a course in New Testament while studying for a Science degree in Mathematics and Botany. We soon went on several dates, but she was not particularly interested in me. She did, however, invite me to meet her family during my first Christmas vacation when she heard that I planned to spend six weeks in Johannesburg's northern suburbs, working in a new church extension project. Isobel, who was of Cornish and Methodist stock, had meanwhile started going out with John Borman, a Methodist theological student. I myself had several girlfriends, though none of those relationships lasted very long.

Visiting the Dunstan home was an enjoyable diversion from walking in the summer heat to innumerable houses guarded by large dogs and separated by extensive gardens, to invite largely uninterested people to come to church. Another welcome distraction during that long, hot summer was watching South Africa play Australia at cricket at the Wanderers. In addition, I began Hebrew lessons with a sage-like Jewish scholar and, for the first time, experienced the awe with which Orthodox Jews regard the name of God given to Moses at the burning bush. Soon, however, it was time to return to Rhodes for my second year.

Our professors and lecturers were mainly expatriates, and the curriculum was based on the traditional Scottish model: Systematic Theology, Church History and Biblical Studies, each divided into various sub-disciplines. In addition Biblical Studies required Hebrew and Greek. I came to understand the Bible with fresh eyes, relishing the prophets and wisdom literature. It was an eye-opener to learn, for example, how the Synoptic Gospels came to be written, and how such knowledge helped one to comprehend them.

There were some attempts to give us training in pastoral care, but as this was not part of the university curriculum, it did not amount to much.

Looking back, I now know that our courses could just as well have been taught in Edinburgh, Zurich or New York, for there was little attempt to relate them to South Africa; although I did learn much about our social and missionary history, as well as the wrongs of apartheid, from Leslie Hewson, a South African Methodist.

Despite the curriculum's shortcomings, I received a reasonable theological grounding and was introduced to some of the major themes and challenges facing Christian faith in the twentieth century, such as the relationship between faith and science. I was also encouraged to read widely and well. I enjoyed the work of the Scottish Congregationalist theologian P.T. Forsyth and that of another Scot, John Baillie, who, I later learnt, had been one of Bonhoeffer's teachers at Union Seminary in New York. The major European theologian I studied was the Swiss Emil Brunner, whose controversial disagreement with his compatriot Karl Barth over the problem of natural theology exercised our minds. I also read Brunner's massive book on ethics, *The Divine Imperative*, which was on our reading list. Barth himself, the most significant Protestant theologian of the twentieth century, was not a big part of the curriculum, and Bonhoeffer was an unknown name. It was only during my final BD year that I read the latter's *The Cost of Discipleship* as part of a student reading group convened by Peter Storey, who went on to became a Methodist bishop and president of the SACC.

During my final two years, despite being part of a denominational minority, I was elected chair of Livingstone Fellowship, which comprised all theological students and represented them more widely. Livingstone Fellowship did much to foster a sense of ecumenical belonging, even though denominational identities were strong. It also brought me personally into contact with theological students at Fort Hare who would later become church and political leaders. I travelled there on several occasions – a two-hour journey by car – in order to discuss issues that threatened to destroy the already tenuous relationship between us at Rhodes and those studying Theology at Fort Hare. Although I always felt welcome, anger at both the injustices of apartheid and our liberal white paternalism was palpable.

Another task allotted to me as fellowship chair was attending the centenary of the Faculty of Theology (or Kweekskool) at Stellenbosch University in 1959 at the invitation of the Students' Council. This turned out to be the beginning of a long relationship, which was uncomfortable at first, but enriching eventually. I went to the celebrations with James Elias, my Presbyterian friend from Cape Town. We were, I think, the only English-speaking guests among the students who joined the procession from the stately Kweekskool to the nearby and beautiful Moederkerk (Mother Church). There I listened to Professor B.B. Keet, doyen of the theological professors, who gave an overview of Reformed theology during the past century. Keet was one of the few Dutch Reformed theologians who had openly criticised apartheid, notably in his book *Suid-Afrika – Waarheen? (Whither South Africa?)*, which I had read the year I was at UCT.

I made many friends in Livingstone House and by my third year, Isobel Dunstan and I had also become good friends. By this time she had broken off with her Methodist suitor, John Borman, and it was he who suggested that I should court her again. It was 1959 and Isobel was now in her final honours year. We began going out again, grew closer, felt attracted to each other, and discovered that we shared a similar spiritual journey and sense of humour. We were, in short, falling in love.

One weekend, I had to go to preach in Port Elizabeth, so we went together. We borrowed the minister's small car on the Saturday evening, and went out to have supper on the Humewood Beach front. All we could afford were hamburgers and chips. It was then, in that "romantic" setting, that I proposed. Isobel later told me that she had anticipated my doing so. That evening we were young and I impetuous, the moon was full, and the future stretched invitingly before us.

Over the years of our now long marriage, Isobel and I have often commented that both our upbringings mitigated against expressing romantic feelings in overt ways. We had difficulty baring our souls or hugging and kissing exuberantly in public, simply because that was not done in our families. But reserve did not mean that love was absent or intimacy avoided. Years later, Isobel expressed this in a poem:

> Mine was a loving, caring home
> but not of demonstrative love …[7]

It is true that on the night I proposed to her I did not have a love poem to recite or a bunch of roses to give, nor did I fall on my knees; nor was her response a spontaneous hug and sensuous kiss, such as we had already shared aplenty while we walked and talked and lay on the grass on the hills above Grahamstown. Instead her response was a thoughtful pause and a request for time to think. She kept me hanging on a thread for two days. Then she accepted with hugs and kisses. Many years later, while looking back, she captured our relationship in another poem:

My love for you never was
an exotic brilliant-hued bloom,
or a heady-scented rose,
never a story
to catch the imagination
of the whole world.
Not Iseult loving Tristan,
nor Juliet with Romeo.

More like an acorn,
or the fleshy, round seed
of a yellow-wood,
small and insignificant,
but falling on dark, rich soil
and growing to a mighty tree –
deep-rooted and firm,
stretching arms to pluck
the rainbow from the sky.

Isobel's love for me was immediately tested. Her parents were visiting Grahamstown with her younger sister, Elsie, soon after our decision to get married. I approached Mr Dunstan while he was alone and asked him if I could marry his daughter, and he agreed right away without more ado. But Isobel's mother, Lilian, upon hearing the news later that day, was appalled. She flatly refused to give her support. My Congregational affiliation was unacceptable (surely there were enough eligible Methodists!) and I was far too young, which was true. Isobel dug in her heels. We were in love and she was going to marry me. That was that. In December 1959, we got engaged in Cape Town. Our photograph was taken by Happy Snaps while we walked arm in arm down St. George's Street, with Isobel sporting her modest diamond engagement ring, paid for with money I borrowed from my father. I must remember someday to repay him.

After completing her Honours degree in Mathematics, Isobel went home and taught at a high school in Johannesburg. Unfortunately, her mother died suddenly on 16 March 1960, in the same week that I turned twenty-one. Preparations were hurriedly cancelled for celebrating this traditional rite of passage in Grahamstown, and I hitched a long overnight ride to Johannesburg to be at the funeral. Not only did Isobel now have to mourn the sudden loss of her mother, but she also had to take over the responsibilities of running the family home. This meant caring for her much younger sister, and managing a household for a busy father and two very active brothers, who were just a year or two behind her. Thus she was plunged into shopping and cooking, for which she had very little preparation, while I, 1 500 kilometres away, completed my BD.

The week of Isobel's mother's funeral and my aborted twenty-first birthday was made far more ominous by the Sharpeville massacre on 21 March 1960. The terrible events that occurred that day rudely awakened many to the inherent violence of apartheid and the challenges facing the country. It happened just as I was finishing my studies and about to begin my ministry. I was one of a handful of theological students who signed a protest letter to the prime minister, Hendrik Verwoerd.

During that final year at university, I learnt much from Professor W.D. Maxwell, an authority on Calvin and Liturgy; studied Paul Tillich's *Systematic Theology* in detail; and wrote a dissertation on Congregational Ecclesiology, tracing its roots in both the Calvinist and Anabaptist traditions, and showing how it had developed since then. I completed my BD with a first class honours at the end of 1960.

I had now satisfactorily concluded my training for the ordained ministry – at least, that's what I thought. I was soon to be proved wrong, but for now my thoughts were fixed on my impending marriage.

Isobel and I were married in Johannesburg on 7 January 1961 in her home Methodist Church in Parktown North. Ian MacDonald, later professor of Philosophy at Rhodes, was my best man, and Jean Pyle, a close friend of Isobel's, was her bridesmaid. After a fun-filled and adventurous honeymoon that took us 6 000 kilometres around South Africa in a second-hand Fiat 600 that regularly broke down, we arrived in Cape Town where I was ordained to the ministry in my home congregation in Cape Town. There was a power failure that evening at the beginning of the service, so all the ministers processed into the church by candlelight. I don't recall much else, except that Basil Brown preached, and at one point, as I removed my handkerchief from my suit pocket, I dislodged a wad of confetti that had become embedded there at our wedding. Not a very auspicious incident on that otherwise solemn, important and joyful occasion, which concluded with a party back at my parents' house.

4

On a sharp learning curve

I'm wondering what you've got in your veins these days, you young priests! When I was your age we had men in the church – don't frown, it makes me want to clout you – men I say – make what you like of the word – heads of a parish, masters, my boy, rulers. They could hold a whole country together, that sort could – with a mere lift of the chin.

(Georges Bernanos)[8]

During my final year at Rhodes, I received and accepted a call to the Sea View Congregational Church in Durban. I had previously visited there to preach with "a view", as it is said, and liked the congregation. I also liked the attractive red-bricked church with its stained-glass windows, bell tower and lych gate at the bottom of the garden path that led onto Sarnia Road. The recently built manse was situated beyond an old hall on the same property, awaiting our arrival. We moved there at the beginning of February 1961. Soon afterwards, I was inducted on a very humid evening, perspiring heavily beneath my black Geneva gown – a gift from my parents. In those days, such garb was expected, as was the wearing of a suit and clerical collar when doing pastoral visits. It was madness in Durban's sub-tropical climate, and I would soon get out of the habit.

Apart from the assurance of a warm welcome, my letter of call informed me that my annual salary would be 550 pounds (1 100 rand), and that I would get an extra 36 pounds each year for travel, but no car. Not much of a salary after five years of studying, even in those days. But my father, in an attempt to change my mind some years before, had warned me not to expect to make money in the ministry. We had a free manse, though, and the telephone and electricity were covered. Isobel had saved enough money during her teaching year to purchase furniture, and I was able to buy basic tools for my rudimentary workshop. A Zulu family, the Mbathas, who also lived on the church premises, cared for the grounds and helped in the house.

Back then, there were no supermarkets in town; only some local grocery stores, a hardware shop, chemist, post office and garage. Each week, we bought our fruit and vegetables from the Indian market in Durban. Our monthly groceries cost ten rand a month on average, and I could fill the tank of our car for two rand.

As the custom still was, Isobel, as wife of the minister, was expected to fulfil certain roles in the congregation, which she gladly did, but from time to time she also did some relief high school teaching.

Compared to the Dutch Reformed Church (DRC) down the road, whose members seemed to control the community, ours was a small congregation of not more than a hundred members. It was all white, all English-speaking, and most members were getting on in years. But there were some ex-servicemen, a sprinkling of young families, a vibrant youth fellowship, and a committed and caring leadership. Whatever anybody else thought, to my mind the congregation had a future.

So what did I have to offer in return for my monthly stipend? I felt I knew much about theology, understood the Bible, and could explain the Trinity, but I had virtually no training in pastoral care, and almost zero life experience. I was, to state it bluntly, a naive young minister, despite a projected image of competence and my BD certificate hanging on my study wall. I am now appalled at how I was let loose on the congregation, but some said they found my sermons helpful, and several of the young men in the youth group subsequently went into the ministry.

Our son Stephen was born in November 1961. I was present at his birth before the doctor arrived, and had a good look at him before Isobel cuddled him in her arms. So within one year I had graduated, married, been ordained, started my ministry and became a father. I still can't quite understand how that all happened in such a short space of time, but it seems that we took it in our stride, as though it was perfectly normal. We got on with what had to be done; Isobel far more than I in the parenting arena, aided by Benjamin Spock's now discredited guide to child-rearing. Isobel's sister, Elsie, who became a boarder at Epworth Girls School in Pietermaritzburg following their mother's death, often spent weekends with us and helped to look after Steve. Athanasius, our mongrel dog named after the fourth-century Orthodox bishop of Alexandria, made up the family complement.

I soon became involved in the regional affairs of the denomination, and got to know some of the congregations in Durban and elsewhere around Natal. I was appointed convenor of youth work, and organised several camps and conferences. Most memorably, I was a delegate to the Natal Congress, a week-long gathering in Pietermaritzburg, organised by the Liberal Party of which Alan Paton, Peter Brown and Archie Gumede were the leading figures. The congress was intended for the discussion of opposition to apartheid in the province, and the delegates did so with a defiance and clarity I had not experienced before. I was a junior delegate and had little to add to the discussion, but I listened to some of the most progressive and articulate political leaders at the time, both black and white. More than ever before, I became aware of the gaps in my political knowledge. There were some senior church leaders present whom I would later get to know well, including Catholic Archbishop Denis Hurley, and the Presbyterian minister Calvin Cook, whose intellectual stature I soon came to admire.

Other defining experiences were the two visits I made to Chief Albert Luthuli, the former president of the ANC, Nobel Peace Prize laureate, and a deacon in the Groutville Congregational Church. Luthuli was already banned and confined to his magisterial district. My first visit was in February 1962, and the second a few months later. I still have a photograph of Luthuli standing alongside my bright-red VW Beetle outside his home. His book *Let My People Go*, which I was reading at the time, was a life-changer. But try as I then did to encourage other white ministers to read it, I failed. To them, Luthuli was a communist. I suspect they thought I was one as well.

I was happy in my work in the congregation, and gladly accepted the extra responsibility of a new extension charge in New Forest about eight kilometres away. Preaching at least twice on Sundays was a challenge, but a good discipline. I enjoyed confirmation classes and Bible study groups, but pastoral care was a burden. What could I say to the parents of a five-year-old boy who was killed by a drunken driver while crossing the road near our church? How was I to counsel the teenage daughter whose parents thought she should seek an illegal abortion? How could I help a victim of polio and another of bilharzia, who asked me to pray for their healing? Little of what I had learnt as a theological student equipped me for such tasks. Today there are internships, continuing education programmes, and other support or mentoring structures. I am sure some senior ministers wondered whether I would go the distance.

Perhaps it was my pastoral inadequacy that led me to think about further study – largely as a distraction. As my BD was the equivalent of a master's degree, I registered for a PhD at the University of Natal. And, because my congregation was located in an area with a large Indian population, I decided to explore the growing dialogue between Christianity and Hinduism. Professor Alfred Rooks in the Department of Theology suggested that I begin by reading the writings of Sarvepalli Radhakrishna, the well-respected Hindu Oxford philosopher of religion. This I did, and began to have occasional conversations with swamis in local ashrams and priests in nearby temples. None of this held much promise for my work as a pastor, though, nor did I feel equipped to pursue research at the required level.

In my second year at Sea View, I applied for and received a World Council of Churches (WCC) scholarship to study at Chicago Theological Seminary (CTS), which was then linked to the University of Chicago. WCC scholarships were not intended to further academic careers, but to widen horizons and change perspectives. I looked forward to that, but in preparation for a PhD, I hoped to focus on Christianity and World Religions – a subject well catered for in the Divinity School at the university.

My congregation gave me a year's leave of absence, and we promised to return. So we made preparations to leave Durban for Chicago – a city associated in our minds with Al Capone, corrupt politicians, and a bloody massacre at a barber shop on St. Valentine's Day.

5

Chicago, Chicago!

> Departure and arrival, the path and the goal, all are part of the adventure, and if you leave on such a journey, you will return as a different person.
>
> (Christopher Engels)[9]

In July 1963, Isobel, Stephen (now twenty-one months old) and I set off on the *Southern Cross* for Southampton. We crossed the equator – Stephen and I for the first time – and I was ceremoniously dunked into a tub of water. Stephen spent much time in the crèche, but when on deck he would occasionally break free from my grip and, to my horror, run to the railings. I came second in the table tennis tournament, led an evening service at the request of the captain and, on a more sombre note, conducted two funerals – one that of a New Zealand diplomat. We called in at Las Palmas, one of the Canary Islands, and spent an interesting day exploring its mountainous interior.

Once we had arrived England, we stayed some days with friends in London. Visiting the city's well-known tourist sites (usually with Stephen in tow) was exciting, despite the rain. We then toured the Oxfordshire countryside in a small Morris Minor station wagon, cooking our meals on a gas cooker perched on the lowered back door of the car, again in the rain. We visited Cornwall and Isobel's relations whom she had last seen when she was twelve. This was her ancestral home and remains close to her heart.

We crossed the Atlantic on the old *Queen Mary*, deep in the bowels of steerage class. En route we experienced an Atlantic storm, and generally had a dismal time in a tiny cabin whose single light went off the moment we closed the door. But apart from seeing the iconic Table Mountain in the distance as you arrive in Cape Town, few things can compare to arriving in New York for the first time by sea. After disembarking, we sat on the quayside with our luggage for several hours, having no idea as to how we would get from there to Chicago. Leaving our trunks in the care of officials who promised to rail them to us (the trunks arrived three weeks later), we took a cab to a dodgy downtown hotel where we spent the night. The next day, a South African student friend who was studying at Union Theological Seminary, Bob Hammerton-Kelly, introduced us to Union and helped us catch an overnight train to Chicago.

We were met at Chicago Central Station by Jo Davis, a warm and generous staff member at CTS, and were soon settled into our apartment in Hyde Park on Kimbark Avenue. The house, which we shared with three other families, had once been the residence of the philosopher-educationalist John Dewey, whose famous experimental school was across the road. The University of Chicago's Rockefeller Chapel towered close by. It was all invigorating and exciting.

I registered for a one-year Master of Theology (MTh), which required a dissertation and six semester courses, at least two of which had to be taken at the university. I did courses in Constructive Theology, Cultural Anthropology, Social Psychology, and one on the Ministry of the Laity. I also did a course on Ministry to the Mentally

Ill, and an experimental course in Leadership Sensitivity Training. I learnt much from this eclectic assortment of courses, but ached to do some "serious" theological study. Therefore, I attended as many additional lectures a possible. These included a series by the French philosopher Paul Ricœur on Hermeneutics, and a weekly seminar by Paul Tillich on his major works. I also learnt much from Franklin Littell, a noted Methodist historian, about the German church struggle. In January 1964, I was a delegate at the Ecumenical Student Conference held in Athens, Ohio, where I heard daily lectures by the Yale church historian Roland Bainton, and the Russian Orthodox theologian Alexander Schmemann. Most importantly, it was in Chicago that my interest in Bonhoeffer began in earnest.

Two things accounted for this interest: Firstly, on the boat from Durban to Southampton, I read *Honest to God* (a media sensation at the time) by John Robinson, the Anglican bishop of Woolwich. Robinson, who years later visited us in Cape Town, drew somewhat randomly on Bonhoeffer's theological ideas in his letters from prison. I had read these before as part of a ministers' study group in Durban, but only now did I begin to glimpse their possible implications. Robinson visited Chicago while we were there, and I heard him lecture, as well as give a seminar on *Honest to God*. At the latter, Tillich made the comment that, while Robinson might not have fully understood Barth, Bultmann and Bonhoeffer, he had certainly understood him and his books were now selling better than ever before.

The second and most important reason for my interest in Bonhoeffer, was the fact that Eberhard Bethge, Bonhoeffer's close friend and biographer, had given the Alden-Tuthill lectures on "The Challenge of Dietrich Bonhoeffer's Life and Theology" at the seminary in 1961. I soon devoured these, and discovered what I really wanted to do. There were no courses on Bonhoeffer, but I made a special study of his doctoral dissertation, *Sanctorum Communio*, which became a major source for writing my own dissertation under the supervision of Ross Snyder. Ross (as he insisted on us calling him) and I were not on the same page theologically, but he was a gifted teacher who encouraged me to do independent study. I soon learnt that he had no time for any theological humbug.

Although our ability to explore the rich cultural offerings available in Chicago was limited by lack of money and looking after Steve, Isobel and I met many interesting people, and on occasion I preached in churches in other parts of the Midwest. We attended various churches in Hyde Park on Sundays and always felt welcome, but while usually impressed by their social concern and Christian education programmes, we were not particularly taken by the standard of preaching.

A weekend we spent at Reba Place Fellowship in Evanston stands out in our memory, because it was our first experience of Mennonites and their pacifist commitment. During our short visit, I had a heated exchange with a militant pacifist about Bonhoeffer's role in the plot to assassinate Hitler. This challenged me to think more deeply about the Christian peace witness and non-violent resistance. That was a timely development, because in the same year President John Kennedy was assassinated, and the Civil Rights Movement reached its climax. Protest marches and the murders of social activists down south were daily news, and the campus community was abuzz with heated debate. For light relief, we watched The Danny Kaye show on TV each week, saw news clips of the Beatles arriving for their first American tour, and ate hamburgers at the very first McDonald's, not far from where we lived.

Most of my time and energy, however, went into writing my dissertation on *The Local Church and the Race Problem in South*

Africa. In writing it, I was undoubtedly influenced by what was happening in the US, but I also drew on my course work and wider reading, and was greatly stimulated by weekly sessions with Ross Snyder. Using insights from my course in Cultural Anthropology, I began the dissertation with a case study of my congregation in Sea View. I then examined the relationship between theological and racial/cultural identity, followed by a study of the problem of white racial prejudice, using Gordon Allport's masterly *The Nature of Prejudice* as a guide. Then followed a chapter on racial anxiety, based on Paul Tillich's book *The Courage to Be*, in which I examined how change in patterns of behaviour and attitude are inhibited by a deep-seated, irrational anxiety. Using Bonhoeffer's *Sanctorum Communio*, I concluded by developing an ecclesiology of personal and social transformation. The manuscript was longer than required, and I had to work late into the night on my manual typewriter to meet the deadline and provide additional carbon copies. I was awarded a summa cum laude for my efforts.

Towards the end of our stay in Chicago, Isobel and I discussed whether or not we should return to the United States in a year or two so that I could do a PhD. Ross offered to arrange for an assistantship and to help in whatever way he could to make this possible. The prospect was tantalising, but we could not postpone our return to Sea View. In any case, three months of summer lay ahead of us in which to explore America and widen our experience. I also had the great fortune of being invited to be the summer supply pastor of the First Congregational Church (UCC) in Stockbridge, Massachusetts.

After a long overnight ride on Greyhound buses, we arrived in Albany, New York, where we were met by the minister of the church and taken through the beautiful countryside to one of the loveliest places we had ever seen. Stockbridge is the quintessential New

England rural town, located in the Berkshires, an area renowned for its fall colours in the autumn, and for being transformed into a fairyland when the snow covers the landscape in midwinter. We had no idea what to expect, but our eyes opened wide as we were driven up the long road, then still lined by elm trees, which led to the red-bricked church with its white steeple and stone bell tower nearby, and to the large manse adjacent to the church where we would live for the summer.

In his reflections on his first visit to America, Bonhoeffer observed that "American Christianity remains concealed from those who do not know from the beginning of the Congregationalists in New England, the Baptists in Rhode Island, or the revival movement led by Jonathan Edwards."[10] Edwards, so we discovered, was the second of a series of distinguished ministers in Stockbridge when the church was founded in the eighteenth century. Without knowing it, we had arrived in the heartland of historic American Protestant Christianity and Congregationalism. And being a Congregational minister in New England, where the Congregational Church had once been the established church, I had certain privileges. Among them was a free family pass to Tanglewood, the summer home of the Boston Symphony Orchestra, and membership to the golf club. I relished these, despite my nonconformist conscience.

Stockbridge was full of notable personalities, both past and present. The painter Norman Rockwell was one of the town's most celebrated citizens, and our family doctor, while there, was depicted in one of Rockwell's most famous paintings. Then there was Daniel Chester French, who carved the nineteen-foot-high marble figure of President Lincoln for the Lincoln Memorial in Washington DC. The Austin Riggs psychiatric centre, established by Erik Erikson whose book on identity and the life-cycle I had read in Chicago, was a short walk from the manse, close to the iconic Red Lion Inn in the centre of town. And the distinguished theologian Reinhold Niebuhr, along with his wife, Ursula, and son, Christopher, were all members of the Stockbridge congregation. I visited Reinnie (as his students at Union Theological Seminary knew him) several times. Although he was recovering from a stroke, we had lively discussions about South Africa, apartheid and the Civil Rights Movement.

After concluding our enchanted stay in Stockbridge, we drove south to Georgia, to visit Koinonia Farm, a multi-racial Christian community. We went all the way in a borrowed VW Beetle, staying en route in Washington DC with a Mennonite scholar, Paul Peachey, and his family. When we eventually arrived at the farm, well known for its pecan nuts, we found out that it had been attacked by the Ku Klux Klan the week before. My recollection is that a burnt-out cross was still standing near the gate. This was the Deep South about which we had heard so much. Racism in Chicago's South Side was real; here it was raw.

The second day we were there, I went to the bank in Americus, the nearest town, to cash a cheque. The teller, immediately suspicious when I opened my mouth, refused my request because, she said, the cheque was from a bank in Massachusetts. I asked to see the bank manager, who told me that he had noted my car's Yankee number plates, so what was I doing down south and why did I not speak like "one of them northerners"?

I explained that I was visiting and came from South Africa.

"Okay," he replied. "You people know how to treat N.....s, so we'll give you the cash."

I took the money and fled, cowardly reasoning that that was not the time to take a stand.

Back at the farm, we gathered each evening in the kitchen with those who had remained after the Klan's attack. After the meal, Clarence Jordan, the leader of the community and a New Testament scholar, would read from the *Cotton Patch New Testament* he was busy translating at the time. The Jordans visited us years later when we lived in Johannesburg, and told us about their new initiative called Habitat for Humanity. Sadly, Clarence died shortly after his visit, but I suspect not before he had encouraged Habitat for Humanity to consider working in South Africa at some time in the future.

The time came for us to return to South Africa and the Sea View Church. It had been a good year, but we were ready to go home. By this time, it was cheaper to fly than travel by sea, so late in August we boarded a new Pan Am Boeing 707 from New York to London. Isobel and Stephen then went on to Johannesburg, while I made a detour of several weeks visiting Paris, the WCC and Calvin sites in Geneva, the Ecumenical Institute at Bossey, and the Taizé Community near Cluny in France. Taizé made a lasting impression on me, as it did on Steve many years later, for it was there that he decided to go into the ministry. Having lugged my suitcases up from the train station in this seemingly isolated rural community, I arrived at the monastery door and rang the bell.

A Dutch monk bade me welcome, sat me under a nearby tree and asked, "Why have you come here?"

"I was interested to see the place," was all I could think of saying in reply.

"That's not good enough!" he replied. "You shall go on a five-day silent retreat, and I shall be your leader. You will worship with the community three times a day. I shall give you some reading for reflection. And on the fourth day you will make your confession. There is no talking over meals." With that he led me to my room.

A week later, suitably chastened by that monastic experience,

I arrived in Rome, eager to visit St. Peter's Basilica for the first time. But the Second Vatican Council (Vatican II) was in session and St. Peter's was closed to visitors. Despite that, I fell in love with the city and, casting a few coins into the Trevi Fountain, vowed to return.

It was time to end my year of travelling abroad, but I don't think I fully grasped how different a person I was now from the one I had been just a year before.

6

A Confessing Church?

It should be clear to anyone who is familiar with the developments of the church situation in the Third German Reich ... that there are more and more parallels between Nazi Germany and present-day South Africa ... If you think about all these signs, then it is clear that the time has arrived for a Confessing Church in South Africa.

(Beyers Naudé)[11]

While still in Chicago, I had a phone call from a visiting South African who introduced himself as Beyers Naudé. His name rang bells. I had briefly met him in Johannesburg once before, and knew him as the DRC minister who had become an outspoken critic of apartheid and the government. On the phone, he told me that he had established an ecumenical institute, one of whose tasks was to provide support for South African theological students with WCC scholarships. After enquiring how I was doing, he invited me to visit him upon my return to South Africa.

Naudé had been a committed member of the Afrikaner Broederbond – the secret society in the vanguard of Afrikaner nationalism – and was destined for high office. At the time of Sharpeville – an event which deeply shocked him – he was a senior minister in his church and a leading figure at the Cottesloe Consultation convened by the WCC in response to the massacre. The subsequent failure of his church to honour the decisions of Cottesloe angered him. This led to his resolve to establish the Christian Institute (CI), even though it meant losing his status in his church. As a former student of Professor Keet in Stellenbosch, Naudé was inspired by the church struggle in Germany, especially the legacy of Bonhoeffer, and would often write about the need for a "Confessing Church" in South Africa in the CI journal, *Pro Veritate*.

Soon after my arrival in Johannesburg from Rome, I visited the CI's offices and met Naudé again. He was in his forties, a graceful person interested in what I had done in Chicago (not everyone back home was), and what I was planning to do in my future ministry. I mentioned that I was hoping to take my studies in Bonhoeffer further, and to become involved in the ecumenical struggle against apartheid. He invited me to join the CI, which I did, and to keep in touch. He also asked me to write some articles for *Pro Veritate* based on my dissertation. I subsequently did this, too.

A few days later Isobel, Stephen and I returned to Durban and were warmly welcomed back into the Sea View congregation. I had kept my promise to return. But what awaited us as we settled back into the manse and returned to the daily routine of ministry? I had much more clarity on how to resume my ministry, although I was aware that the challenge facing me was not going to be easy if I followed path I had set out in my dissertation. There was no denying that we had been changed by our year abroad, and South Africa had become a different country in our absence.

The ANC and the Pan Africanist Party (PAC) had been banned, and in June 1964 Nelson Mandela was found guilty of treason and imprisoned for life. The armed struggle had begun, and most of the ANC and PAC leaders were either in prison or in exile. The significance of this change dawned on me with considerable force when, soon after returning to Durban, I was invited to dinner at the home of one of our American Congregational missionaries, Bob Bergfalk. There I met the newly arrived US consul and two black lawyers, both of whom were members of the ANC. Soon the discussion turned to the armed struggle, and eventually to the question: Will the US government support the armed struggle? The consul's answer was evasive, but clearly negative.

As I drove home that night through the peaceful streets of Durban's white suburbia, I knew that we were all in for a rough time. How could I convey this to my congregation? How could I help them overcome the racial prejudices and anxieties that I had described in my dissertation? More broadly, how was I to participate in the emerging Confessing Church struggle about which Naudé was speaking so courageously? One of my deacons told me that I had changed as a result of being in America, and he was not sure he liked it. I could only nod in agreement; it would've been surprising if I had stayed the same.

Our daughter, Jeanelle, was born on 5 March 1965, so there was much to keep us busy on the home front. We regularly went to the beach and visited relatives. I did carpentry projects in my workshop, and we often spent Saturday evenings with George and June Booth and their family. George was our church secretary and June a surrogate mother to our children. We also had a close circle of friends outside the congregation; among them were Einar and Inger-Elise Ims, Lutheran missionaries from Norway, who were working in the Indian community in Chatsworth. We also found time for holidays down by the south coast with our friends Duncan and Naomi

Davidson. We had known them for a long time, and Duncan was now the Congregational minister in Glenashley, north of Durban.

In June 1965, with Steve and a three-month-old Jeanelle, we drove through southern Natal and the Transkei to the Federal Theological Seminary (FEDSEM), located in Alice near Fort Hare. FEDSEM had only recently been built to train black students for the Anglican, Congregational, Methodist and Presbyterian Churches. It was a pioneering ecumenical initiative, made essential because the government had taken control of Fort Hare. As a result, there was a very uneasy relationship between the two adjacent institutions, and ominous political clouds on the horizon did not bode well for the future. The seminary had an excellent faculty, good library, and the academic standards were high, as was the spirit among the students. I gave a lecture on Social Ethics and addressed many questions about the implications of what I had said for the struggle against apartheid. I was also introduced, in passing, to a young Desmond Tutu for the first time, though he probably doesn't remember me from back then. He had just returned from studying in London and was teaching at the seminary. On our way home, we had to drive through snow in the Transkei, but a winter in Chicago had prepared us well for this.

Pastoral life continued, but I increasingly felt unchallenged by the daily routine of ministry. I once again considered the possibility of returning to Chicago as Ross Snyder's teaching assistant and to work on a doctorate; but that was not financially feasible. In any case, we had resolved to stay put in South Africa. So instead, we established a Christian Institute study group, which attracted an interesting range of people, including several Catholic priests who were relishing their post-Vatican II freedom. On one occasion, Naudé visited our congregation and preached at an evening service. He also invited me to become a member of the editorial board of *Pro Veritate*. This frequently took me to Johannesburg, where I got to know others involved in the work of the CI, including its dynamic Cape Town director, Theo Kotze, a Methodist minister.

In the meantime, I became actively involved in the work of the Natal Council of Churches and got to know Philip Russell, who later became the Anglican archbishop of Cape Town. On several occasions, I attended Faith and Order discussions at the Lutheran Seminary in Maphumulo, Zululand, and at St. Joseph's Catholic Seminary in Cedara outside Pietermaritzburg. Father Garth Michelson, who taught Theology at St. Joseph's, became a good friend and was, in my book, a saint. St. Joseph's considered asking me to teach at the seminary, but Archbishop Hurley did not think a married Protestant could be easily accommodated. It was a nice idea, nonetheless.

In 1966 I was appointed as part-time chaplain at the University of Natal, along with Alex Boraine, director of the Methodist Youth Department. Alex and his wife, Jenny, had recently returned from the United States where they had lived for five years, during which time Alex did his doctorate at Drew University. We were kindred spirits. For two years Alex and I gave extra-mural evening lectures in Theology and on the Bible. These lectures took place on the university campus and were attended by over a hundred people, twice a week during term time. In addition, Isobel and I joined the Boraines in developing a multi-volume Sunday school curriculum project called *Breakthrough*. This was an ambitious venture, partly inspired by Ross Snyder, who visited Durban with his wife, Martha, at the invitation of the Methodist Youth Department.

An important ecumenical initiative among the churches during this period was the Christian Education and Leadership Training programme (CELT). CELT used insights gathered from sensitivity training to change perspectives and leadership styles in working for social transformation. I went to an early CELT course and suddenly realised that I was participating in something that I had experienced earlier at the University of Chicago. I kept this knowledge to myself, but evidently acted and spoke as someone who had good insight into what was going on. When it was later learnt by my group that I had "insider knowledge" I was shunned for the rest of my time there. Isobel, who was much more committed to CELT, still thinks I deserved what I got for not being upfront about my previous experience.

This was also the age of newfound sexual freedom, as the birth-control pill became readily available, and couples living together before marriage became widespread. *Playboy* magazine, which was banned in South Africa, and the British movie *Alfie* starring Michael Caine, which we saw in 1966, were chauvinistic trendsetters. In developing my understanding and critique of what was happening in secular culture, I read Harvey Cox's *The Secular City*, published in 1965, in which he argued that the process of secularisation was partly a result of the biblical tradition, but he was critical of the values of secularism. *The Secular City* is undoubtedly dated now, but it still has something important to say in today's world of religious fundamentalism.

Early on in my ministry, I had become friendly with several American Congregational missionaries, Lawrence and Carol Gilley among them. In turn, they introduced me to ministers in what was then known as the Bantu Congregational Church (BCC). Congregationalism, as I mentioned earlier, had been planted in South Africa by the LMS. In Natal and Zululand, however, it was established by missionaries of the American Board of Commissioners of Foreign Missions. The first mission station was established in Umlazi (now a township south of Durban) in 1836. Others soon followed and some fine schools, such as Adams College and Inanda Girls Seminary, were founded. John Dube, one of the first leaders of the ANC, was a

Congregational minister, and, as already mentioned, Albert Luthuli was a deacon at the Groutville Congregational Church where I preached on one occasion. Both had attended Adams.

In April 1966 I was invited to a pastors' conference in Mfanefile College, a small village deep in the heart of Zululand, to give a series of Bible studies on Law and Grace. This was a difficult assignment, because the theme challenged the legalism that had characterised Mission Churches ever since the early missionaries had formulated rules governing their life. I am not sure what the pastors made of my talks. Most of them were older than me and they all had more experience. In any case, the life and culture of their congregations were very different from that with which I was familiar. But it was a good experience for me, and my lectures were all translated and printed in Zulu.

A few months later, I was invited to give another series of Bible studies at the Annual General Conference of the African Independent Churches Association (AICA) held in Umlazi. This was even more challenging, because I had very little knowledge of what was then referred to as the AICs. However, the CI had begun a programme to help them improve their theological education, and a good friend from my Rhodes days, Danie van Zyl, was the programme's director. During the conference, Danie asked me whether I would consider joining the staff of the CI to help him in his work. There had already been some tentative enquiries from Beyers Naudé about my availability to join the CI staff, but now I had the chance to discuss the possibility with one of my peers who had already done so. It was an opportune moment, because I was feeling that my years at Sea View were drawing to a close, and there was no indication that I would soon receive a call to another congregation. But I was not ready to make any decisions.

With the ANC and PAC banned, the anti-apartheid ecumenical

churches had to take on some of the responsibility of leading the above-ground struggle against apartheid. Some churches and church leaders rose to the challenge, which was increasingly coordinated by the CI and the SACC. Since 1967, the latter was led by a new general secretary, Anglican Bishop Bill Burnett.

Burnett and Naudé attended the Church and Society Conference in Geneva in 1966, sponsored by the WCC. Upon their return to South Africa, they convened a number of conferences around the country to discuss the Church's role in the struggle, in the light of what had transpired in Geneva. They also established a working group to draft what became the *Message to the People of South Africa*. I participated in one of the conferences in Johannesburg and another at the Catholic monastery in Mariannhill, and once again felt attracted to joining the staff of the CI or maybe the SACC. Soon afterwards, I met Bishop Burnett in Durban and discussed the latter possibility with him.

At the beginning of 1967, Steve started his first year at the Sea View Primary School, virtually opposite our garden gate. On the day, Isobel and I, with two-year-old Jeanelle, gathered in our driveway to wave him goodbye as he set off across the narrow road, carrying his small brown school case and proudly wearing a school uniform for the first time. Isobel was heavily pregnant, as photographs of that auspicious day remind us. In due course, Anton was born on 5 March, and a few weeks later he was baptised by Alex Boraine in our church. Isobel and I agreed that our family was now complete. From birth, all three children were different in character, but they were all born in Sea View and baptised in the church there, so for that reason alone it has always had a special place in our hearts.

In October 1967, CUSA united with the churches established by the LMS in Botswana, as well as with the Bantu Congregational Church, to become the United Congregational Church of Southern

Africa (UCCSA) – a denomination that extended into Namibia, Zimbabwe and Mozambique. The new church elected Joseph Wing as its general secretary, and it was largely due to his selfless devotion that the UCCSA began to play a more important role in the ecumenical and social witness of the Church in South Africa.

Joe Wing was one of the last of a great line of life-long LMS missionaries who had come to southern Africa from Britain. He arrived in 1951 and spent his whole life completely dedicated to the sub-continent, its peoples, the UCCSA and their wider ecumenical family. He was one of the unsung heroes of the church struggle, and was widely and highly respected. I had the privilege of working closely with him, and he had a great influence on Steve. After Joe's untimely death in 1992, Steve wrote a fine and extensive biographical essay in his memory.[12]

Early in 1968, I received a phone call from Beyers Naudé formally inviting me to join the CI staff in Johannesburg. I was honoured and keen to accept, but at the same time Bishop Burnett asked me to join the staff of the SACC as director of Communication and Studies. I agonised over this dilemma for several weeks and had several more phone conversations with Naudé and Burnett. But then, after consultation with Joe Wing, who was both a CI member and an executive member of the SACC, I accepted Burnett's invitation. The position at the SACC provided an opportunity to work more directly with the churches, and it was combined with the role of secretary of the recently formed Church Unity Commission (CUC). I had already become involved in the work of the CUC, which was tasked with seeking the union of the Anglican, Congregational, Methodist and Presbyterian Churches, and I was excited about serving it in this way. I was about to become a full-time ecumenical activist, and to be thrown in at the deep end.

7

Thrown in at the deep end

> During the years of the struggle against apartheid it was increasingly clear what was required of us, and we found our unity in that struggle ... we became the ecumenical church in South Africa ... a community of churches and Christians who were united in our witness to the gospel around a common cause.
>
> (From my essay "Becoming the Ecumenical Church")[13]

We moved to Johannesburg in August 1968 and lived in a modest house in Blairgowrie, a new suburb then, without any tarred roads. It was a good place to bring up our family, with schools conveniently nearby. Life in suburbia was different from life in a manse adjacent to the Sea View Church. I had a long bus commute every day to work and back home again. Isobel had to carve out a new existence for herself, and now lived near her father, stepmother, brothers Alan and John and their families. We had to establish a garden and find a niche for ourselves in the community. For the first time, I was able to buy some power tools, and in no time I had my workshop up and running.

Soon after we settled in, Isobel's sister, Elsie, and her husband, Ron Steel, came to live in Johannesburg. Like us, they had courted each other at Rhodes, and Ron had now accepted a call to the Florida and Turffontein Congregational Churches. We would spend many a Sunday afternoon together, and formed a very close bond that has lasted throughout the years.

The same week that we arrived in Blairgowrie, I began work at the SACC. Its offices were located in Dunwell House, Braamfontein, one floor below the CI, and within walking distance of the centre of Johannesburg and the University of the Witwatersrand. My first assignment was to arrange a press conference at which the *Message to the People of South Africa* was to be launched. The boardroom was crammed with newspaper reporters listening to Burnett and Naudé. I had to chair the event, and I remember thinking to myself that I was suddenly sitting in a very hot seat.

During the next few days, the *Message* made headlines around the country, and soon provoked an angry response from Prime Minister B.J. Vorster. He warned us not to try and follow the path taken by Martin Luther King, Jr. in the United States.

The *Message* pronounced that apartheid was a false gospel contrary to the Christian faith, and declared that the Church had an obligation to reject segregation and seek reconciliation across the racial and ethnic divides. Not since Cottesloe was there such a furore around a church or theological statement. It was not a revolutionary document, but its rejection of apartheid was unequivocal. By no means were all churches in agreement with what it said. The DRC was clearly opposed, and so was the Baptist Union, which withdrew its membership from the SACC. Many white members of SACC churches were also critical.

My immediate responsibility, together with staff members from the CI, was to respond to these criticisms and to work out ways to distribute the *Message* more widely. This involved travelling to various parts of the country – something I usually combined with my work for the CUC. I also edited and published a book of essays entitled *The Message in Perspective*, in which the issues were explored in some depth. So within a few months of joining the staff of the SACC, my life as an ecumenical activist was in full swing. But my commitment to the task was suddenly put to the test by an unexpected turn of events.

On one of my early trips, I found myself sitting next to William Maxwell, my old professor at Rhodes, on a plane from Durban to Port Elizabeth. He invited me to visit him and his wife for dinner in Grahamstown, which was on my schedule. I did so, and during the evening, right out of the blue, he asked me to apply for a vacant position as lecturer in Theology at Rhodes, and virtually assured me of an appointment. I was honoured but had a sleepless night. The next day, I was encouraged further by Professor Hewson to accept the offer. He and Maxwell even introduced me to the vice-chancellor as their preferred candidate.

It was outrageous of me to contemplate doing this, but I was so excited by the possibility that I threw common sense and caution to the wind. Phone calls, first to Isobel, and then to Bishop Burnett, soon brought me down to earth, as did a conversation in which I learnt that Basil Moore, a far better candidate than me, had applied and been rejected for being "too radical". I hastened back to Johannesburg, and within a matter of days informed Maxwell that I could not let my name go forward. I was disappointed, but soon glad that I had withdrawn. It would have been morally wrong, both in terms of my contractual obligations to the SACC and what I now knew about Moore's application; it would also have prevented me from participating in the life and work of the SACC just as the church struggle was moving up a gear; and, in any case, I was not yet adequately equipped or ready to enter the academy any more than I had been to become a pastor when I did.

While at the SACC, I continued my pastoral ministry as part-time minister of a congregation in the semi-urban northern suburb of Bryanston. After a few years, our congregation united with the local Presbyterian congregation to become St. Mungo's United Church, and I became an honorary associate minister. The united congregation had more than a thousand members and forty elders. Des Clynick, a Presbyterian, was the senior minister and a good, caring pastor. Isobel and I found a home in the congregation and made many friends, some of whom have remained so over the years, amongst them Mike and Marijke Kirby, and Alan and June Wentzel.

As if I did not have enough to do, I also decided to register at the University of South Africa (UNISA) in Pretoria to obtain a doctorate. This time I determined to do whatever it took to complete it, and to do so within three years. I took the preliminary oral examinations and submitted a proposal. The topic was a critical comparison of the ecclesiologies of Karl Barth and Dietrich Bonhoeffer within the framework of the South African church struggle. This was prompted by a question in Bethge's Alden-Tuthill lectures as to whether Bonhoeffer's engagement with the WCC in Geneva – especially with its general secretary, W.A. Visser 't Hooft – could inform the post-Cottesloe church debate in South Africa. My topic was approved and Professors Johannes Lombard (a former student of Barth's) and Brian Johanson were appointed as my co-supervisors. Burnett was understandably unhappy about this extra commitment, but I argued that it was important for my work at the SACC.

In 1969 I was a delegate to the All Africa Conference of Churches'

(AACC) Assembly in Abidjan, Ivory Coast, and was elected an alternate member of the council of the AACC. I subsequently participated in several meetings in other parts of Africa that were closed to most, especially white, South Africans.

On one occasion I went to Liberia. Although I had been refused a visa, in those days you could board the plane without that being checked, so I simply went ahead. On arrival in Monrovia, however, the passport control officials laughed in my face for thinking that I could enter. The situation was becoming tense when, out of a side door, Burgess Carr, the general secretary of the AACC and a Liberian himself, appeared, grabbed my arm and hurried me through the door into the outside car park.

During a banquet in honour of the council members, I was invited to sit next to William R. Tolbert, Jr., the president of Liberia. He warmly quizzed me about the situation in South Africa. He also asked me if I had had any difficulties at the airport, and I thought it best to assure him that I had not.

A few days later, as I once again went through passport control, I encountered the same official who was on duty when I tried to enter. He looked at my passport, informed me that it had not been stamped, so he could not stamp it now, because, he said, "You have not been to Liberia." Then he added, "Have a good flight!"

Following the publication of the *Message,* the CI and SACC jointly initiated a project to work out its practical implications. Named Sprocas (Study Project on Christianity and Society), it brought together many leaders from universities, churches, business, political parties and NGOs to debate the issues and make concrete proposals. There were six commissions: political, education, law, economics, society and church; each worked independently, but they were co-ordinated by Peter Randall, a well-informed director based at Dunwell House.

I was secretary of the church commission and would eventually draft the report, together with Douglas Bax and Brian Johanson.

Spro-cas was an ambitious undertaking, which took several years to complete. In the process, they also launched the Black Community Programmes initiative, led by Bennie Khoapa, as well as a variety of action-orientated projects across the country. Spro-cas demonstrated that the *Message* was not idealistic theological rhetoric; it could inform concrete practice. Whether or not its proposals had any impact on the political process is difficult to say, but it might well have done.

Working at the SACC, in close proximity to the CI and the Black Theology Project, daily brought us in contact with what was going on in the country. Dunwell House was a convenient meeting place for activists and many international ecumenical and anti-apartheid visitors. Among them were the general secretary of the WCC, Visser 't Hooft, and Michael Ramsey, the archbishop of Canterbury, who smuggled some highly confidential documents through customs under his purple cassock.

But Dunwell House was also a "one-stop" place for the security police. On several occasions, our offices were raided, our phones were tapped, my mail was regularly opened, and although I was never personally assaulted or imprisoned, there was a file on my activities in the security police head office at John Vorster Square. According to my informant, it was reasonably fat.

Discussions with members of the Black Theology Project – notably with one of its leaders, Basil Moore – introduced me to Gustavo Gutierrez's *A Theology of Liberation* and some of James Cone's early writings on black theology. At the same time, my involvement in the AACC introduced me to developments in African theology around the continent, as expressed in the work of John Mbiti, John Pobee, and Gabriel Setiloane, later a colleague at UCT. I was entering a new world of theological enquiry for which my own theological education had not really prepared me.

Sometime in 1969, I was approached by a Johannesburg travel agency to join a group of church editors on a tour of the Holy Land. There were two from DRC magazines, a Seventh Day Adventist and myself as editor of the monthly SACC ecumenical broadsheet, *Kairos*. The only condition was that we should write and publish articles on our visit after our return. I guessed, rightly, that the tour was being funded by some Israeli government agency committed to improving Israel's image abroad within Christian circles after the Six-Day War in 1967. But as I had long dreamt of doing what pilgrims have done over the centuries, I was delighted to accept without too many reservations.

We had a wonderful ten days in Israel. Led by a well-informed guide, we were taken to most of the main historic sites, from Galilee to Jerusalem. We visited the Dead Sea, Masada and the Qumran caves. We stayed on kibbutzim, toured the Golan Heights, and after our arrival in Jerusalem we had dinner with some high-ranking official at the King David Hotel. We had arrived late on the Saturday evening, and briefly visited the Western Wall below the Dome of the Rock, but I had no real sense of the city. Early the next day, I woke to discover that my room looked down on the city from the Mount of Olives, and I saw the ancient walls flooded in sunlight. It was an unforgettable sight.

As our tour progressed, I was increasingly bothered by the plight of the Palestinians and sometimes annoyed by the presentation of the "Israeli point of view", which glossed over many questions. One evening, in discussion with a venerable leader at a religious kibbutz, I asked what he thought the prophets of old might say to Israel today.

I asked it diplomatically, sensing that as a Christian I probably had no right to ask such a loaded question. I was still taken by surprise by his angry response. I later wrote two articles about the visit, both of them positive about the experience, but I could not avoid raising my concerns about the Palestinian question.

In April 1970, I revisited FEDSEM in Alice to give the graduation address, which I entitled "From ferment to growth: Today's challenge to the Ministry." By then the campus was well-established. That was the hey-day of FEDSEM's life and the hall was packed with students, faculty members and guests for the occasion. I have often wondered what has happened to all those who graduated that day, and whether my words were of any help as they began their own journey into the ministry. Not long afterwards, the FEDSEM campus was expropriated by the government and, after a sojourn in Umtata, was relocated to Pietermaritzburg.

During my years at the SACC, I was a consultant for the WCC Faith and Order Commission. One of the first conferences I attended was in Limuru, Kenya, where I met and became friendly with Martin Cressey of the United Reformed Church in England and Wales. He later became the principal of Westminster College in Cambridge. I also got to know Lukas Vischer, the secretary general of the commission. He was an excellent scholar and theologian, proficient in several languages, and remarkably clear and precise in his formulation of issues.

In 1970 Isobel and I received a travel fellowship from the CI, which enabled us to visit Europe for six weeks during August and September. I went ahead of Isobel to participate in a Faith and Order Conference in Louvain, Belgium. At the conference I heard, among others, a presentation by Professor Joseph Ratzinger, later Pope Benedict XVI, and a sermon by the graciously ecumenical Cardinal

Suenens. Looking again at the list of participants, I must have rubbed shoulders with many of the leading theologians of the time, often without knowing it. But I did briefly get to know the Latin American liberation theologian, José Miguéz Bonino, an Argentinean Methodist, whose work I had already read with interest. Years later, I hosted Míguez when he visited Cape Town in the early 1990s, and wrote an essay for his Festschrift when he turned seventy.

Isobel joined me in Brussels, and from there we went to various ecumenical and university centres in Holland, Sweden, Hamburg, Berlin and London. Those were heady days in the ecumenical and anti-apartheid movements, and the two often intersected. We met many interesting people and I spoke at various meetings about the church situation in South Africa. Among these was one in Uppsala at the Church of Sweden Mission house, where several missionaries who had worked in Natal were present. That was when I first became aware of the significant role that Sweden and the Church of Sweden were playing in the anti-apartheid movement.

At the end of our visit to Europe, we travelled by a winding route to the home of Eberhard and Renate Bethge in Rengsdorf, Germany, where Eberhard was in charge of a continuing education programme for ministers. I had been in correspondence with him about my dissertation, and we were warmly invited to visit. We stayed in the nearby church hotel for a week, during which time I had several discussions with Eberhard and was privileged to see the originals of some of Bonhoeffer's letters from prison. This visit led to a friendship of many years. Without him knowing it, Eberhard became my unofficial *doktorvater*.

Not long after this overseas trip, I received a call from Alex Boraine, who was then president of the Methodist Church. He was phoning from Jan Smuts Airport (now named O.R. Tambo) outside

Johannesburg, and was on his way home to Durban from a meeting in Geneva. He asked me to meet him, as he had some important information to share with the SACC, which he could not divulge over the phone. I hastened out to the airport – a long trek by car – and we had coffee together. He then told me that, at the meeting, the WCC had decided to launch a Programme to Combat Racism (PCR), which would financially support liberation movements, including the ANC. The matter was hush-hush, as no official announcement had yet been made. We both knew what the implications of this decision would be for the member churches of the WCC in South Africa, as well as for the SACC. When I told Bishop Burnett, he informed me that he had some inkling of this, but had received no official word.

Shortly after my meeting with Boraine, we had a fraternal visit from Eugene Carson Blake, who was the newly appointed general secretary of the WCC. In anticipation, I travelled to Stellenbosch to meet J.S. Gericke, a member of the Moderature of the DRC and rector of Stellenbosch University. My task was to ask him if he would invite Blake to meet with the rest of the DRC leadership in Cape Town. Gericke agreed to do so, and after Blake's arrival I accompanied him to Cape Town for the meeting. It was held at the synodical offices in Queen Victoria Street, in the office of Koot Vorster, the elder brother of the prime minister, and an arch-conservative defender of apartheid. I was not included in the discussion, but Blake had told me that he was making an effort to restore relations between the WCC and the DRC which, after Cottesloe, had collapsed. On the plane back to Johannesburg, Blake said that his mission was worthwhile and he had been invited to return.

It was only after Blake had left the country that an official statement was made in Geneva about the launch of the Programme to Combat Racism (PCR) – something he had not mentioned to the

DRC leadership or the SACC. Virtually everyone was taken by surprise. Now we had to deal with angry attacks from the government, with Prime Minister Vorster taking the lead, as well as attacks from the DRC. The member churches of the WCC and SACC were in crisis. While their black constituency was hugely supportive of the WCC decision, many white members were horrified: Their churches were supporting terrorism! Sensing a growing split in their ranks, the prime minister turned the screws more tightly, demanding that the church leaders withdraw their churches' membership from the WCC.

To their credit, none of the churches withdrew, though some came close to doing so. Many white members, however, decided that this was an opportune moment to leave their denominations or withdraw financial support, and some migrated to more conservative churches that, they said, were not "involved in politics". They were, of course, for by being silent or siding with the government, also being political. Sadly my old home congregation, Union Church in Cape Town, along with a few other congregations, decided to leave the UCCSA, under the influence of the Gospel Defence League. From then on, I was an *enfant terrible*, labelled a communist, and no longer welcome in any of these congregations.

At this time, the Charismatic Renewal Movement was rapidly spreading through many of the mainstream denominations in South Africa, as it was across the world. Emphasising the power of the Holy Spirit to transform Christian life and renew the Church, the movement encouraged speaking in tongues and other more ecstatic gifts of the Spirit. In some ways, it was a reaction to the political engagement of those denominations who were politically active in the church struggle against apartheid.

In 1970 Bill Burnett resigned as general secretary of the SACC to become the bishop of Grahamstown. It was there that he unexpectedly became a leader in the Charismatic Movement, partly in reaction to the extent to which politics had come to dominate much of church life. For him, the Renewal was not an escape from the struggle for justice, but engaging in it differently. I was not too convinced about this. On one of my subsequent visits to Grahamstown, I stayed with Burnett and his wife, and after dinner he shared his experience of "baptism in the Spirit" with me. I was moved by what he said, but not able to respond in the way I think he had hoped.

Burnett was succeeded at the SACC by a dynamic Methodist lay leader, John Rees. John had little theological training, and in addition he was working for the government in what was then called Bantu Administration; so there was some reservation about his appointment. He did, however, have extensive connections with people living in the black townships. He had also been to the WCC Assembly in Uppsala in 1968 as a Methodist delegate, and he had caught something of the ecumenical and social vision of that milestone event. The SACC staff members were pleased that, after several months, we had a new leader who brought fresh energy to the job, and who was an excellent administrator and good colleague. John eventually left the SACC to work in the NGO sector, and some years later he died relatively young of cancer.

My work, both for the SACC and the CUC, took me to all parts of the country, which gave me a better perspective on what was happening – something I would never have had gained otherwise. I came to know virtually all the church leaders of that time, including some rather dour and blinkered Dutch Reformed ones (so different from Naudé and the DRC leaders of today, many of whom are my good friends). I must have preached in virtually all the Anglican cathedrals in the country and attended more synods and conferences than I care to recall.

Every year we held a full meeting of the CUC, which brought together around forty or fifty church leaders and scholars from the participating denominations. These week-long residential gatherings were stimulating, and there was a great willingness to overcome the centuries of division that had kept the churches apart. Given our South African context, there was an urgency to do so.

During these years I became close to Anglican Archbishop Robert Selby Taylor, president of the SACC and chair of the CUC. I had first met him at an exploratory church union conference held at Modderpoort in the Free State, back in 1967. I arrived late at this remote mission school complex after a long and hot drive from Durban. I was hot, my suit looked shabby, and I hastily put on my tie as the dinner bell rang. The only seat available in the dining hall was next to this distinguished-looking prelate, who beckoned me, the youngest delegate by far, to occupy it. When I sat down the tip of my tie promptly dropped into the soup in front of me. Selby Taylor raised his impressive eyebrows, but said nothing. Embarrassed, I gingerly lifted my tie, rung it dry and continued to eat. From then on, until the end of Selby Taylor's life, we were on friendly terms.

Selby Taylor was one of the last of a long line of aristocratic high-church bishops who initially came to Africa as missionaries. A shy person, he was deeply concerned about racial justice, and equally committed to church unity. He would later support the ordination of women, even though it went against the grain of his own high-church ethos. He was firm in his opposition to apartheid and his commitment to ending it. I should mention that Mandela, on the day of his release from prison, visited Selby Taylor in the company of Desmond Tutu (then archbishop of Cape Town).

Our family connection with the Mennonites was unexpectedly renewed when, in December 1971, I was invited to lecture at the

Mennonite Southern African Workers' Retreat in Mbabane, Swaziland. These workers from the US and Canada were involved in various rural development projects. As a result, there was growing contact between them and my colleague at the SACC, Ron Legg, who was in charge of the development desk. Ron could not go to Swaziland for the retreat, so I was invited in his place. As always, we found these mostly young and always energetic Mennonites exceptionally fine people, and enjoyed being with them. My lectures must have been well received, otherwise the consequences of our visit would not have been what they were. I will say more about that shortly.

For political reasons, the South African government was loath to introduce television in the country, even though its advent was inevitable. With this in mind, the executive of the SACC asked me, as director of communications, to convene a workshop on the role of the churches in television in South Africa. I was able to invite Ronald Faulkner, a Church of Scotland minister who directed religious TV for the Scottish BBC, to visit South Africa and lead the event. There was widespread interest in his visit, and the workshop proved to be a success. The South African Broadcasting Corporation (SABC) sent their religious programmes director (a DRC minister), and I was hopeful that there could be an ecumenical approach to religious television in due course. Following his visit, Faulkner invited me to Scotland and introduced me to his work. But soon after my return I was told in no uncertain terms that the government would not allow the SACC to play any role in religious TV.

In April 1973 I arranged for the Bethges to visit South Africa for a month, under the auspices of the SACC. Eberhard had met Beyers Naudé at the founding International Bonhoeffer Congress in Düsseldorf, Germany, the year before, and he was keen to renew contact. I was with them when they met at Naudé's office. Afterwards,

Eberhard told me that Naudé reminded him of Bonhoeffer; he was, in fact, South Africa's Bonhoeffer. During his stay, Eberhard gave a series of lectures that I later edited and published as *Bonhoeffer: Exile & Martyr*. At his invitation, I included an essay on "Bonhoeffer in South Africa" – my first Bonhoeffer essay to be published.

Meanwhile, I had completed my doctoral dissertation,[14] graduating in April 1972. At the same ceremony in Pretoria, Isobel obtained her Higher Education Diploma with six distinctions, for which she received much more applause than I did. My parents came from Cape Town for the occasion, so we had a good family celebration. Having earned a doctorate in Theology I was entitled to become a member of the Dogmatologiese Werkgemeenskap van Suid-Afrika (Theological Society of South Africa). The society was one of several catering for the various theological disciplines. Established mainly by DRC theologians, Afrikaans was the default language of communication. I joined partly because I thought membership was necessary if I was to understand the mind of Afrikaner theology. One of the major figures in the society was Professor Johan Heyns from the University of Pretoria, who was beginning play an important role in ecumenical and political developments within his church.

I had previously joined the more progressive Missiological Society, which had been founded and was led by the well-respected DRC missionary scholar David Bosch. I regularly attended the society's annual conference and discovered it to be far more contextually engaged and progressive. This was partly due to Bosch's leadership, but also because many white DRC missionaries were acutely aware of the harsh realities of apartheid through their work alongside black colleagues in the DR Mission Churches in black townships and rural areas.

Through these engagements, I became increasingly aware that there was a lack of English-speaking theologians doing serious theological work in South Africa. Indicative of this was the fact that there were several theological journals published in Afrikaans, there were none in English, apart from two which focused on mission work. To rectify this glaring gap, I founded and launched the *Journal of Theology for Southern Africa* (*JTSA*) in December 1972, and became its first editor. The *JTSA* has, I think, fulfilled its purpose and played an important role in the development of theology in South Africa.[15]

Shortly before launching the *JTSA*, I visited UCT to publicise it and elicit contributions. During my conversations with John Cumpsty, head of the recently established Department of Religious Studies, I was asked if I would be interested in teaching at UCT. He was particularly interested in the fact that I had done some graduate work on the Indian religious tradition. As academic positions in Religious Studies (to say nothing of Theology at English-speaking institutions) were few and far in between, and as I was beginning to think that maybe my future lay at the university, I let my name go forward for consideration. Perhaps now was the opportune moment to enter the academy.

There was a risk involved, though: The position being offered was for a one-year contract in a field of study in which I was not a specialist. Not only would Isobel and I have had to sell our house in Johannesburg, but we would also have had to move with our three children to Cape Town without any promise of a permanent position. And if I was to have a long-term future at UCT, I would have to research and publish in a relatively unfamiliar area.

The thought of going was tough for Isobel, not least because it meant leaving her wider family behind. She had also developed other interests that made her reluctant to leave. I was chauvinistic enough to assume that she would dutifully follow, which she did, though not without voicing her misgivings.

I had yet to conclude my work at the SACC and tender my resignation to John Rees and the executive committee. When I did so, I was asked to continue as editor of the *JTSA* on condition that it maintained its ecumenical and scholarly character. I was also asked to stay on as caretaker secretary of the CUC for the forthcoming year, which I agreed to do.

There were also a few other things to wrap up before my work at the SACC was complete. The evangelistic organisation African Enterprise (AE) – led by the widely respected lay-Anglican evangelist Michael Cassidy – along with the SACC under John Rees's leadership, had long envisioned a major Congress on Mission and Evangelism. I was a member of the planning committee, which included a number of church leaders and theologians selected from the SACC and AE ranks, most notably David Bosch. The congress was held at the Durban Central Methodist Church, and was attended by over five hundred participants, spanning almost all the denominations and theological perspectives in the country, as well as representing the various racial groupings. But unfortunately the DRC and the Roman Catholic Churches declined to participate officially. There were many overseas visitors, including Hans-Ruedi Weber of the WCC, whose daily Bible studies set the tone for each day's proceedings. Justice du Plessis, well-known as "Mr Pentecostal", was among the speakers, as was Billy Graham, who also preached at a mass rally in the rugby stadium. I had an opportunity to meet Graham briefly. He certainly had an aura about him, but his staff seemed to be constantly protecting him from engaging with others.

For me, the most noteworthy moment at the congress was the paper presented by a staff member of the CI and the leading black theologian of the time, Manas Buthelezi. Buthelezi set out six theses on what evangelisation meant in South Africa from the perspective of a black Christian. He declared that it was "time for the black man to evangelise and humanise the white man". This required, inter alia, taking over leadership in the churches and shaping policy. It must have been the first time that some conservative white church leaders had heard anything like this. Immediately after Buthelezi spoke, there was an uproar that led the black delegates to withdraw and meet elsewhere, while the rest of us heatedly engaged with one another over apartheid. Eventually black and white came together again, but the gulf remained.

There was one overseas journey to be made prior to our departure to Cape Town. At the invitation of Desmond Tutu, I went to Bromley in London at the end of 1972, to participate in a meeting of the Theological Education Fund, of which Tutu was then the African secretary. This arose out of my increasing involvement at the SACC in helping to coordinate an ecumenical approach to theological education. When I arrived in Bromley, Tutu met me at the station and insisted on carrying my suitcase to the taxi! I was understandably delighted when he became dean of Johannesburg in 1975. Soon after, he invited me to lunch in a "whites only" hotel restaurant. We walked in together, much to the consternation of the white patrons but to the applause of the black waiters. After all, he was dean of Johannesburg.

Axel-Ivar Berglund, a Swedish Lutheran missiologist of note who had long been involved with the African Independent Churches and in theological education in Zululand, was appointed my successor at the SACC. And so, after four and a half very eventful and formative years in Johannesburg, we set off by car on the long journey south into an uncertain future. But I had my doctorate, and we were headed towards the city I loved.

PART TWO

Through extraordinary times

1973-1990

> There comes a time in history, in the history of the church ... when words must end and be transformed into deeds. And if that time is serious enough, the deed will be an extraordinary one. We are living in such a time. We do not know whether there is still time, but we must hurry – the bell has already tolled.
>
> (B.B. Keet)[1]

8

An aspiring academic

> Academic work is one of those fields which contain a pearl so precious that it is worthwhile to sell all our possessions, keeping nothing for ourselves, in order to be able to acquire it.
>
> (Simone Weil)[2]

I started at UCT in May 1973. The Department of Religious Studies was in the Arts building, and my office was near the lecture room where I had heard my first lectures in Philosophy seventeen years ago. Soon after my arrival, there was a knock on my door. In walked "the boss", my old SACS headmaster, Robin Whiteford, who taught me Latin and coached me at cricket and hockey. Back then, he was feared by all and could be excessively sarcastic. But not on this day.

"De Gruchy," he declared, "the tables have turned. I am now a part-time junior lecturer in Classics, and you are a senior lecturer!" Wishing me well, he was soon gone.

I never saw him again, but I was grateful for his affirmation. I always thought he regarded me as intellectually challenged.

The department was established in 1969. Apart from me, there were only two on the teaching staff. John Cumpsty, a Yorkshire man, was the head. He had a brilliant mind and soon built up a strong medium-sized department. John Painter, an Australian New Testament scholar, returned to a distinguished career "down under" a few years after I arrived, and was replaced by Chuck Wanamaker, an American.

I already had good friends in other departments. Among them were the sociologist Mike Savage, whose irreverent humour has always attracted me; the economist and keen ecumenist Francis Wilson, whose work on poverty has become a benchmark; and the anthropologist Martin West. I was invited to share the Social Anthropology common room. Monica Wilson, professor and head of the department, made me feel welcome and hosted a dinner for us. A distinguished scholar and devout Anglican, Monica had attended the Second Assembly of the WCC in Evanston, Illinois, in 1954, when apartheid was first debated. Upon her retirement, she gave me all her ecumenical conference papers, which subsequently came in useful in my own work.

My main task was to teach the Indian Religious Tradition to undergraduates. During the five years I did so, the first-year class generally numbered about 250 students, and there was a lecture every day, sometimes given twice. At that time, when some students were turning eastwards in search of a guru, there was considerable interest in my lectures on the *Upanishads* and *Bhagavad-Gita*, as well as the history and tenets of Buddhism. But the latter's psychological depths required more expertise than I had. As the students were from diverse backgrounds, I considered it inappropriate to foreground my own faith convictions. When a student asked me what I was, I simply said, "Listen to what I say and see if you can work that out." I am not sure if she ever did.

Apart from teaching Religious Traditions, each member of the department had to lecture on a variety of other subjects. My favourites were those on the Secular Critique of Religion, and the Psychology of Religion. But I soon had numbers of graduate students interested in Christian Theology, so most of my research and writing began to focus in this area.

Soon after arriving in Cape Town, I became the honorary associate minister at the Rondebosch Congregational Church (which later became the Rondebosch United Church, as I shall tell), located near UCT. The minister was Geoffrey Dunstan who came from London. He confided in me that I had been considered by the church prior to them calling him, but they had decided I was too young. As he was only two years older than me, I suspect what really counted was that he came from the "home country". I couldn't complain, though. I had become an academic, and an associate minister at the church that had turned me down. From then on the Rondebosch Church became our spiritual home, but I will refrain from trying to describe our involvement from week to week, the high and low moments in worship, the friends we made, the tears, joys and laughter we shared, the meetings we attended and the sermons I preached.

I immediately agreed when Archbishop Selby-Taylor invited me to join the board of the newly formed St. George's Cathedral Centre, tasked with fostering fresh initiatives in ministry to the city. The board, chaired by the outstanding Dean Ted King, was made up of a creative group of people. On occasion, the nave became a theatre in which thoughtful productions were staged, including Beckett's *Waiting for Godot*. We recommended plans for extending the cathedral building, turned the crypt into a coffee shop and introduced an additional monthly Sunday choral Eucharist. We initiated a series of evening public lectures, and I taught some courses in Theology for lay people. Soon we were able to appoint a Methodist minister, Jim Leatt, to develop a ministry to the business community (he later joined our department at UCT). The centre was an exciting venture, but the congregation was ambivalent, as was Bill Burnett who succeeded Selby-Taylor as archbishop in 1974. Eventually the centre was disbanded before it could fully achieve its goals.

I decided to grow a beard and join the Progressive Party. These were unrelated, but I mention the first because, like my grandfather, I have had a beard ever since. The Progressive Party, or Progs, had had some success in the elections in 1973, and my friend Alex Boraine was elected to Parliament. Alex, Jenny and their family then moved to Cape Town and lived relatively close to us. I was elected chair of the Rosebank branch of the party and served in that capacity for two years, during which time I was also part of a monthly think-tank convened by Colin Eglin, the party leader. The Progs had some fine, hard-working members committed to a more just society, but I resigned when the party united with Harry Schwarz's Reform Party to form the Progressive Federal Party.

Those who opposed apartheid in Parliament achieved some minor successes, but the cards were stacked against them. Unlike Parliament and its political parties, the churches I was associated with were at least racially mixed, and provided me a better space within which to participate in the struggle against apartheid.

In October 1973 I went to Spain for a WCC Faith and Order Conference held in Salamanca. En route, I visited the Bethges in Rengsdorf. They took me to Schwäbisch Hall, the Bonhoeffer ancestral home. On our way there, we visited the cathedral in Worms where Martin Luther defied the Roman Catholic authorities in 1521. In Tübingen we visited Jürgen Moltmann, whose *Theology of Hope* taught me that Christian hope is a way of living and acting in anticipation of what God intended the world to be. I invited Moltmann to visit South Africa, which he did in 1975, and we became good friends.

The Bethges finally took me to Frankfurt Airport, from where I left for Spain. As we said our farewells, Eberhard reminded me that Bonhoeffer always refused going to Faith and Order meetings, because they avoided debate on social and political issues that divided the churches. That was still the case, but it was becoming an untenable position.

During the conference, we were taken to Avila to visit St. Theresa's convent, and then to the Spanish Civil War headquarters of General Franco. Such excursions are great conference perks, but the relics of saints and the memorials of generals are not to my taste. More to my liking was walking around the colonnaded piazza in the old city of Salamanca one Friday evening with hundreds of others, deep in conversation about family and business transactions. Years later, while writing *Christianity, Art and Transformation*, I recalled that evening and bemoaned the fact that the road systems in modern cities have largely destroyed such communal spaces.

Soon after starting at UCT, I received an invitation to speak at a meeting on conflict resolution. There I met two DRC scholars, Jaap Durand and Bernard Lategan, from the Faculty of Theology at the University of the Western Cape (UWC). I spoke on relationships between the DRC and English-speaking churches. This later became my first academic journal article[3], and my meeting with Durand and Lategan turned into life-long friendships.

I also visited the Kweekskool in Stellenbosch that year in order to continue my membership in the Dogmatologiese Werkgemeenskap. I had not been back there since I went as a student to attend the Kweekskool centenary celebrations. My memories are of sitting in the curatorium around a massive boardroom table, observed by illustrious and heavily bearded professors of past generations whose photographs covered the walls. I was invariably the only

AN ASPIRING ACADEMIC

other bearded person in the room, as short-back and sides was the order of the day in such conservative circles. The senior theologian, Professor F.J.M. Potgieter, was a learned gentleman, but a dedicated apartheid apologist with whom I disagreed about most things. I was made welcome, but sensed I was an outsider. At the Kweekskool I also came to know the professor of Missions, Nico Smith, who was appointed as a "safe candidate", but then broke with the Broederbond and joined the CI. He did not last long at Stellenbosch. Another good friend was the more cautious but excellent and gracious professor of Theology, Willie Jonker.

For several years, I was a regular participant in the *gespreksgroep* (dialogue group) hosted by Johan Degenaar, a philosopher of note at Stellenbosch University. As a result, I was privileged to meet other Afrikaner academics – few of them theologians, but all invariably (if cautiously) critical of apartheid. There was a handful of UCT academics who shared in these evenings, marked almost as much by good wine and food as they were by lively discussion and provocative papers. Degenaar was a brilliant Socratic conversationalist, who kept on posing questions rather than offering solutions. I think I was a little arrogant in my certainties, and probably reinforced the impression that Stellenbosch academics then had of English-speaking academics.

I visited Degenaar at his home one afternoon. Suddenly a furious Professor Keet burst into his lounge. He had been attacked for his enlightened views in the *Kerkbode* – a DRC monthly – by the editor Andries Treurnicht, an arch-apartheid ideologist and church leader. It was a venomous article and Keet wanted advice on what to do. I was introduced to this legendary man, and spent the rest of the afternoon listening to him and Degenaar passionately discuss the issue over coffee.

One evening I was invited to dinner in Stellenbosch by Jaap Durand and his wife, Randu, who, sadly, died of cancer a few years later. The occasion was the visit of American theologian Paul Crow, who asked me to arrange a meeting with Afrikaner intellectuals. It was a fine evening, the *bobotie* (a Cape speciality) was delicious and the conversation lively. But then, in order to help Paul better understand Afrikanerdom, I remarked that those from the Orange Free State were usually more conservative or *verkramp*, than the *verligtes* (enlightened ones) from the Cape.

In his amiable manner, Jaap interjected to set the record straight: "You should know that all of us here this evening come from the Free State."

My education into the mind of Afrikanerdom was growing exponentially as stereotypes collapsed.

This prepared me for writing *The Church Struggle in South Africa*, the book that launched my publishing career and established my reputation as an academic. In it I would express strong criticism of the DRC, but in a way that did not close off dialogue or descend into an anti-Afrikaner diatribe. By then I knew better than that. Years later I learnt that some Afrikaner theological professors – among them former Prime Minister Verwoerd's son-in-law, Carel Boshoff, who strongly disagreed with me – even made *The Church Struggle* required reading for their students. I was told it was a life-changing experience for some. But I had yet to write that book.

9

To leave or to stay?

I have come to the conclusion I have made a mistake in coming to America ... I will have no right to participate in the reconstruction of Christian life in Germany after the war if I do not share the trials of this time with my people.

(Dietrich Bonhoeffer)[4]

The time has come to tell about the consequences of my participation in the conference of Mennonite missionaries in Swaziland, shortly before I left the SACC. Firstly, I received an invitation to teach a winter semester course at Bethel College in North Newton, Kansas, in 1975. Although the college was relatively small and geographically isolated, it was progressive and intellectually stimulating. Early on in my stay, I was told there would be a place for me at Bethel if I ever needed to leave South Africa. As I could probably have manufactured a reason to leave, it was another tempting invitation to move to the US. This touched me at a brittle spot, which became evident when I went to Stanford University, California, for a few days at the invitation of my old friend Bob Hammerton-Kelly.

On the plane to San Francisco, I sat next to a young woman who was avidly reading the *Bhagavad-Gita*. I enquired whether she was finding it helpful. In response she told me her sad life story of drugs and divorce. I don't normally spend flights engaged in conversation with strangers, but sometimes they take me by surprise and become thought provoking. Here was a young white American woman of Christian background, who was finding spiritual help in the *Gita* rather than in the New Testament. Before the flight ended, she invited me to stay with her in San Francisco. Whatever her motives, I was glad that Bob was there to meet me at the airport.

Bob was now dean of the university's Memorial Church where I preached that first Sunday. Inspired by St. Mark's in Venice, the church is full of beautiful mosaics, stained-glass windows, frescoes and other artworks. I had never seen anything like it before, or preached in any comparable church. Bob, a distinguished New Testament scholar, also taught in the Department of Religion at Stanford, along with Robert McAfee Brown, a former president of Union Theological Seminary, who invited me to dinner at his home one evening. I had previously read some of Brown's books and admired him as a scholar-activist. I also renewed acquaintance with Ernlé Young, a South African Methodist theologian who had relocated to California, where he was assistant dean of the chapel.

Sunday luncheon in the Hammerton-Kelly home was a good time for catching up, but it was marred towards the end when we started discussing the pros and cons of staying or leaving South Africa. Bob and Ernlé had made the decision to leave, and I was once again personally uncertain whether to do the same. I did, however, express my mind rather strongly when they claimed the moral high ground for their decision. Of course, as a white person living in South Africa, I've made compromises; but living in the US did not automatically prevent anyone from doing the same, or exonerate them from responsibility for what was happening in the land of their birth.

TO LEAVE OR TO STAY?

At the end of the winter term, I lectured at several other Mennonite colleges, including the Associated Mennonite Biblical Seminary in Elkhart, Indiana, as well as Goshen College nearby. On my way there, I stopped in Chicago for a weekend to visit my mentor Ross Snyder, who invited me to give a seminar presentation to his class. He was enthusiastic about what I said and asked me to write it up as an article for publication. I spent the weekend doing so and gave him the result before I left, with the proviso that I wanted to edit it further before he submitted it. He was reluctant, as he liked it just as it was. But I felt it needed tightening up to meet academic requirements. He was unimpressed with the result, as to his mind it had lost its freshness. I still had to learn how to write with my own voice.

While at the seminary, I met Jim Cochrane for the first time. He was a fellow Capetonian and member of the CI, who was working as Snyder's assistant while completing his master's in Divinity. We talked about him returning to South Africa to do his PhD and finding a pastoral position in the UCCSA. I promised to do what I could to make this possible. On his return to South Africa shortly afterwards, Jim started his PhD under my supervision and became the youth minister at the Rondebosch Church. Steve, then in his mid-teens, was particularly influenced by his ministry, in which Christian faith was explained with honesty and connected to the struggle against apartheid. This attracted many thinking young people who might otherwise have drifted away from the church.

After visiting Elkhart, I went to Bluffton College in Ohio, where I remember preaching four times on the Sunday morning, beginning at the Catholic Church and then being whisked away to the next church immediately after the sermon, and so on throughout the morning. I clearly remember the burly Irish Catholic priest telling me to "keep it short and sweet, sonny boy". Good advice for preachers,

I guess. And yes, there was an embarrassing moment when, after I had preached, I went up to say farewell as he stood in front of the altar before continuing with the Mass. I held out my hand to shake his, but instead he took out an envelope containing a cheque from beneath his chasuble, and placed it in my open palm. For seven minutes worth of sermon, it was more generous than what I probably got from the Protestants down the road.

On my way to Pennsylvania for my last Mennonite engagement, my luggage was misplaced and I was rerouted to Washington DC. Alone in a strange city, I went out to dinner in a nearby restaurant. Sitting close by, was a lonely American who suggested we dine together. Without blinking he told me that he was a salesman who sold intercontinental ballistic missiles. I drew a deep breath. I had just spent six weeks with committed Christian pacifists. But before he could ask me what I did, I asked him, "Does your work selling weapons of destruction ever make you feel guilty?"

His reply startled me: "I've never thought about that."

I went back to my hotel and phoned Larry Rasmussen, a Bonhoeffer scholar I knew by reputation, who was teaching at Wesley Theological Seminary. He invited me to a meeting of the steering committee of the English Language Section of the International Bonhoeffer Society (IBS), which I had recently joined. At the meeting I met Larry, Clifford Green, Burton Nelson, John Godsey and Geoff Kelly for the first time, resulting in lasting friendships and scholarly cooperation ever since. That evening I returned to South Africa, aware that my life would have turned out very differently if my luggage had not been lost in transit somewhere in Pennsylvania.

At the suggestion of the Mennonite Central Committee, on my journey back home, I spent a day at London's Heathrow Airport getting to know the American Mennonite scholar John Howard

Yoder, who was then living in Switzerland. I had read his well-known *The Politics of Jesus* at Bethel College and was keen to meet him in person. I had also been asked by the MCC to persuade Yoder to visit South Africa at their expense. I don't know if he knew about this sub-plot. He had no small talk, so it was a difficult day as we moved from one coffee shop to another, thinking of things to say. He did agree to come to South Africa, though, and I agreed to organise his programme. He came in 1976, stayed with us, and gave some lectures on Christian Pacifism. These evoked a heated discussion led by the doughty Margaret Nash, who gave moral support to the armed struggle against apartheid. They were formidable opponents.

Shortly before Yoder's visit, television was finally introduced in South Africa, so he had an opportunity to witness a crude piece of military propaganda on SABC, which left us all bemused. But there was nothing amusing about the escalating war on the Namibian border. The conflict was taking place thousands of kilometres away, but no one with any political awareness was oblivious to its reality. Military conscription was affecting more and more families, daily coming closer to our own two sons. Was this the time to leave the country?

When I first began to teach at UCT, the only crisis that occurred, I once jokingly remarked, was when the kettle burnt out and we could not make tea. Another was when the photocopier broke down. How different this was from my previous life at the SACC, where we lurched from one crisis to the next as the struggle escalated. Dunwell House was no ivory tower, but UCT could easily become one. I had little illusion that I was working in a bubble of privilege that would soon burst. The bell had begun to toll, as Professor Keet had already written in the aftermath of Sharpeville.

In May 1976 I attended the Second International Bonhoeffer

Congress in Geneva. This coincided with the seventieth anniversary of Bonhoeffer's birth. On the way there, I again visited the Bethges in Rengsdorf, where I participated in a seminar in Eberhard's continuing education programme. Peter Beyerhaus, a theologian from Tübingen challenged what I said about the situation in southern Africa, and we exchanged heated words. He had been a Lutheran missionary in Natal, but since his return to Germany had spearheaded a German group opposing the PCR (Programme to Combat Racism) on the grounds that the WCC was supporting terrorism. He also became a supporter of the reactionary Christian Defence League in South Africa, which had divided some congregations in the UCCSA, and whose leader regularly reported on my activities to the security police.

On the train to Geneva, the Bethges and I were joined by Ernst Feil, a Roman Catholic theologian from Munich who, Bethge told me, had written the best Catholic study on Bonhoeffer's theology. Feil and I stood for much of the way in the corridor of a crowded coach talking about Bonhoeffer. Feil had considerable difficulty in understanding how it was possible to do theology in dialogue with Bonhoeffer in relation to the South African context. I think he thought Bonhoeffer's theology could be interpreted without too much reference to his biography, something that I found equally difficult to comprehend. By the time we reached Geneva, the problem remained unresolved.

I had spent a great deal of time thinking about this problem in preparing my paper for the congress. How could I appropriate Bonhoeffer's legacy in a context that wasn't his own? It was clearly important to understand Bonhoeffer in his own context, but it was equally necessary to engage his legacy critically through an informed analysis of other contexts and the witness of the Church within them.

This was a tricky hermeneutical challenge, but I could not engage in a scientific study of Bonhoeffer's writings in isolation from the church struggle in South Africa.

The Geneva congress was a remarkable experience. It attracted some of Bonhoeffer's former students, members of his family (including his twin sister, Sabine) and his former fiancée, Maria van Wedemeyer. Many notable theologians and academics also attended, including the distinguished physicist Carl Friedrich von Weizsäcker, whose work had so profoundly influenced Bonhoeffer in prison.

At the concluding service, I was asked to read a passage from Bonhoeffer's letter to Reinhold Niebuhr, in which he told him about his decision to return to Germany from New York in 1939. He had gone to the States, specifically at Niebuhr's invitation, to avoid military conscription in Germany and to escape the clutches of the Gestapo. The moment he arrived in New York, however, he became uncertain. Was his place not back in Germany with his compatriots fighting Nazi tyranny? It is a poignant passage that spoke directly to my temptation. Should we as a family leave South Africa, or stay? Those listening to me reading the passage asked me the same question. In response, I said that the question bothered many South Africans, but I felt committed to being in South Africa. It was where I belonged.

Even so, the Soweto uprising, which erupted on 16 June 1976, freshly raised the question for many South Africans. Ever since the banning of the liberation movements after Sharpeville, black-led political opposition had been in the doldrums, and the armed struggle was getting nowhere. But now the situation changed dramatically as a younger generation of black leaders, inspired by Steve Biko's Black Consciousness Movement, entered the fray. I recall the Assembly of the UCCSA in Durban in 1976, when young people from Soweto told their stories about what had happened to them during the uprising. The situation was tense as we discussed ways for the Church to express solidarity. In the wake of the uprising, there was an exodus of panicking white South Africans who sought security elsewhere, and angry young blacks who went into exile to join the liberation army.

I have never questioned the decision of those who, for reasons of conscience or real danger, chose to leave. I know something of the struggle involved in making that decision. But I decided to stay each time the opportunity arose. So South Africa has remained home, as much a part of my Christian faith and commitment as anything else. I learnt from Beyers Naudé and Bonhoeffer to be a critical patriot. Those who truly love their country are those who challenge its failures even as they proudly applaud its achievements.

10

Becoming an author

> At many times during the writing of this book, I have been conscious of my identity as a white, English-speaking South African, and the limitations that this inevitably means in terms of insight and perspective. I cannot speak for either Afrikaners or blacks, nor, indeed, for the English-speaking community … But I have written as one involved in the situation, and out of the conviction that the Christian gospel contains the word of hope for present and future South Africans.
>
> (From *The Church Struggle in South Africa*)[5]

I was invited to return to Bethel College in Kansas for the Fall Semester in 1977 to give the annual Menno Simons Lectures, named after the seventeenth-century Dutch Anabaptist leader. The prospect of spending an eight months sabbatical in the US was eagerly accepted by the whole family. This would be Jeanelle and Anton's first experience of America, but not Stephen's, though he had only been two years old when we went to Chicago. We visited the Bethges in Germany on our way to the States. How they coped with us five I don't know, but they insisted on us staying with them and taking us around the countryside. The children were mightily impressed by Renate's speedy driving on the autobahn.

Our US visit began in Stockbridge where I again served the Congregational Church, this time for six weeks. It was good to renew friendships and revisit the beautiful Berkshires. Rozelle, who had been divorced several years before, had recently remarried an American, Bill Putnam, and they also visited us from Atlanta. Steve started playing and composing songs in earnest, and I remember going to the Folksong Club at the Lion's Den to listen to him play and sing. One of Steve's heroes, Arlo Guthrie, had written "Alice's Restaurant" in a restaurant in an alley just off High Street. Whether this anti-war ballad influenced Steve, we don't know, but it is likely.

At the end of our stay in Stockbridge, we set off by car for Washington DC. There I taught a summer course at Wesley Seminary, at the invitation of Larry Rasmussen. The weather was hot and humid, so when I wasn't teaching we spent much of the time visiting air-conditioned museums. Then we travelled across the Midwest to Denver, Colorado, where I taught for several weeks at Iliff School of Theology. A week in a cabin in the Rockies followed before we drove back east to Kansas. Along the way we heard that Elvis Presley had just died. Soon the music in our car switched from the songs of John Denver, Paul Simon and Neil Diamond to those of the king of rock.

Sabbaticals might appear to be glorified vacations, but academics are meant to come back refreshed and energised, with new insight and acknowledged outcomes. The official term used these days is "research and study leave". In order to get a sabbatical, you have to have served a certain length of time, have a proven research track record, have an acceptable research proposal, and at the end achieve your stated goals. A sabbatical is not just meant to serve an individual academic's career, but to enhance the life of the university.

Universities cannot function in isolated silos or ghettoes. That is also why academics often travel a great deal, both to conferences and on research visits. But in 1977 "research and study leave" was less codified than it is now. What I did with my time abroad was largely up to me.

After our long journey from Denver, we were welcomed into the Bethel community by Jim and Anna Juhnke, whom we had first met in Swaziland in 1972. Our sabbatical home was next door to theirs. Isobel attended art classes, and the children all went to school; we attended the local Bethel Mennonite Church and enjoyed many social events. I spent the first weeks finalising my Menno Simons Lectures. And then the time came to give them. I am still amazed how, in that rural college town in the Midwest, several hundred people came for five evenings in a row to hear about the church struggle in South Africa. But South Africa was much in the news after the Soweto uprising, the death of Steve Biko during the very week of the lectures, and the subsequent banning of anti-apartheid organisations and activists, including the CI and Beyers Naudé.

As Naudé could not now travel abroad, I was invited to go to Seattle in his place one weekend to speak at a conference on South Africa. To my surprise, I found myself sharing a platform – and a cathedral pulpit – with Alan Paton, the author of *Cry, the Beloved Country*. I had met him the previously at his home outside Durban, but now I had a chance to get to know him better and to appreciate his sharp mind – also his gruffness in response to adulation.

Upon my return to Bethel, I completed a rough draft of a book based on my lectures and set about finding a publisher. Eerdmans in Grand Rapids, Michigan, came to mind. They had published Yoder's *The Politics of Jesus*, and I suspected that they would be interested in what I had written. Then, out of the blue, came an invitation to go to Grand Rapids to take part in a conference organised by the United

Church of Christ (UCC), the American equivalent of the UCCSA. I accepted and made an appointment with Eerdmans to deliver a draft of my manuscript for consideration. Once there, I met members of the editorial staff (including Bill Eerdmans himself), and had dinner at the home of Nicholas Wolterstorff, then a Philosophy professor at Calvin College. Nick would become a good friend over the years.

Our stay in Kansas soon came to an end. We travelled east to Erie, Pennsylvania, for Christmas with Isobel's brother Alan, his wife, Nancy, and their family. They had been transferred there by Alan's company several years before, and we had not seen them since they left Johannesburg. We awoke to snow on Christmas Day, which made the family reunion and celebration particularly memorable. But then I had to go to San Francisco to attend a Congress of the American Academy of Religion (AAR) on 28 December.

Isobel and the family were going to spend New Year with friends in Sturgeon Bay, Wisconsin, so we drove together to O'Hare Airport outside Chicago. The highway was iced over and, coming down a side ramp, I applied the brakes too sharply. The next thing we knew, we were careering uncontrollably towards a VW Beetle that had stalled ahead of us. We watched in horror as we slid uncontrollably into it, badly damaging its rear. Our heavy-metal Chevrolet came off without a dent. The young lady driver was understandably shaken and angry, but there was not much we could do other than apologise profusely and wait with her for the next patrol car.

"This is a minor accident compared to the many others we have had to deal with today," declared the officer.

After taking details for the insurers and checking my driver's licence, we were soon able to continue to the airport, where I caught a flight to San Francisco and Isobel drove north along Lake Michigan (more cautiously than she might have done previously) to our friends Don and Katharine Olski, who had lived next door to us in Chicago.

This was my first attendance at a congress of the AAR. These days it attracts many thousands of participants from across North America and the rest of the world. Back then it was more modest, but still, for me, a large event. I was one of the first South Africans to join the AAR, and I have participated in many of its congresses. On this occasion I gave my first paper on "Bonhoeffer and South Africa", and to my delight the respondent was Robert MacAfee Brown from Stanford University. I also spent an evening with Ross and Martha Snyder, who had retired to nearby San Anselmo. As young in spirit as ever, they were involved in ministry to older folk. I now have better appreciation for the importance of what they were doing.

My return flight to Chicago was uneventful, but not so the flight from O'Hare to Sturgeon Bay. The runway itself had been cleared of snow, but the snow on the tarmac was still higher than the wings of our twenty-seater plane, which was also dwarfed by the Boeing in front of us and another one on our tail. The pilot jokingly asked us if we had put on an extra pair of socks. I didn't think that was very funny. We flew low over the dark countryside and eventually landed at the airport in Sturgeon Bay, its runway piled high with snow, with just enough room for us to land. The next day I discovered that the airport was also the railway station.

After New Year we returned along the way Isobel had come, and, after a long drive without any further mishaps, we arrived at the Associated Mennonite Biblical Seminary in Elkhart, Indiana, where I taught for a month and Steve took a course in Biblical Archaeology, while Jeanelle and Anton went off to the local school. We came to know John Yoder better, met his family, and appreciated their hospitality greatly. John was then teaching at the University of Notre Dame. His influence on my own thinking at that time was evident in the final chapter of the book which I was still hoping Eerdmans would agree to publish.

Towards the end of our stay, Isobel and I were invited to a restaurant about eighty kilometres north of the town. Our hosts were Calvin College philosopher Richard Mouw and his wife. We enjoyed the dinner and conversation without knowing that Mouw had been a reader of the manuscript I had submitted to Eerdmans, and that he had actually come to tell me it had been accepted for publication. He kept that news to himself until we were having coffee. I was ecstatic. We drove back to Elkhart in high spirits, looking forward to sharing our news with the rest of the family.

During the next few days, the Midwest was hit by a massive blizzard. The seminary campus and our apartment were soon deep under snow. The roads were impassable, lectures were cancelled, schools shut, and our toilet froze. O'Hare Airport also closed down, so we had to renegotiate our return flights home several times. The fun of Christmas in the snow turned into anxiety about how we would ever get out of Elkhart, let alone America. We finally made it to the airport in a roundabout way and were able to fly out of a chaotic air terminal. Our sabbatical had come to a dramatic end.

Back home, life continued much as before for me, but Isobel was busy with some new ventures. Among them was the Centre of Concern at the Rondebosch Church, which she started with Jenny Boraine. The project's aim was to teach skills to domestic workers, and it continued for many years. Isobel was also a part-time teacher at St. Cyprian's Girls' School.

Alan Paton wrote the foreword to *The Church Struggle in South Africa*, which was published in 1979, launching my career as an author in earnest. Eerdmans and David Philip in Cape Town, who co-published the book, became wonderful supporters of my work, for which I remain deeply grateful. And Bill Eerdmans became a supportive friend over the ensuing years. I only recently discovered that, shortly after its publication, *The Church Struggle* was classified as "objectionable literature" in the National Archives.

Soon after our return to Cape Town, Archbishop Burnett invited me to speak at a two-day Anglican Diocesan conference on the Church's political witness and Church-State relations. As I have said, my thinking at the time was much influenced by Yoder's *The Politics of Jesus*. I still stand by much of what I had said then, and what I wrote in the final chapter of *The Church Struggle*. The Church "has no vocation frantically to shape history, control the cosmos, and ensure that the Kingdom arrives on time", but it does have a responsibility to work for justice, to proclaim truth to power, and to foster a more humane and compassionate world.

11

A church leader of sorts

> It is easy, you know ... to get sentimental and rhetorical and rhapsodical about the Church when you think of it in general ... You say you love Christ's Church. Well, here it is: Tom, Dick and Harry, and the rest; a funny lot of lame ducks, but they carry out the conditions we have laid down ... they have, in their own odd ways, heard Christ's call.
>
> (Bernard Lord Manning)[6]

The Church is a funny institution. Yes, I know it is meant to be holy and all the rest, but when you truly belong to it and survive the journey as a member over many years, you come to appreciate something of God's humour. For the Church as I have experienced it, whether at a local level or more broadly, is made up of very ordinary people, some of whom have become extraordinary without knowing it. The Church is God's experiment in creating a new community out of a mixed bag of people from all cultures and backgrounds whose only commonality is their humanity in its brokenness, their sometimes faltering faith and shaky hope, and, more often than some critics give them credit for, their desire to serve others in love. The Church has often frustrated and annoyed me, but I would never leave it because among the dross I have discovered diamonds. Whatever its faults, I have learnt that they are often my own.

In January 1979 Douglas Bax succeeded Geoffrey Dunstan as minister of the Rondebosch Congregational Church. I had known Doug since my student days at Rhodes. He was a Presbyterian minister who, after Rhodes, had studied at Princeton and then in Göttingen in Germany. Under his ministry, the congregation became increasingly involved in social and political issues, attracted young people who (like Steve) were committed activists and conscientious objectors, and became well known for its opposition to apartheid. I continued as an associate minister under his leadership.

In March I turned forty. I am sure we celebrated that in some worthy way, but all I can recall is that I went that month to a conference in Pretoria on "The Meaning of History". Held at the University of South Africa, it was in honour of the doyen of Afrikaner historians, Professor F.A. van Jaarsveld. The main item on the agenda was the interpretation of the Battle of Blood River, the formative myth in the development of Afrikaner nationalism. The opening ceremony was held in the plush Senate Hall, which was filled to capacity with dignitaries drawn largely from the upper echelons of Afrikaner society. I was sitting next to Jaap Durand, when suddenly the main doors burst open and in came khaki-clad young men who strode to the podium and literally feathered and tarred Van Jaarsveld. The group's leader grabbed the microphone and shouted that they would not allow their sacred history to be trampled underfoot. This was the first public performance of Eugène Terre'Blanche and his militant right-wing Afrikaner Weerstandsbeweging (Afrikaner Resistance Movement or AWB). We were frozen to our seats, mesmerised as though face to face with a spitting cobra. Our sense of impotence was as frightening as the violent intrusion. The congress continued the next day, but this demonstration of brutal power left an indelible impression on the proceedings, and the AWB soon became part of the shadow side of South African politics.

In June 1980 I attended the Third International Bonhoeffer Congress held in Oxford. My paper, in dialogue with Bonhoeffer, was on civil disobedience against tyranny and an illegitimate regime. I argued that Christians had a responsibility to oppose unjust regimes and work for their downfall. By now I knew many members of the International Bonhoeffer Society (IBS), but there were always new people to get to know. One was Dan Hardy, who had organised the event. He had a remarkable theological mind, though he was not always easy to understand. It was also at Oxford that I first met Don Shriver, then president of Union Theological Seminary.

I returned to Pretoria in July to attend the South African Christian Leadership Assembly (SACLA). This remarkable event, sponsored by the AE under the leadership of Michael Cassidy and David Bosch, brought Christians and church leaders together from across racial, denominational and theological divides to discuss the urgent issues facing South Africa. Desmond Tutu set the tone for the gathering in his opening address. Although he was like a red rag to a bull for some, he had a way of winning hearts and minds. There was considerable opposition from the government, security police, right-wingers and conservative churches. But six thousand of us attended the ten-day event held at the Pretoria Show Grounds. Isobel and Stephen were there with me; as were civic, political and business leaders; students (some from Soweto); and ministers and members from churches ranging from the DRC to Pentecostal. For many participants it was an eye-opener to discover that many international evangelical and charismatic speakers were critics of apartheid.

Visiting Pretoria, as I regularly did, brought me into contact with Denise and Laurie Ackermann. Denise, who would later become the leading feminist theologian in the country, was then completing her doctorate in Practical Theology at UNISA, and Laurie was a judge. I much appreciated their hospitality, and the friendship that developed as a result would last over the years, especially after they came to live in Cape Town.

In 1979 I was elected chairman of the UCCSA to serve from 1980 to 1981. As chairman-elect, I received an invitation from the chaplain general of the South African Defence Force to join a delegation of church leaders on a visit to the troops on the Namibian border that November. There was some opposition in the UCCSA leadership to my accepting the invitation. But I was keen to see for myself what was happening in the war zone and sufficiently alert not to be seduced by military-speak. Once there, I saw soldiers recently returned from skirmishes in a state of shock. In contrast, a major told me over drinks in the mess that God was "on our side". When I asked him what gave him that idea, he replied that it was because "our troops" always survived these engagements with "the godless communist enemy". I enquired whether there ever were casualties, and he admitted there were some. I suggested that God was then not always on "our side", something he reluctantly conceded. After a week spent in camps on the border and in the Caprivi Strip, meeting with chaplains and officers, my conviction that the war was futile, politically unwise, and morally wrong was reinforced.

I was inducted as chairman of the UCCSA at the 1980 assembly held that September in Cape Town. Archbishop Burnett was one of several church leaders who participated in the service. In my address I brought together themes that were too often kept apart: bearing witness to the gospel, working for justice, and being open to the Spirit. I remember walking out of the service in the robes of my new office and being given a suitcase in the vestry by the general secretary, Joe Wing, to keep them in.

"You'll be doing a lot of travelling this coming year," he said. How right he was.

I had to get permission from the university to become the UCCSA chairman. Fortunately my teaching responsibilities could be arranged so that I could be away from time to time. Apart from chairing various meetings, taking part in ordinations, and leading a convention of all the ministers of the Church held at Rhodes University, my main assignment was making pastoral visits to the Outeniqua, Natal and Zimbabwe regions. My visit to Zimbabwe was particularly interesting, because the country had only recently become independent from Britain, with Robert Mugabe as president. I had a meeting with the new minister of education to discuss issues affecting our mission schools, but this was not very helpful. I guess mission schools were a little suspect in the new dispensation. I also spent a few days at the majestic Victoria Falls which I saw for the first time.

Shortly before I left, I preached in a Harare township. The large congregation was made up of members of different local churches who had gathered for the occasion, but sat together in separate groups. I still had a great deal of money in my pocket that I had received for incidental expenses. When the collection was taken, I put it all into the offertory bag, not realising that it was the bag that had also been sent round the poorest of the groups. Later, before the service ended, an announcement was made that the poorest of the poor had given the most to the work of the Lord. This led to an outburst of praise and adulation.

Such occasions made it all worthwhile, but it was a difficult period in which to be a church leader. The PCR was still divisive, and we had to deal with the crisis created by the Soweto uprising and the government's increasingly violent response. The Conscientious Objection (CO) issue was also a hot topic as the armed struggle gathered momentum and the war in Namibia escalated. Even some of us "older" men were beginning to get call-up papers. These came in registered letters which we had to collect from the post office. We soon got wise to this, and simply ignored the registered slip informing us that our call-up was waiting to be collected. But younger white males were obliged to register while still at high school. Several of my students, as well as others in our congregation, decided to become COs, but initially the penalties for doing so were two years in prison.

During my term in office as UCCSA chair, I worked hard to achieve the union of the UCCSA and the Presbyterian Church of Southern Africa (PCSA) that had eluded the denominations since the beginning of the century. We had already achieved a great deal and even made it possible for congregations to unite ahead of the anticipated union, such as happened at St. Mungo's in Bryanston in 1973 when I was associate minister there. In 1980, at the invitation of the moderator Alan Maker, I was the guest preacher at the PCSA General Assembly held in Port Elizabeth, and optimistic that the union would be achieved. But apart from establishing new united churches in some places, or some congregations voting to become united churches as happened at Rondebosch and Stellenbosch, all hopes for the uniting of the two denominations were dashed when negotiations failed at the final stage in 1988.

I had equally high hopes that the CUC would fulfil its promise of uniting the Anglican, Presbyterian, Methodist and Congregational Churches. I preached at the service in St. George's Cathedral in 1980 when the covenant that made intercommunion possible was finally ratified. It was a momentous occasion, presided over by Archbishop Burnett. This prepared the way for the mutual acceptance of ministries in 1986 – a first in ecumenical relations worldwide. This now meant, for example, that I, as a minister of the UCCSA, could preside at an Anglican Eucharist, something I cherished as the years passed. But the actual uniting of the CUC churches has eluded us despite all the efforts made.

In November 1980 Archbishop Burnett invited me to address the Anglican Synod in Pietermaritzburg on "The Present Crisis and the Task of the Church". I began by listing non-negotiables. The first was the social responsibility of the church; the second the immorality of apartheid; and the third was the need to combat racism within the Church itself. I concluded that the liberation of Mozambique, Angola and Zimbabwe, together with the escalation of the war in Namibia, the rise of black trade unions, the students' uprising, the escalation of rural poverty, militarisation, and President P.W. Botha's proposed reforms, had created a new agenda for the churches in the struggle against apartheid. The synod was serious in its attempt to engage with these issues. Burnett, who was in the chair, was not happy with all I had said, but afterwards Desmond Tutu, David Russell and other (mainly black) delegates, told me that I had hit the nail on the head.

I was becoming a regular speaker at such Anglican events, and some thought that I had become a crypto-Anglican. This was not surprising, because Congregationalists were nonconforming Anglicans in the seventeenth century in England, refusing to accept the monarch as head of the Church or the Prayer Book as the only liturgical text. Neither of these, however, are issues in South Africa. Whether I am a crypto-Anglican or simply an ecumenical hybrid does not compromise my convictions in the slightest; it only enriches my faith.

Burnett resigned as archbishop in 1981 and was succeeded by Philip Russell that September. He was regarded as a "stop-gap" appointment. Desmond Tutu was the other candidate, but he was not elected because many white Anglicans, who still had control of the elective assembly, were unwilling to support him.

Russell proved to be more than a caretaker. During his enthronement service in St. George's Cathedral, which I attended as his guest, he gave a clear warning to both Church and State that he committed the church under his leadership to fighting racism and working for common citizenship, and that he rejected the notion that the Church should keep out of politics. The only thing that I objected to in the magnificent service, as I told him afterwards in a letter, was the choice of a Psalm which seemed to exalt him to the status of a Messiah. But I was a Congregational nonconformist after all.

My term as chair of the UCCSA ended in August 1981 at the assembly held in Pietermaritzburg. The emerging "Young Turks" in the denomination, among them our Steve, gave me an uncomfortable time in the chair when they demanded that we all march to the local prison to demand the release of some political detainees. The decision was not mine to take, but the assembly decided not to. In retrospect, I don't think I was much of a church leader. Maybe you can't be that in a one-year term in office, for no sooner are you in it than you are out of it again. These days, the office of president of the UCCSA is two years, and is preceded by a year of induction. I had learnt much, however, and met some wonderful people working under the most difficult circumstances in churches across southern Africa. If it had not been for the indefatigable and clear-sighted leadership of Joe Wing, it would have been a far more burdensome task.

At the UCCSA Assembly I was asked to join Archbishop Russell, together with the president of the Methodist Church and moderator of the PCSA, to meet with President Botha. Our brief was to demand that he repeal the Mixed Marriages Act and the Immorality Act – both racist pieces of legislation that caused great hurt to people. We had submitted a strongly worded statement to him prior to the meeting. But before we could speak, Botha, flanked by several heavyweight cabinet ministers, gave us a "history lesson" to explain why these Acts had come about. Then he ended by saying that he would withdraw both if we could convince his church, the DRC, to support him doing so. We, and I suspect others around the table, were taken by surprise. There was not much more to be said, except to ask for his support in approaching the leaders of the DRC, which we later did. I do not know whether this contributed to the repeal of the Acts in June 1985.

Looking back, however, it is clear that Botha's surprising announcement that day reflected his so-called reformist strategy: the creation of a tricameral parliament, which would include "coloured" and Indian chambers alongside the white one. But, as this excluded Africans, it was nothing more than a way of maintaining power through co-option, without any sharing of power.

By the beginning of the 1980s, our department at UCT had grown considerably, and most graduate students were in the Christian Studies programme. Several new faculty appointments had been made, and others were in the offing. Among them were the American David Chidester, who soon achieved an international reputation for his work in comparative religion, and Charles Villa-Vicencio, who joined me in teaching Christian Studies. Itumeleng Mosala came to teach Old Testament and Black Theology, along with Gabriel Setiloane, who taught African Religions. There was a part-time lecturer in Judaism, and to complete the complement Abdulkader Tayob and Ebrahim Moosa were later appointed to teach Islamic Studies. By then I was fortunate to have the secretarial assistance of the wonderful Nan Oosthuizen, who was the manager of the *JTSA*.

Charles Villa-Vicencio was a Methodist minister who had obtained his PhD at Drew University. Upon his return to South Africa, he served various congregations and taught Theology at UNISA, prior to coming to UCT. Together we pioneered a new master's degree based on coursework and a dissertation, developed graduate research seminars, and encouraged students to participate with us in various research and publishing projects. We had a great deal of latitude in developing our courses, largely because we did not have to conform to the training requirements of any church. We worked hard to achieve high academic standards, though, and I think we complemented each other rather well. Not only did we teach courses together, but we jointly published several books as well. We also developed the Research Institute on Christianity in South Africa (RICSA), which was funded by the Human Sciences Research Council and subject to its annual audits and independent reviews every few years. Duncan Forrester from Edinburgh University served in this capacity on two occasions.

Charles and I were blessed by a continuous stream of bright, committed and enthusiastic students. Most of them were also political activists, and some served jail sentences as a result. On one occasion five students of my class of eight were in jail at the same time (even if only for a few days), and Charles was among them.

In January 1982 I attended yet another congress in Pretoria, this time at the University of Pretoria. My fellow attendees were church leaders and theologians from the DRC and SACC churches. The theme, "Practical cooperation between the Churches", may sound innocuous, but sparks soon began to fly. In my paper, I expressed scepticism about cooperation without consensus on what it means to witness to God's justice. I concluded by saying that we were facing a crisis that was tearing our society apart and driving many to acts of fear and desperation. The ecumenical officer of the DRC, Pierre Rousseau, presented his paper after me. It was nothing but a whitewash of reformist government policy with a Christian veneer. During the heated discussion that followed we traded verbal blows. I recall he was wearing grey shoes, and ever since I have had an antipathy towards grey shoes. The time for nice words had passed.

12

Nothing but a heresy

The Afrikaans Reformed Churches have only to return to their roots to discover that what they now cherish is nothing but a heresy that strikes at the foundation of the Church.

(David Bosch)[7]

In 1982 the DR Mission Church, at its synod in Belhar near Cape Town, adopted the Belhar Confession, declaring the theological justification of apartheid nothing but a heresy. This was strong ecclesiastical language, but the political implications of the Belhar Confession were soon recognised by the government: A daughter church of its own DRC had rejected the claim that apartheid, whether reformist or not, could be defended on Christian grounds. Sensing the importance of this decision, Charles Villa-Vicencio and I produced a book of essays entitled *Apartheid is a Heresy*, which was published in 1983. Allan Boesak, Desmond Tutu, Douglas Bax and David Bosch were among the contributors.

Despite such opposition, President Botha steamed ahead in an effort to sell his reforms. Even Alan Hendricks, a formidable "coloured" minister in the UCCSA with solid anti-apartheid credentials, was co-opted. At the UCCSA Assembly in Kimberley in September 1982,

Alan opposed my appointment as the church's delegate to the WCC Assembly to be held in 1983 in Vancouver, Canada, on the grounds that a black person should be elected. That was a good reason. But when it came to the vote I was elected, even though the vast majority of the assembly was itself black. I had lunch with Alan after the debate. He confided in me that he had been approached by Chris Heunis, the government minister of constitutional development and planning, to participate in the new political dispensation, and he was thinking about doing so. I was taken aback as this was clearly against the sentiment in the UCCSA. When Alan eventually decided to participate, his name was taken off the role of ministers. By then, such participation had become a disciplinary matter. It was a sad day for him and the church he had served well.

In January 1983 Isobel, Jeanelle, Anton and I set off for Princeton in the US for a sabbatical year. Steve was a graduate student at UCT and engaged to Debora Patta, a vivacious young woman who was involved with him in the youth ministry at the Rondebosch Church and in the Student Union for Christian Action (SUCA). On our way to the States, we stayed with Debora's father in Rome where he owned a small hotel. We had fun exploring the city, as well as Assisi and Florence. The life-long impact of such cultural experiences cannot be easily measured. By contrast, after we arrived in Princeton, we regularly heard from Steve about protests in which he and Debora were involved at Crossroads, a township that had become a notorious site of struggle against government policy that excluded Africans from living permanently in the Western Cape.

Resistance against reformist apartheid was gathering momentum, led by a new movement, the United Democratic Front or UDF. This coalition of faith communities, civic organisations, trade unions and NGOs, had been initiated by Allan Boesak and was officially launched in Cape Town that September. While acting in consort with the ANC, the UDF was a separate organisation with its own democratic structures and ethos. Besides Boesak, several other church leaders played important roles in this new phase of the struggle, including Desmond Tutu, then general secretary of the SACC; Catholic Archbishop Hurley; and Frank Chikane, the director of the Institute for Contextual Theology (ICT) in Johannesburg. By the time we returned from our sabbatical at the end of 1983, the UDF had become a formidable force in the country. For the moment, however, we could only look on from a distance.

I had been invited to Princeton Theological Seminary by James McCord, who was about to retire as president. We went for a walk one day during which he shared with me his dream for what later became the Princeton Center of Theological Inquiry. Both he and Charles West, well known in ecumenical and Bonhoeffer circles, who was the dean at the time, made us very welcome.

I had long concluded that the theologians at Stellenbosch had a distorted understanding of Calvin's theology and ignored the prophetic trajectories in the Reformed tradition, of which my own Congregational heritage was a part. Therefore, exploring the Reformed tradition more thoroughly became my sabbatical project, and Princeton was an ideal place for it. With that in mind I attended Edward Dowey's graduate seminars on Calvin's *Institutes of the Christian Religion*, which gave my work a solid foundation in this key Reformed text.

Isobel audited a course in Spirituality, Jeanelle attended Princeton University for a semester, where I was also a visiting fellow, and Anton attended high school. And as a family, we renewed our Mennonite connection by joining a house fellowship.

I taught two courses at the seminary: one on Bonhoeffer (which

I also gave at Drew University in nearby Madison) and the other on the Church in South Africa. There were other South Africans on sabbatical at Princeton, including Makhenkesi Stofile. He was a Presbyterian minister from the Eastern Cape and a Theology lecturer at Fort Hare. A student in my class on the Church in South Africa would go to him after each lecture to find out whether I was telling the truth. That resulted in lively discussion. Stofile later became minister of sport in the new post-apartheid South African government.

While at Princeton I was invited to the Center for African Studies at Yale University in New Haven to speak at a seminar on the church struggle in South Africa. I also spoke at the Divinity School where I renewed contact with Burgess Carr, who was a visiting professor, and recalled with him how he had rescued me from the passport officials in Liberia years before.

My UCT colleague Mike Savage was on sabbatical at Yale that year, so I stayed with him, and the two of us went and bought our first computers from the university bookstore. Today those Kaypro word processors are crude artefacts from an ancient past, but back then they were the best piece of affordable technology for academics. Keep in mind that up until then I had only used a manual or electric typewriter, and that all copies were made by using sheets of carbon paper or cutting stencils. I cannot now imagine my life in writing without the increasingly powerful computers that I have had since those days. And it all began for me – and for Anton, who is now an IT software developer – with that Kaypro, which used two floppy disks and boasted 64k of memory.

During the summer Isobel, Jeanelle, Anton and I drove from Princeton to Montreal, then across Canada to Vancouver for the WCC Assembly. The majestic beauty through Banff National Park and the Rockies was only spoilt by innumerable mosquitoes that attacked us at each picnic place. Vancouver was everything the tourist brochures described, and the University of British Columbia campus on which the assembly was held was a fine location.

The event was memorable for many reasons, among them the daily services in the huge Tent of Worship and meeting so many people and friends from across the world. There were special sessions on the debate about apartheid as a heresy, and I was part of a group of South Africans who met with some observers from the ANC to discuss matters relating to the Church in South Africa. Another memorable event was the evening that Desmond Tutu made a dramatic appearance in the Tent of Worship, having belatedly received his passport from the South African authorities.

On the way back from Vancouver, we spent a fortnight at Holden Village, a Lutheran conference centre in the Cascade Mountains in Washington State. This was such a fine experience that Jeanelle decided to stay there for the rest of the year as a volunteer. The Rasmussens were in residence, and John Yoder was one of the guest teachers, as was I. On one occasion I went climbing up a mountain ridge towering over the magnificent landscape below, but I found it a frightening experience. Although I have loved hiking all my life, the fear of heights was becoming an increasing problem.

After Holden Village, we passed through Minneapolis to visit Jim and Dolores Burtness who taught at the Lutheran seminary. We had come to know them at various Bonhoeffer Society events. Together we began to plan a visit to East Germany, in conjunction with the next Bonhoeffer Congress to be held in East Berlin in June 1984.

Shortly before my sabbatical ended, I went to New York to have dinner with publisher Bill Eerdmans. We were meant to go to a Broadway show, but our conversation developed wings, and we ignored the bells which rang to inform patrons that the show would soon begin. Bill asked me what I was working on, and I told him about papers I had written on Bonhoeffer and South Africa.

Without a moment's hesitation he said, "We will publish them!" I was taken aback, but delighted.

Soon after our return home I edited the lectures, added some introductory material, and *Bonhoeffer and South Africa* was speedily published in 1984, with a foreword by Eberhard Bethge who commented that the book proved Bonhoeffer's relevance for South Africa[8]. I was privileged to have several distinguished guests at its launch at UCT the next year, including the member of Parliament Helen Suzman who was the speaker for the event. Specially bound copies were presented to her, the Roman Catholic archbishop of Cape Town, UCT Vice-Chancellor Stuart Saunders, Alex Boraine and Jaap Durand. The book was not without its critics. In a review in *Die Burger*, a leading DRC minister expressed anger that I had used Bonhoeffer to criticise apartheid. I visited him later, but failed to convince him otherwise.

In 1984 I was appointed deputy dean of the Faculty of Social Science and Humanities. For much of the rest of my time at UCT, I was either an acting dean or a deputy. I became involved at higher levels in academic administration and familiar with the university's inner workings. This did not lessen my teaching responsibilities, or unduly restrict my research and participation in conferences. I was not particularly interested in some of the essential nitty-gritty administrative tasks in the faculty office, nor particularly good at budgets. Fortunately, there were always competent people around without whom a university would grind to a halt. I did, however, enjoy policy discussions and planning, and being available for members of the faculty.

One of my tasks as acting dean was to host visitors. Two of the more famous were Connor Cruise O'Brien, the Irish scholar and United Nations diplomat, and Jesse Jackson, the US civil rights leader. O'Brien's visit became notorious after he made some off-the-cuff caustic remarks about students who had disrupted a meeting arranged by the Student Jewish Association, at which he was the speaker. In the heated faculty and senate debates that followed, I was not prepared to condone what either party had done, so I refused to support O'Brien against the students as some faculty members demanded.

Jesse Jackson's visit was arranged by the former president of the Chicago Theological Seminary, Howard Schomer, who asked me to host him. I was startled when Jackson's security team came to check out my office before his arrival. He held court over a luncheon that included Frederik van Zyl Slabbert (then a professor of Sociology at UCT) and various other individuals I respected for their political insight. Jackson asked us to tell him how we understood the political situation. But I don't think he was listening as he stood by the window looking into the distance.

After seven years under house arrest, Beyers Naudé's banning order was lifted in 1984, and he was able to re-enter public life. During his banning, he had been allowed to meet with only one person at a time, but he often disregarded the rule, as when Steve and I visited him in 1980. During those years he was an important communications link between South African anti-apartheid activists at home and those abroad. In May 1985, a year after his unbanning and in celebration of his seventieth birthday, he was awarded an honorary doctorate by UCT. In a lecture at that event entitled "My Seven Lean Years", he spoke, with all the vigour that we remembered from the past, of his experiences as a banned person and his hopes for the future. For his birthday, Charles and I edited and presented him with a *Festschrift* entitled *Resistance and Hope*.

On the family front, Steve and Debora, who were "really meant for each other" as some friends told us, were married in our church in April 1984. It was a wonderful occasion. Sadly the marriage only lasted eighteen months. We were bewildered by their decision to separate, though we had begun to sense that things were not well between them. Steve, who was busy writing his master's dissertation under my supervision, went to live temporarily in Johannesburg, while Debora's life took a new direction. She later became a celebrated TV presenter. Meanwhile, Isobel was teaching Mathematics at an informal school in Nyanga township to students who were either kicked out or dropped out of school because of their protest against apartheid.

In May 1984 Isobel and I set off for the Bonhoeffer Congress in East Germany. Beforehand we drove from Frankfurt along the Romantische Straße to Bavaria. We visited Augsburg, the Benedictine monastery in Ettal where Bonhoeffer wrote much of his *Ethics*, then Oberammergau – famous for its Passion Play. We met an old monk walking in the hills above Ettal.

"Do you remember a young *Evangelische* theologian called Bonhoeffer who stayed here in 1943?" I asked.

"No," he replied, "but we could visit the room of a Jesuit priest who did stay and who was martyred during the war."

Perhaps, I thought to myself, if they knew that Bonhoeffer was also martyred they might even find his room and make it a pilgrimage site.

Getting into the German Democratic Republic (GDR) on a South African passport was a challenge, but the congress organisers had an undertaking that all participants would be welcome. So Isobel and I joined several other Bonhoeffer friends in West Berlin and caught the train east. There were armed guards at the station, but we had no difficulty at passport control. Our host was Martin Kuske, a Lutheran pastor who later participated in the democratic revolution in East Germany, but soon became disillusioned and, driven to despair, took his own life.

The day after we had arrived, Kuske took us by bus along a pre-war autobahn for the fifty-kilometre trip to the church conference centre in Hirschluh. Bishop Albert Schönherr, one of Bonhoeffer's students, welcomed us on his own turf.

One evening we returned to East Berlin for a reception hosted by the minister of cultural affairs – a Jewish communist named Klaus Gysi. Gysi was an intelligent and gracious man. In his speech of welcome, he extolled the achievements of the GDR, and acknowledged the importance of Bonhoeffer in the struggle against Nazism, as well as his significant influence on the Church in East Germany. I was asked to respond, but the irony of a white South African doing this was not lost on me, and probably not on him either.

After the congress we, together with the Burtnesses and Greens, set off by train on our visit to Luther country. In Wittenberg we saw where the Reformer nailed his ninety-five theses to the Castle Church door to launch the Reformation, and in Erfurt we visited the monastery where he was a monk, prior to that decisive moment. In Leipzig we visited St. Thomas' Church, where J.S. Bach was the organist for many years. We stayed in the opulent Mercure Hotel, set aside for foreign visitors, and had a fine meal at Goethe's Auerbachs Keller, which cost us virtually nothing, given the exchange rate between the US dollar and the East German mark.

After Leipzig we visited the notorious Buchenwald concentration camp outside Weimar, and were surprised it was portrayed more as the place where communists, rather than Jews, had been incarcerated and murdered by the Nazis. Either way, it was a sobering reminder of those crimes against humanity.

Our last stop was Eisenach and the Wartburg Castle. Expecting to go on a Luther tour, we discovered that the castle was more famous as the residence of Heilige Elisabeth (St. Elizabeth), the Catholic queen who became a saint for her work among the poor. But we did visit the dark turret room, perched high above the forest below, where Luther translated the New Testament into German and hurled his inkpot at the devil in a moment of despair.

Back in West Germany, we visited the Bethges in Villiprott and, as always after dinner, the men had to smoke the obligatory Cuban cigar – one of Bonhoeffer's and Bethge's less salubrious habits. Even though I had smoked a pipe as a student, this always left me in a state of nausea, but the lively conversation made it worthwhile.

My travels for the year concluded with another visit to the US, this time to Seattle for a symposium celebrating the fiftieth anniversary of the Barmen Declaration – the charter of the German Confessing Church. The chairman was my former professor in Chicago, Franklin Littell, who had first taught me about the German church struggle. Also present were the Bethges and one of Bonhoeffer's close friends from the Barmen period, Franz Hildebrandt.

I had several lengthy conversations with Hildebrandt, who was now in his late seventies. He had been a Lutheran pastor in Germany, but, being partly Jewish, had fled into exile in England in 1935, where he became a Methodist minister. In Seattle I was asked to write an introductory essay for the publication of his Cambridge doctoral dissertation, *The Gospel and Humanitarianism*, but his son-in-law who piloted the project was unable to find a publisher. That was a great pity for Hildebrandt had shown that Luther's rejection of the Anabaptists had serious negative repercussions for the social witness of the Lutheran Church in Germany. I had long thought this was the case.

The well-known German feminist theologian Dorothee Sölle's lecture at the Seattle symposium preceded mine. It was a difficult act to follow. I agreed with most of what she said, but felt that she had not done justice to Barmen's Christological core; so I took her up on that in my lecture. Fortunately she was gracious, and I even ended up being invited to a small party in her room that evening. As I was already in bed when Eberhard Bethge phoned to ask me to come, I declined at first. But he insisted, so I sneaked down the hotel stairs in my pyjamas for what turned out to be a hilarious party, punctuated by reflections on a memorable conference about more sober times and issues.

13

A moment of truth

> South Africa has been plunged into a crisis that is shaking the foundations ... It is the KAIROS or moment of truth not only for apartheid but also for the Church and all other faiths and religions.
>
> *(Kairos Document)*[9]

As 1985 dawned, the future of South Africa looked bleak, but still Botha refused to accept the need for genuine change. Even so, we hoped he might have the sense to grasp the nettle in an eagerly anticipated speech to be made in Durban. But he failed to cross that Rubicon, became more intransigent, and belligerently declared a general State of Emergency. This was renewed in 1986 and lasted until 1989. A new wave of State terror and violence was unleashed in an attempt to crush the UDF and the Mass Democratic Movement led by COSATU, the nationwide trade union. There was violence in the townships as the police brutally sought to halt protests; scores of activists were arrested and thrown into prison, many of them kept in solitary confinement and tortured, and some murdered. But resistance only hardened.

A few personal memories resurface. One is of a prayer service I conducted in a small shanty of a church building in Crossroads – one small way in which some of us tried to show solidarity. I walked through a muddy, dirt-strewn path to get there late in the afternoon. The church was dark and dank and half filled with people who had gathered to remember the victims of police brutality. I felt depressed. Then the door creaked open and in walked a young girl dressed in white, carrying a candle which she placed on the crude altar. My spirits lifted. This simple act was one of defiant hope.

On two occasions the Rondebosch United Church, as it was now known, was surrounded by armed police preventing the holding of meetings by the UDF in our hall. I recall Doug Bax striding up to the church door through the police cordon and tearing down the notice which forbade the meetings.

Then there were the services we held in our church to celebrate the Soweto uprising each year, usually attended by young black activists from the townships. On one such occasion the police raided the church after the service looking for banned pamphlets and questioning several worshippers. On another occasion, at a memorial service for an activist, the visiting black participants burst into a struggle song in Xhosa. I asked those next to me what the words meant.

"It is better you don't know!" was the reply.

During the State of Emergency, there were the Wednesday late-afternoon services in the Buitenkant Street Methodist Church in the city. Crowds came to pray for the release of detainees. It was illegal to publicise their names, but they were defiantly read out in front of a candle burning inside a spiral of barbed wire. I was there one afternoon at the same time as Steve was in the holding cells of the police headquarters across the road, having been arrested during a street protest. The police demanded that we all leave the church. A major pulled by a snarling dog on a leash tried to disperse us. I crossed the road to the police station and demanded to see Steve. Permission was reluctantly given, and I was taken through dark passageways and several cells before finding him sitting on the concrete floor in the company of hardened criminals – but "whites only". All I had time to do was to tell him we were trying to get him released.

On the ninth anniversary of the Soweto uprising, 16 June 1985, a mass service was held at the African Methodist Episcopal Church (AME) in Hazendal to pray for an end to unjust rule. This was in response to a theological rationale that had been issued by the SACC, whose general secretary was now Beyers Naudé. What it called for was treasonable; today we would call it a demand for regime change. This anticipated the publication of the *Kairos Document*, which was then already in the process of being drafted.

Early in 1985, in the midst of all this, I received a surprise invitation to have dinner with Willie Esterhuyse, professor of Political Philosophy at Stellenbosch University and a leading Afrikaner intellectual. I knew him from a UCT-Stellenbosch fellowship group to which we both belonged. Initiated by John Reid – then the deputy vice-chancellor of UCT – the group met monthly on a Sunday evening to discuss our concerns. I soon sensed that Willie had an insider's knowledge about what was going on within the government and Afrikaner establishment. One day he phoned and asked me to meet him at the Southern Sun Hotel in the city for Sunday evening dinner. I accepted on the assumption that there was no such thing as a free dinner.

Dinner and small talk behind us, Willie asked, "If you were to invite two African-American scholars to visit South Africa, John, who would they be?"

I was completely taken aback. After a few moments of thought,

I mentioned James Cone and Cornel West, both of whom I knew. Cone was the leading black theologian in the US, and taught at Union Seminary; West was a philosopher who had taught at Yale and Princeton Universities, as well as at Union.

"But they will never get visas," I added.

"What if they did?" Willie responded. "And what if all their expenses were covered?"

"Perhaps," I said, "but I do not think they will come to apartheid South Africa in any case."

Nonetheless, I promised Willie that I would approach them. I discussed the proposal with Charles Villa-Vicencio, and we approached Allan Boesak for his support.

To my surprise, Cone and West, after consulting with each other and noting that the proposal gave them freedom to go anywhere they wanted and meet anybody they chose, accepted the invitation. It came formally from the US-South Africa Leader Exchange Program (USSALEP) of which Willie Esterhuyse was a board member. But the invitation and the obtaining of visas would never have been possible without the support of the relevant authorities in the government.

Cone later gave an account of their visit in his book *Speaking the Truth*. The trip was made in July 1985 and took them across the country to meet with theologians engaged in the struggle – especially black theologians. I was part of a small group who met with them for three days at the Vineyard Hotel in Newlands, Cape Town. Apart from Charles, Allan Boesak and myself, the group included Takatso Mofokeng and Bonganjalo Goba, both from UNISA. The conversation focused on the role of the churches in the struggle, the morality of violence in a just revolution, and the possibilities of radical change. We were all convinced opposition to apartheid would soon erupt even further, but were hopeful that this would be non-violent and soon lead to the end of apartheid. I have often thought of the irony that our stay at the Vineyard was made possible with some official connivance.

A few weeks earlier, in April, I was asked by the SABC to give a radio talk on "Dietrich Bonhoeffer: Christian, Theologian and Martyr". I was *persona non grata* with the SABC at the time, so this was a surprising turn of events. But I still have the lengthy script of my talk on Bonhoeffer's role in the German Resistance.

In July I gave two addresses to the Anglican Students Federation meeting in Modderpoort in the Free State. The first was on "Christianity and Patriotism" and the second on "Christianity and Culture". Again there was lively debate in this non-racial student environment, as white students wrestled with conscientious objection and black students expressed their anger with the inadequate way in which the church was responding to the crisis.

On 28 August 1985 there was a mass protest march on Pollsmoor Prison outside Cape Town where Nelson Mandela was taken after being on Robben Island. The march was part of the Free Mandela campaign led by the UDF, and involved many Christian clergy members and leaders of other faith communities. It started some kilometres from the prison, but was soon brutally halted by riot police. Many protesters, including Steve and Debora, and some of my students, were arrested. A second march on the same day had been planned, but kept secret by the organisers.

I was not in Cape Town that day. Early in the morning I flew to Pretoria to give the C.B. Powell Lecture at the University of South Africa. En route I met with Beyers Naudé at the airport in Johannesburg, with a message for him from Charles updating him on the planned secret march. This smaller event, led by Naudé, Boesak and other church leaders, started nearer the prison and managed to hand over a memorandum.

Those on the main march, when they heard about this later, felt they had been left isolated without any high-profile leadership. In his diary, which he kept in Pollsmoor Prison after his arrest, Steve wrote, "When the chips were down where we the leaders?" He then went on to say the fact "that some ministers were willing to step in to a violent and ugly situation speaks volumes for the church, and gives one hope".

The atmosphere was tense in Pretoria that night as I gave my lecture on "Standing by God in His Hour of Grieving", influenced by one of Bonhoeffer's prison poems. I repeated it a few days later in Cape Town and dedicated it to those in prison, who were released four days later.

Soon after the first State of Emergency was declared in 1985, Frank Chikane as director of the ICT, together with Catholic theologian Albert Nolan and other theologians associated with the ICT, drafted the *Kairos Document*. I first became aware of the document when Nolan, who was on the run from the security police, came to Cape Town and gave a clandestine seminar on the document in our department.

The document rejected the "church theology" of the more liberal English-speaking churches that were accused of putting reconciliation ahead of justice, and the "state theology" of those churches that gave legitimacy to apartheid. Instead it proposed a radical prophetic theology that encouraged church participation in the struggle to bring the illegitimate apartheid regime to its knees. In doing so it implied that the apartheid government was a tyrannical regime, with which Christians could not collaborate in any way.

When the *Kairos Document* was published in September 1985 with my name appended, Willie Jonker, the DRC theologian at Stellenbosch, was aghast.

"How could you sign it, John?" he asked in a phone call the next day.

I replied that neutrality was not an option. But then I had less to lose than him in signing it.

14

Some kind of expert

Professor (n.) late 14c. ... from Latin professor "person who professes to be an expert in some art or science; teacher of highest rank," ... As a title prefixed to a name, it dates from 1706.

(Online Etymology Dictionary)[10]

During the first State of Emergency I was promoted to full professor with the title professor of Christian Studies. It sounds surreal looking back on those tumultuous days, but life continued, lectures were given and essays marked, church meetings were held, friends came to dinner, we made love, we went hiking and swimming, we went to movies and the theatre, we repaired our houses and walked the dogs. I also played squash, and tennis on Saturday afternoons with Geoff Burton, Heribert Adam, Mike Savage and Alex Boraine, when politics and pleasure mixed in equal doses. Bonhoeffer did the same in the time of the Third Reich. In abnormal times you try to live normal lives, even if a dark cloud of political madness is always hovering over you, and you're guiltily aware of the pain of so many for whom any normality is a distant dream.

In South Africa the title "professor" is reserved for those who have been appointed to the position as acknowledged leaders and experts in their field. The normal progress up the academic ladder is from lecturer to senior lecturer, then associate professor, and finally appointment to a professorial chair. Later, in 1994, my chair was named after Robert Selby Taylor, the former archbishop, who had been responsible for the original foundation of the Department of Religious Studies. The chair was designated Christian Studies, not Theology. My expertise, if I may call it that, was at the interface of Christianity, history and politics.

In confirmation that I was also regarded by some as a Bonhoeffer scholar, I was invited by the Lutheran Bishop Martin Kruse to give a lecture at a conference in Berlin, in celebration of Bonhoeffer's eightieth birthday in February 1986. Upon my arrival I was taken to a radio station for an interview. I had agreed to do this on the understanding that, while the interview would be in German, I would respond in English. What I did not know was that the interviewer would be in a studio in Hanover. This meant that I could only hear his voice but not read his lips. This is very difficult when conversing in another language. I had been given the questions in advance, but halfway through the direction of the interview changed tack. All of a sudden I had to make sense of unexpected questions fired in rapid succession. It was a tough conversation, as these questions were about the situation in South Africa and I could not afford to misunderstand them.

I gave my lecture on the opening day of the conference on Bonhoeffer's influence on confession and resistance in South Africa. Just before doing so, all the students in the auditorium stood up and staged an angry demonstration, which erupted into trading blows with some of the professors who tried to intervene. They were not protesting my presence as I had assumed, but that of the mayor of

SOME KIND OF EXPERT

Berlin who had been invited to open the event despite suspicions of fraud and corruption. Later that evening I enjoyed a lively discussion with some of those same students, drinking beer and talking theology with much passion.

From Berlin I flew to London for the launch of my little book *Cry Justice!* Intended as a devotional manual and comprised of prayers, meditations, poems and some artwork, I had put it together in one month at the request of the publisher William Collins. *Cry Justice!*, soon translated into German, related the theology of resistance and protest to Christian spirituality. The launch was presided over by Bishop Trevor Huddleston, who wrote the classic *Naught for Your Comfort* in which he tells the story of his ministry as a priest in Johannesburg in the 1950s. This was the first time I met him. A few years later, on a cold winter's Sunday morning, I went to a very early Eucharist in St. James, Piccadilly, at which he presided. I was the only person present other than a sidesman, who took my pittance up to the altar during the offertory with great reverence. But the service proceeded with dignity, as though we were surrounded by a great cloud of witnesses – which we probably were.

While in London I was also interviewed on BBC Radio and preached in Westminster Abbey on the Sunday morning. My sermon was on the revolutionary power of the Word, recounting at the beginning how, when I had gone through the security check at Heathrow on a previous visit, the zip on my travelling Bible had set off the alarm. I informed the officer that it was only a Bible.

He immediately retorted, "Yes, but that can be a very dangerous book!" "Especially for tyrants and oppressors," I retorted, as I swiftly took my leave.

Soon after I had preached, we processed down the nave and gathered for a closing prayer in the sacristy, famous because it was there that the Authorised Version or King James Version (KJV) of the Bible was translated. King James had handpicked the translators to ensure that the KJV would not be quite as revolutionary a document as I had suggested in my sermon.

That Sunday was memorable for another reason. While I was having breakfast at the Royal Automobile Club (RAC), where Collins had kindly arranged for me to stay, and enjoying the beauty of the snow gently falling outside, I noted the headlines in one of the newspapers on a nearby table: "South African opposition members of Parliament resign". The article reported that the leader of the Progressive Party, Frederik van Zyl Slabbert, and his colleague Alex Boraine, had resigned from Parliament, believing that it was impotent in dealing justly with the crisis in the country. I had some prior knowledge that this might happen, but was still taken by surprise. Van Zyl and Alex's resignation was a shock to many white South Africans, and led to harsh words directed at the two politicians. But they were right to my mind. Soon after their resignation, they founded the Institute for a Democratic Alternative in South Africa (IDASA)[11] to help achieve a non-racial society. I thought they should have called it the Institute for Social Democracy to signal the direction that democracy needed to take.

Three invitations took me back to the US in April 1986. Steve joined me for sections of the trip, as he was keen to find a place where he could do further graduate study. By this time he was already going out with Marian Loveday, a physiotherapist in Cape Town, and they were soon to be engaged. Steve was with me when I began my visit with a lecture at a National Conference on Faith and Learning at Bethel College in Kansas. – an event at which I first met the theological ethicist Stanley Hauerwas. Steve and I were delighted to return to a place we had come to know well, and to revisit friends from our sabbatical almost ten years ago. I was asked to speak on "Christian Liberal Learning in an Unjust World," but spoke instead about "Education at the Cape of Storms". I described the multicultural changes taking place on the UCT campus and how we were responding to them. There was some debate as to whether it was possible to do so without losing institutional identity. My response was that justice demanded it and, in any case, we had no alternative.

The second invitation was from the dean of the Divinity School at the University of Chicago. There my lecture was on theological developments in South Africa relating to the *Kairos Document*. Catholic theologian David Tracy, whose book *The Analogical Imagination* had influenced my thinking at that time, presided.

The third invitation was to a symposium at the Center for Humanities at Wesleyan University in Middletown, Connecticut, where I was asked to speak on "Religion, Tradition and Transformation". While there, I met Gene Klaaren from the Department of Religion, who would become a close friend. I also met his son, Jonathan, who later came to do graduate work in our Christian Studies programme. He then studied law at Columbia University, and ended up teaching at the University of the Witwatersrand in Johannesburg.

My travels for the year were only halfway through. In June Isobel and I went to Cambridge, where I gave the Reid Lectures at Westminster College at the invitation of the principal, Martin Cressey. My book based on the lectures, *Theology and Ministry in Context and Crisis*, was published soon after by Collins and Eerdmans. During my visit I had the pleasure of visiting the dean of Clare College, Rowan Williams, who later became the archbishop of Canterbury. When Steve died years later, he wrote us a very gracious and supportive letter.

I dedicated *Theology and Ministry* to Desmond Tutu. He came for dinner to celebrate its publication, arriving a little later than the other guests. As he came into our sitting room, our usually benign Labrador, Tamba, jumped to his feet and snarled at him. We were deeply embarrassed. But the genial archbishop patted him on the head and calmed him down with the words: "You racist dog, you!"

My father died in Cape Town on the day of my final lecture at Westminster College, though I was only told after giving it. He was eighty-four years old. We had visited him in hospital just before we left for England, and he was then only barely conscious. His death struck me very hard, especially as we could not get back for the funeral. Isobel and I were scheduled to go to Greece, and my mother insisted that we should do so. Steve took my place, and he, Marian and Jeanelle made all the arrangements, and did so with great maturity. On the day, Isobel and I went to a village parish church, St. John the Baptist in Finchingfield, Suffolk, where I wept tears in remembrance of a wonderfully kind and generous father. But I still regret that I was not there for him that day.

The distinguished University of Chicago church historian Martin Marty, together with his wife, Harriet, spent six weeks in the Department of Religious Studies during July to August 1986. Marty had edited one of the earliest books in English on Bonhoeffer's theology, which I read while studying in Chicago. I had invited him to come to UCT when I met him during my sabbatical in Princeton in 1983 and was delighted when he finally managed to do so. He gave several lectures during his stay and preached in St. George's Cathedral. He and Harriet joined Isobel and me when we first visited Volmoed at the suggestion of our son Anton.

Volmoed had just been established as a retreat and conference centre in the Hemel en Aarde Valley near Hermanus, about 120 kilometres from Cape Town. Little did we know at the time that it would eventually become our home. Shortly after our visit, I was invited to be the master of ceremonies at the launch of the Volmoed Trust at a fundraising dinner in Cape Town. This was not a great financial success, but helped launch Volmoed as a place of multi-racial reconciliation and healing. The founding of Volmoed was a remarkable act of faith at a time when the future of South Africa looked decidedly bleak.

I began this chapter by saying something about my new status as professor of Christian Studies. While Theology as such was not meant to be taught in the department, I could not deny that I was a theologian or confine theology to some religious sphere or spiritual dimension. For me, doing theology meant crossing boundaries and disciplines in an attempt to understand life in all its complexity from the perspective of faith in God. It was with such reflections in mind that I gave my Inaugural Lecture on "Doing Christian Theology in the Context of South Africa, or, God-Talk under Devil's Peak". Isobel helped me conceive the title, which of course refers to the peak on Table Mountain which towers above UCT.

My final journey, in November of that eventful year, was to New York where I participated in Bonhoeffer's eightieth birthday celebrations at Union Theological Seminary. After Union, I went with Steve, who was now studying at Union, to give a lecture at the Karl Barth Symposium held at Stony Point in upstate New York. This was a relatively small event, but the papers and discussion were stimulating. My paper on "Racism, Reconciliation and Resistance" engaged Barth's theology in relation to the issues raised by the *Kairos Document*. I concluded by saying that, because many of us believed that apartheid was destructive of human life, "a form of disorder rather than order, lawlessness not law", it was the duty of the Church to resist the State and, through both prayer and action, work for change and transformation.[12]

15

Not only a tourist

> Bonhoeffer left for Italy on the afternoon of April 3, 1924. Toting his leather-bound Baedeker, his pens, books and writing paper ... he appeared in every way the sophisticated traveller ... Bonhoeffer was ... following family tradition, but he was also expressing a more personal desire to cross borders and make discoveries in his quest for originality.
>
> (Charles Marsh)[13]

Bonhoeffer was an inveterate traveller, but he was more than a tourist. He was always reflecting on what he was seeing and experiencing. In a prison letter he confided that he had only significantly changed once in his life, and that was due to the influence of his father and his early travels to Italy, North Africa and America. Without travelling he would not have become the person he was.

My travels have undoubtedly also changed me, my outward journey influencing my inner journey. And while they have put considerable strain on family life, and especially on Isobel at times, she tells me that they have also enhanced our lives as a family in many ways.

In 1987 I went to Bulawayo, Zimbabwe, for the UCCSA Assembly.

Not much had changed since my visit in 1980, but now it was possible to meet, as we did at the assembly, with representatives of the ANC in exile – one of many such gatherings that were taking place around that time. Afterwards, Isobel and I, together with her sister Elsie and brother-in-law, Ron, who had just been inducted as chair of the UCCSA, went for a holiday to the Victoria Falls. Once again I was overwhelmed by their awesome beauty. David Livingstone, one of the ancestors of the UCCSA, was evidently the first European to set eyes on them, so we paid homage at his statue nearby.

Also in 1987, I was elected president of the Theological Society of South Africa. The society was a very different organisation from when it had been the Dogmatologiese Werkgemeenskap. I guess I can take some credit for its transformation, and my election for two terms (1987 to 1989; 1990 to 1992) was some vindication of my decision to join the society in the first place. Sadly, some of the senior Afrikaans theologians had meanwhile withdrawn their membership, but a younger generation soon took their place.

A young American couple, Suellen and Don Shay, came to spend 1987 in Cape Town doing youth work at the Rondebosch United Church, and walked into our lives. They became friendly with Steve and Jeanelle, settled in Cape Town, and have since only returned to the US for the occasional visit. Don and Suellen eventually became our grandchildren's godparents, and Steve and Marian became the godparents of their three daughters, Charissa, Danielle and Emily. Then Suellen's missionary parents, Ron and Carolyn Butler, left Zaire to settle in Cape Town in 1996, and we became close friends with them as well. We have become extended family to each other. After Ron's untimely death in 2008 from cancer, I felt I had become a surrogate grandfather as well.

At the beginning of 1988 I went to lecture for a month at Fuller

Theological Seminary in Pasadena, California. I knew of Fuller by reputation as a fine evangelical seminary with a good faculty, which included Geoffrey Bromiley, the translator of Karl Barth's multivolume *Church Dogmatics*. Walking on the hills above Pasadena, I listened to Bromiley reminisce on his role as one of Barth's translators.

"His Latin and Greek quotations," he said, "were generally from memory and not always accurate, so I had to spend much time tracking them down and checking them." He was obviously not as divinely inspired as some ardent Barthians might think.

A few weeks prior to departing for the States, Fuller sent me a statement setting out its beliefs and asked me to sign it as an affirmation that I was in agreement. I understood why Fuller felt the need to protect its evangelical integrity, but I declined. I have a respect for creeds as doxological expressions of faith, and for confessions of faith as prophetic declarations in contexts that demand them. But I have a dislike of statements that reduce faith to propositions and are used to control belief. This in no way affected my stay at Fuller, where I felt very welcome.

I introduced my class to the idea that doing theology is a way of reflecting critically on contemporary issues in the light of scripture, and in the process retrieving traditions within Christian history that are transformative. One student belonged to the Foursquare Gospel Church of God. She was concerned about the male dominance in her church. At my suggestion she explored the origins of her church and discovered, to her surprise, that it had been founded by a woman, Aimee Semple McPherson. For her, that "aha" moment was transformative.

My UCT colleague David Chidester, who was originally from California and was home for the vacation, took me to visit the University of Santa Barbara for a day-long seminar on Religious

Pluralism, led by Ninian Smart. Apart from his many academic books, Smart was well known for *The Long Search*, which became a BBC television series. I had first met him when he was teaching at the University of Lancaster in England. Subsequently he came to UCT to teach for six weeks, and took an ongoing interest in the department. We were very privileged in this way, for time and again distinguished scholars from around the world spent time with us, because they were interested in doing so – certainly not because of the paltry amount we could pay them.

On 9 April 1988, Steve and Marian were married in the Rondebosch Church. We were all delighted, and equally pleased that they would be living near us in Observatory. Steve was then serving his internship at Gleemoor Congregational Church in Athlone, writing his doctoral dissertation on Reinhold Niebuhr at the University of the Western Cape, and working part-time as a hospital chaplain at Groote Schuur as an alternative to military service. There had been a change in government policy. If you could convince a tribunal that you were a Conscientious Objector on religious grounds, you could do alternative service in the national interest. Steve applied for this status. I later heard that when his application came before the board, there was strong objection from an Anglican priest, but Professor Johan Heyns, the DRC leader and theologian, with whom I had at best a cool relationship, persuaded the board otherwise.

The Fifth International Bonhoeffer Congress was held in Amsterdam in June 1988. After my lecture, Professor Heinz Eduard Tödt from Heidelberg paid me one of the highest compliments I had yet received. My lecture, he confided to Eberhard Bethge, proved that I was more than a theological tourist. But I must immediately confess that, after the congress, Isobel and I joined Larry and Nyla Rasmussen, along with John and Emilie Godsey, on a barge holiday on the Canal du Midi in the South of France. Godsey had written the first major theological study on Bonhoeffer in English when he was a student of Barth's, and many years later I dedicated my biography of Bethge to him. But on the barge John, who was older than the rest of us by a number of years, was like a child who found it difficult to surrender the wheel. We had great fun exploring the Lanquedoc countryside on bicycles and enjoying rural cuisine in the village restaurants we discovered along the way. We stopped over one day to explore medieval Carcassonne, the refuge of the Cathars during the terrible years of persecution by the Inquisition. When religion goes bad, it is truly awful.

Isobel and I drove back from Marseillan, the port where our barge trip ended, to Avignon, home to an exiled papacy in the fourteenth century, then on to the massive ruins of Cluny Abbey, Taizé, Tournus, Beaune and other delightful places in Alsace. Our journey ended in Heidelberg where we were the guests of Wolfgang and Kara Huber. Wolfgang, who was a professor of Christian Ethics together with Professor Tödt, had invited me to participate in their Bonhoeffer seminar. We stayed at the Internationales Wissenschaftsforum, within walking distance of the town centre and the Neckar River, and beneath the towering castle made famous in *The Student Prince* (a film that was by then a very distant memory).

Sometime during the State of Emergency in 1987, an explosive blew up the bus shelter outside the apartment block where my mother was staying in Rondebosch, directly opposite the president's Groote Schuur residence. The police arrested a group of young "coloured" men led by Ashley Forbes. They were found guilty of treason in the High Court and were liable to be sentenced to lengthy periods in prison. I was requested by their defence counsel to be a witness in mitigation of their sentence. In preparation, I spent a morning with the group in Pollsmoor Prison. They were most anxious that I should not compromise their stand against apartheid or apologise for what they had done. I assured them that I would not do so.

The High Court convened in November 1988 and was presided over by Justice Williamson, a well-informed Roman Catholic. This was fortuitous. As several of the accused were members of churches (a few were Muslims), I was cross-examined on the Christian understanding of resistance against tyranny. The discussion ended up with Williamson engaging me at length about the teaching of Saint Thomas Aquinas and John Calvin. This left those in the dock and the gallery out in the cold. But I think I made a strong enough case for the right for people of faith to resist oppression, even though I did not condone the use of violence. In fact, I told the group when I visited them in prison that I was angry that they had blown up my mother's bus shelter. Their sentence was reduced and in 1989 they were set free.

The year ended with another visit to the US. My first assignment was to give the E.B. Hoff Lectures at Bethany Theological Seminary on "The Challenge of South African Theology". I was honoured to be numbered among several previous lecturers, including the doyen of feminist theologians, Rosemary Radford Ruether, and the psychologist Bruno Bettelheim. Forgive this blatant name-dropping, but I am still truly amazed that I could be included on the same list. After the Hoff Lectures, I went to St. Norbert College in De Pere, Wisconsin, to give the Killeen Lecture at the invitation of another friend from the Bonhoeffer Society, Michael Lukens. My visit ended in Chicago, where I once again attended the AAR.

Over these years Isobel and I often went hiking on some of the wonderful trails in the Western Cape and Karoo, and further afield in the Blyde River Canyon near the Kruger National Park. We also bought a plot of land in 1988, together with our good friends Julian and Judy Cooke, and built a thatched holiday cottage on the banks of the Duiwenhoks River at Vermaaklikheid, about as far away as we could get from civilisation over a weekend. Situated three hundred kilometres from Cape Town along the southeast coast near the famous Blombos Cave, our hideaway has proved its value over the years. Travelling overseas has its great moments and rewards, but nothing can compare to a visit to Vermaaklikheid with family and friends, and the sharing of a glass of wine around a braai under the starlit night sky as the river runs by. It was there that I first heard the news that Nelson Mandela was about to walk free.

1929 My parents' wedding day, St. John's Methodist Church, Port Elizabeth

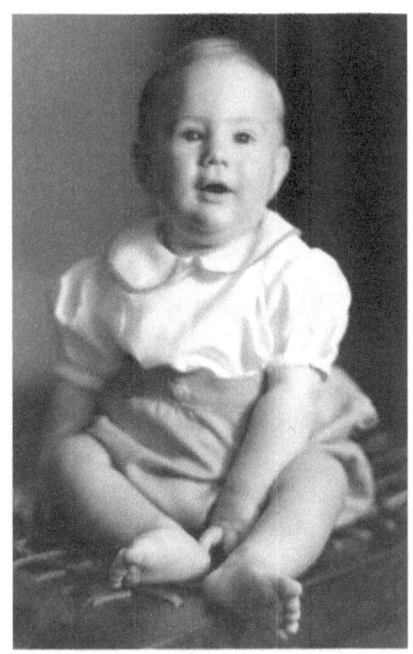

1939 John, aged 6 months

Below: 1944 Rozelle and me walking up Darling Street, Cape Town

Left: 1949 Captain, SACS U11 rugby team

1949 My first bicycle and dog Chippy

Our house. 43 Bellevue Street, at the top of Kloof Street. Table Mountain is in the background.

1959 Going steady with Isobel Dunstan at Rhodes University, Grahamstown

1959 First protest march against the extension of the University Act which segregated "open universities" in South Africa, separating Rhodes and Fort Hare.

January 1961, after my ordination

7 January 1961, Our wedding day

1965 With Jeanelle and Steve in the Manse in Sea View, Durban

September 1966 John and Steven in a boat at Amanzimtoti

January 1964 Shovelling snow with Steve outside our house in Chicago

1964 Talking to Paul Tillich after a seminar at the University of Chicago

1967 Steve's first day of school, Sea View Primary

1971 I was working for the SACC in Johannesburg

1973 Our family outside our home 21 Delta Road, Blairgowrie, Johannesburg

February 1973 With Eberhard Bethge at our home in Blairgowrie when he and Renate visited South Africa

1973 Rondebosch United Church (Congregational and Presbyterian)

February 1986 At the Conference celebrating Dietrich Bonhoeffer's 80th birthday, West Berlin, Germany.

5 December 1976 In the front garden of our home at
10 Vredenburg Avenue, Rosebank, Cape Town

1980 In my study at UCT

1980 Isobel and I in our garden

December 1980 On the front porch of our house in Rosebank

10 May 1985 Beyers Naude's 70th birthday. This was at his first public lecture after his banning ended. He received an Honorary Doctorate and a Festschrift on this occasion.

1986 Steve and John in deep conversation

Above: Grave of John de Gruchy in the Trinity Parish graveyard, Jersey 1993

Right: 1991 Isobel and I on the Great Wall of China

Opposite page: Taken in my study at UCT in 1985 on the publication of *Bonhoeffer and South Africa*.

1997 Anton, Steve and I fixing things at Vermaaklikheid

1994 Establishment of the Robert-Selby Taylor Chair in Christian Studies. Archbiship Philip Russel, Deputy Vice Chancellor Dave Woods, Archbishop Desmond Tutu and Archbishop Selby-Taylor

1999 Pope Shenudoah III, Patriarch of Alexandria, visits Rondebosch United Church

2000 Receiving Karl Barth Prize in Berlin from Dr Huffmeier in the Dom in Berlin

Below left: 2001 Meeting John-Paul II in Rome

Below right: 2004 Receiving an Honorary D.Litt from Chancellor Jakes Gerwel at Rhodes University

2002 Lyn Holness and Ralf Wusternburg presenting my Festschrift at the AAR in Ottawa

Below: 2003 The Volmoed Chapel

Right: 2008 With Desmond Tutu at Volmoed

December 2007 The last photograph taken of the whole family together before Anton and Esther went to settle in Atlanta

2009 Receiving an honorary doctorate from the University of Stellenbosch from Russel Botman

June 2014 Jeanelle, Heidi, Kate, David, myself and Isobel on Jersey Island, before a meal at Crab Shack

2012 Rozelle and I

16

Unforgettable days

Where were you, that unforgettable day when Nelson Mandela walked free?

(The question on everyone's lips in 1990)

On 18 March 1989 I turned fifty. Next to the fall of the Berlin Wall later that year and the release of Mandela from prison early the next, this was not a big deal, but it was a significant moment in my life cycle and appropriately celebrated among friends and family at our home in Rosebank. My mother was there, as were our children, Marian, university colleagues, members of our church, and some of our very special friends. I can still hear Steve making his speech. After he had given me a typical roasting, stressing the "W" in my name, he expressed the kind of relationship we had. "I have been privileged," he said,

> ... to be a full partner in dialogue with you. It has been a blessing to learn so much from you, and I know in my personality and mind that I bear many of your marks; but I also treasure the many things – even theological perceptions – that you have given me the space to share, and you have been willing

to learn from me. Perhaps only you and I will know just how deep we have shared and grappled and learnt from each other. It is a wonderful gift to have a father who is also a friend and a colleague.

It was not always like this. In his younger days I sometimes lost my temper with Stephen (I used his full name when angry). After all, he could be a "cheeky boy" as my mother sometimes said.

A few months after my birthday, Isobel and I made final preparations for a six-month sabbatical at Union Theological Seminary in New York, at the invitation of President Don Shriver. On our way there in August, we visited Athens and the Greek islands, together with Elsie and Ron. Being on Samos, the island of Pythagoras, enabled us to visit the ruins of ancient Ephesus in nearby Turkey – by tradition the place where Mary, the mother of Jesus, spent her last years. From Samos we travelled by ferry to Patmos, spending an uncomfortable night below deck, wondering what would happen if it suddenly capsized. On Patmos we visited the monastery high on the mountain side, and the cave where John the Elder received his mysterious message to the churches of Asia Minor and wrote his Apocalypse.

We then went to Rhodes, an island full of history and places to explore. Our modest hotel advertised a view of the sea from our rooms, but we discovered this required standing on our toes while looking out of the small bathroom window. But a romantic dinner in a restaurant in Lindos, high above the bay where St. Paul once landed, made up for that.

One morning an English newspaper headline informed us that President Botha had resigned and F.W. de Klerk had taken his place. We were not quite sure how to interpret this transition of power. With this unresolved question in mind, we took leave of Ron and

Elsie and set off for New York. As our Olympic Air jet lifted off the runway, we saw peasants working in the fields nearby making the sign of the cross. Maybe they knew something about their airline we did not, but we were grateful for their prayers in any case.

Union Seminary is located in Manhattan between 120th and 122nd Streets on Broadway, in close proximity to Columbia University, with which it is affiliated. Founded in 1836, it has a distinguished tradition of progressive scholarship and teaching. We were within easy reach of all the main attractions in the city, and Riverside Park along the Hudson River was close by. We were on the same campus as our long-time friends Larry and Nyla Rasmussen, close to some great bookshops and restaurants, the Cathedral of St. John the Divine, and right under the shadow of the massive tower of Riverside Church. We were, in short, among friends in a stimulating intellectual, cultural and theological environment.

I had been appointed the visiting Broadway Scholar, which meant I was both on the faculty at Union and an associate minister at Broadway Presbyterian Church a couple of blocks away. Bonhoeffer sometimes worshipped at this church when he was a student at Union, and years later Eberhard Bethge had also been a Broadway Scholar. I could not believe my good fortune. My responsibilities at the church were to preach on occasion and to give a series of evening lectures. I gave these on Bonhoeffer, but had not anticipated that the Bethges, who visited Union during this period, would also be in the audience most evenings.

My sabbatical was timely. I had been asked to give the Warfield Lectures at Princeton Theological Seminary the following year, and Union was an ideal place to prepare them. Soon after our arrival, President Shriver asked me to share what I was doing with the faculty. Jim Cone was not enamoured with my proposal to retrieve the Reformed tradition as a liberating one, and said so with his friendly but blunt frankness. I responded as best I could, recognising the legitimacy of his critique, but determined to do as I had proposed.

During the semester, I went to a meeting at North Park Seminary in Chicago to plan the translation and publication of the sixteen volumes of the new critical edition of the *Dietrich Bonhoeffer Werke* in English. The meeting was convened by the English Language Section of the Bonhoeffer Society. I became a member of the editorial board and remained on it until 2012 when its task was completed – a truly remarkable achievement overseen by Clifford Green and Vicki Barnett. In due course I would edit two volumes, *Creation and Fall (DBWE 3)*, which was translated by Douglas Bax and published in 1997, and *Letters and Papers from Prison (DBWE 8)*, about which I will say more later.

In October I attended a conference at the Columbia Law School to discuss the future constitution of South Africa. The participants included several other South Africans, among them our friends Laurie and Denise Ackermann, along with George Bizos, Arthur Chaskalson, Edwin Cameron, Pius Langa, Raymond Suttner, and members of the ANC in exile. Among the latter were Thabo Mbeki, the future president, and Albie Sachs, a future judge of the Constitutional Court. Sachs was several years my senior at SACS High School, but I had often played chess with his younger brother Johnny at their home, close to my own, when I was at high school. I sensed there was something different about the Sachs household, but only later found out that the parents were deeply involved in the trade union movement and were members of the ANC.

There was an expectant mood at the Columbia conference. The effects of De Klerk's appointment as president, together with the negotiations behind the scenes, were palpable.

Soon after, the dramatic events of political change escalated both in Eastern Europe and South Africa. During that week early in November, when they reached their climax in Cape Town and East Berlin, we hosted a visitor from East Germany at the request of President Shriver. He was a professor of Marxist-Leninist Studies at the University of Rostock. As we watched on TV the events unfold in our respective countries, he assured us that everything was under control, and that the uprising would soon be brought to an end. But Isobel and I were convinced that we were seeing the beginning of the end in South Africa. We could not wait to get back home before Christmas to be part of the drama.

On 2 February 1990, soon after our return, Steve and I joined a protest march which started in Greenmarket Square, then wound its way down Wale Street into Adderley Street, to the Grand Parade. The march was led by UDF activists Cheryl Carolus (the future South African high commissioner in London), Trevor Manuel (the future minister of finance) and Desmond Tutu. It was the opening day of Parliament, and the streets were full of armed soldiers and police. We halted outside Parliament at the very time that De Klerk was making his famous speech, but we were totally unaware of what he was saying. Outside we listened as Carolus stridently read out our demands from the edge of Parliament's precincts.

We continued our march to the Grand Parade where we were to be addressed on the next steps of our protest. Just then a messenger arrived, and instead of hearing rousing calls to action, we were told that De Klerk had decided to unban the ANC, PAC and South African Communist Party (SACP), and to release Mandela on a day to be announced. We were all stunned by the news, and the rally was disbanded. But as we dispersed there was an enormous sense of relief and celebration. Steve and I walked back to my car near the

Company Gardens, and as we passed some heavily armed policemen we gleefully exclaimed, "The liberation movement and communists have been unbanned!" They stared in disbelief. But we hastened on, just in case they arrested us for fomenting unrest.

On Sunday 11 February 1990 Isobel was on a silent Benedictine retreat on the Cape Flats. I was at our remote hideaway in Vermaaklikheid with the Cookes and our friend Mike Savage. We were boating on the river, discussing these recent events, when I suddenly had a gut feeling and blurted out, "Nelson Mandela will be released today!"

Upon our return to the cottage, we heard the news on the radio and decided to return to Cape Town immediately. The news also reached Isobel and her fellow retreatants, who were committed to silence. But as that soon proved impossible, they decided to go to the Grand Parade to witness Mandela's arrival. Unfortunately Mandela arrived too late for them to hear his historic speech to the enormous crowd and the world. I managed to get there a few days later, however, when he again addressed a huge crowd from the balcony of the City Hall. It was electrifying, but also a little terrifying as the crowd shoved and pushed from the back to where I was standing near the front.

A few weeks later I had the privilege of meeting Mandela in person when he came to address a small gathering of clergy who had been involved in the struggle in the Western Cape. I was immediately struck by his towering, graceful presence and the ease with which he related to us. Shortly after, I was again invited to a meeting with him, this time at St. George's Cathedral. There were about fifty of us there to hear him speak about the future of Church-State relations in the new South Africa. I was impressed by his grasp of the issues, the obvious thought that had gone into what he said, and the fact that he addressed us at length without any notes or hesitation. I asked a question in response to his suggestion that there would be a special ministry for religious affairs in the new government. To my mind, this was not something that boded well, I said, because it meant that the churches and other faith communities would not be able to speak directly to specific government departments, but only through this proposed ministry. This could lead to the co-option of faith communities by the government. He was gracious and thoughtful in his response, saying that the matter needed further attention. But he clearly believed that faith communities should play an important role in the process of nation building, along with other agents of change and transformation[14].

During his alternative military service as an ambulance driver, our son Anton had met Esther Marais, a radiologist at Groote Schuur Hospital. He had subsequently graduated in Electrical Engineering at the Technical College and, just before we left on our sabbatical trip to New York, they had begun going out together. But we were totally taken by surprise when, at Union, we heard they had become engaged. On 6 April 1990 they were married in the Rondebosch Church. We were delighted.

Later that month I went to give the Warfield Lectures at Princeton Theological Seminary. The last time I was in the States, just five months previously, Mandela was still in prison and the liberation movements were banned. This was the first time since I went to America in 1963 that I felt an enormous burden had been lifted from our shoulders as South Africans. There was also considerable interest in what I had to say about the role of the Church during this period of transition, but also scepticism among some who thought the transition to democracy would not happen – or at least that it would not happen peacefully.

In my lectures I argued that the Reformed tradition was, at its core, a liberating one, but continually needed liberation from the encrustations of history that had often made it legalistic and sometimes oppressive. Eerdmans agreed to the publication of the lectures under the title *Liberating Reformed Theology*. They were subsequently translated into German and Korean.

On returning home I had to prepare for several speaking engagements, apart from continuing my daily round of lectures, graduate supervision and meetings. In June 1990 I addressed a congress in Pietermaritzburg on "The Task of the Church in the Transition to a Post-Apartheid Society". The congress was arranged by the Pietermaritzburg Agency for Communal Social Action (PACSA), a remarkable faith-based social activist NGO in Natal (now KwaZulu-Natal).

In August Isobel and I, together with Wolfgang and Kara Huber, travelled along the Garden Route on our way to the Annual Congress of the Theological Society, held that year at the University of Port Elizabeth (now named the Mandela Metropolitan University). As president, I gave the opening paper on the topic "From Cottesloe to *The Road to Damascus*". I traced the way in which the churches in South Africa had responded to apartheid from the 1960s until the *Kairos Document* and *The Road to Damascus*. The latter was a document based on *Kairos*, but was more global in its focus.

To round off my travels and conference-going for the year, I, together with my brother-in-law Ron Steel, attended the historic National Church Leaders Conference held in Rustenburg in November. This brought together leaders from across the whole spectrum of denominations. For the first time Christian leaders of such diversity, many of whom had been adversaries during previous years, sought a common mind on the role of the Church in the shaping of a new South Africa. In my address I spoke directly to this subject.

After his lecture on reconciliation, Willie Jonker from Stellenbosch apologised on behalf of the DRC for having given support to apartheid. When P.W. Botha heard about this, he immediately phoned Jonker and gave him an angry telling-off. In contrast, Tutu embraced Jonker at the conference and expressed deep appreciation for what he had said, even though there were some murmurings that Tutu's gesture was premature. But there were hopeful signs of consensus on key issues, reflected in *The Rustenburg Declaration* adopted at the conclusion.

On the sidelines at Rustenburg, I had a conversation with Barney Pityana, one of Steve Biko's former associates. Barney was a lawyer by training and an Anglican priest by vocation, who was working for the WCC and coordinating the conference alongside Frank Chikane, general secretary of the SACC. I had great respect for Barney and believed he had an important contribution to make to the transformation of South Africa. So I encouraged him to return from exile and come to UCT to study for his PhD. He managed to do so and eventually obtained his doctorate under Charles Villa-Vicencio's supervision. Later Barney became director of the Human Rights Commission, and then vice-chancellor of the University of South Africa. Before his retirement, he was rector of the Anglican theological College of the Transfiguration – the successor to St. Paul's College – in Grahamstown. Frank Chikane also enrolled as a doctoral student at UCT soon after, but his studies were cut short when he was invited to become a senior aide to then Vice-President Thabo Mbeki.

Looking back on those momentous days since we set off for our sabbatical in New York and heard about the resignation of P.W. Botha, and then returned to share in the excitement of Mandela's release, we could be forgiven for thinking that, having lived through the worst of times, we were beginning to start living through the best. But we had no idea what was waiting for us on the road ahead. South Africa still had a long way to go.

PART THREE

Embracing the changes

1990-2002

Oh, to be alive amid the Great Turning!
Oh, to be alive in this time of change.
Embrace the changes!
Open new ways for life to sustain.

(Gretchen Sleicher)[1]

17

Transition and travel

> While there have been changes – changes at which we all rejoice – many things remain the same. For as long as there is poverty, as long as there are people without the hope that comes with opportunity for education and housing and security, as long as there are people who struggle for dignity and human rights, there can be no truly acceptable community in the eyes of God.
>
> (Konrad Raiser)[2]

After 1990 we were no longer denizens of a pariah state, but in the process of becoming global citizens. I was past fifty, a grandfather, a senior academic lecturing around the world. I was glad "to be alive amid the Great Turning". Indicative of the changes was a phone call I received that September from one of the programme directors at SABC: "Would you appear on television for a discussion with Joe Slovo about religious freedom in the new South Africa?"

Slovo, chief comrade of the SACP, was the bogeyman of the apartheid regime. I seized the opportunity and several days later found myself in a TV studio in Cape Town, talking to Slovo who was in Johannesburg. Slovo acknowledged the importance of religion in the new South Africa and the right of people to believe in God.

Speaking as a believer, I was critical of the bad track record of some forms of Christianity when it came to religious tolerance. In a light-hearted report in the *Weekend Mail*, Charlotte Bauer said this was a rare event on TV:

> De Gruchy said that Christianity "stands or falls by proving its claims and engaging in a market place of discourse." The atheism debate, he said, was a dead duck. Slovo nodded happily and agreed. Slovo said the fact that materialist atheist communism didn't believe in God didn't mean they would not tolerate Christians. De Gruchy nodded happily and agreed.[3]

Another sign that things were changing was an invitation in 1989 from the WCC to attend a conference in Yogyakarta, the ancient cultural capital of Indonesia. But had things changed enough for me to get a visa? I recalled how, years before, I had tried to visit India, but back then there were signs at Indian airports reading: "No dogs or South Africans welcome". Now India was welcoming South African cricket teams, so surely Indonesia would allow me in. But not even Desmond Tutu could persuade the authorities to do so. Things were changing, but it was not yet certain that either South Africa or the world would fully embrace these changes. Transition did not imply transformation.

Even so, a year later, in May 1990, Isobel and I travelled to New Zealand and China, with a brief stopover in Singapore where a former Singaporean consul-general in Cape Town thought it would be a treat for us to dine at the American Club. We had hoped to experience the local cuisine, but that was not the occasion to do so. And as I observed that bustling city-state, I feared it was losing its soul to global capitalism and consumerism.

Then came the long haul to Wellington and the jump over to Dunedin on South Island for a symposium on Christianity and Culture held at the University of Otago. Prior to its start, I was the convocation speaker at the university's graduation ceremony and was delighted by the blend of tradition and freedom. The symposium itself began with a Maori welcome to Aotearoa (the Maori name for the country), in which the descendants of settlers, or *Pākehā*, acknowledged that they belonged to the land of the Maori. Yet a multitude of contradictions and tensions remained. How could *Pākehā* and Maori cultures co-exist and integrate, and what was their relation to Christianity? What about the status of peoples from the South Pacific Islands? It all sounded very familiar. The organisers had put together an excellent programme. The other invited speakers were Dan Hardy and Janet Soskice from Cambridge, Jürgen Moltmann from Tübingen, and Gustavo Gutiérrez from Peru.

Dan, whom I had first met at the Bonhoeffer Congress in Oxford in 1980, convinced Janet and me to accompany him one afternoon on a flight across South Island to the West Coast, to see the famous Milford Sound. What he did not tell us was that he had hired a small four-seater biplane for the expedition, with canvas sides that flapped in the wind. Neither did he tell us that the pilot was a young fellow who paid little attention to weather warnings that were constantly telling him to return to base. Eventually an approaching storm forced us to do so and, with the gale force wind driving us from behind, our gung-ho pilot gleefully took us back past Dunedin and over the ocean in search of an albatross. On landing we had to jump out of the plane and hold on to the wings to prevent it from being blown over. Ours was the last plane to land before the storm really hit. I feared it was my last day on earth and I had not yet seen an albatross.

My lecture on "Christian Witness and the Transformation of

Culture in a Society in Transition" sparked off a heated discussion about racism and cultural identity in New Zealand, with each side claiming me as a champion of their cause. This convinced me anew that you cannot simply transpose the issues or solutions from one context onto another without serious critical reflection. I spoke on a similar theme one evening at a packed public meeting in a city church. Interest in what was happening in South Africa was at an all-time high. An evening meal in downtown Dunedin with some Samoan conference delegates reinforced my impression that New Zealand and South Africa may face similar challenges, but the differences are greater.

Some years previously a Springbok rugby tour to New Zealand had been aborted after anti-apartheid activists, supported by the churches, forced a test match to be abandoned. There was much discussion now as to whether the situation in South Africa had changed sufficiently to allow a forthcoming tour. The issue clearly divided New Zealanders, and I was asked to debate the matter on public radio one morning with Makhenkesi Stofile back home. Stofile, as I have said, was on sabbatical in Princeton when we were there. He was himself a rugby player and a leading member of the ANC in the Eastern Cape, and he would soon become the minister of sport. On balance, I thought that the tour should go ahead (which it did); Stofile argued otherwise.

After the symposium we headed north to Wanganui, where I gave a weekend workshop on Bonhoeffer's theology at a Presbyterian Church. Then we travelled by car across to North Island and visited traditional Maori sites in Rotorua – the heartland of Maori rugby – where we watched geysers soar and mud pools bubble. Two days later we boarded our flight in Wellington bound for Hong Kong.

Gail Coulson, a good friend from the time I was working at the

SACC, had since become the superintendent of the United Methodist Board of Missions in China. She had arranged our visit to Hong Kong (then still a British colony) and mainland China as the guests of Bishop K.H. Ting and the China Christian Council. Gail was on furlough at the time, but we received orientation for our visit from the staff of the Mission Board in Hong Kong.

We also had conversations with Philip Wickeri, an American scholar, whose fine study of the Three-Self Patriotic Movement in China, *Seeking the Common Ground*, had just been published. The movement was a remarkable ecumenical attempt by former European Mission Churches to become self-reliant and authentically Chinese within the framework of a communist state. This was a different strategy to that of the Underground Church, which refused to relate to the regime and was punished in return; all of which provided some food for thought about the indigenisation of the Church in South Africa.

Our visit to mainland China began in Nanjing, the historic southern capital. We created a stir among the immigration officials on arrival, for South Africans had not been allowed into China previously. But everything was in order. We were met by a young woman, Xui Gu, and were soon on our way to our hotel in a red Jeep. The green leaves of the forest of trees along the roads cast dark shadows, allowing only a glimmer of sunshine to penetrate. That romantic first impression was soon dispelled by the chaotic traffic.

We stayed in a gracious old hotel, located in a walled compound some distance from the city centre. Each day we explored the neighbourhood more confidently and even strolled to the banks of the Yangtze River. We visited Buddhist temples and historic sites; we experienced Sunday worship in a Protestant Church, and learnt about the difficulties of being a Christian in communist China, even in "legal" churches. We had dinner with Bishop Ting and other church leaders who provided us with information, introduced us to the local cuisine, and made us feel welcome.

At Nanjing Union Theological Seminary I gave a three-hour lecture and was asked at the end to sing a song, which I learnt was a sign of student appreciation. The only words that came to mind were *"Daar kom die Alibama"*, which I said was an old liberation song sung by slaves in Cape Town at the time of their emancipation. There was considerable interest in South Africa. I even had to answer a question as to why Nelson Mandela and his wife, Winnie, were separating. I had conversations with some of the seminary's theologians, one of whom was a distinguished poet and victim of the Cultural Revolution – a misnomer if ever there was one.

From Nanjing we travelled to Shanghai by train and were again the guests of the China Christian Council. I gave a lecture at the Protestant seminary and found the faculty well informed about theological developments in the West. We were impressed by the pastor of a large city church and his story of faith during the Cultural Revolution, as well as the signs of new life in his congregation. Like the church, the city seemed to be thriving with its ultra-modern skyscrapers filling the landscape. China might be communist, but Shanghai exuded Wall Street capitalism.

In Beijing we were the guests of Professor Ge from the University of Beijing, who had previously visited UCT. On arrival, she interviewed me about South Africa and then discussed our programme. This included discussions with researchers at the Institute for the Study of Religion. I was amazed at the numbers involved and the range of research being done. Communist China apparently took religion more seriously than the secular West. Even if it was officially bad science and needed to be kept in check, policy makers had to understand it.

On the Sunday, we worshipped with over a thousand others in a large Protestant Church. Our guide brought us to the door where she excused herself, because, she told us, she was a communist. But she then changed her mind and sat with us. I have no idea why she did so and what she made of the service. The hymns were Mandarin translations of well-known pious Western ones, sung to tunes familiar to us. Our interpreter translated the long evangelical sermon which, it seemed to me, had little contextual relevance and could have been preached anywhere.

We spent a day at the Great Wall of China, marvelling at its massive construction as we walked along its top well beyond the tourist crowds. Back in Beijing we went to the Forbidden City and other tourist and cultural attractions, including Tiananmen Square, the day before the second anniversary of the 4 June student uprising. One evening we went to an international club to watch a theatrical performance by young people. The acrobatics were astounding. Afterwards we could not find a taxi, so we hailed a bicycle rickshaw which took us to our hotel through the backstreets of Beijing. En route we were given a commentary in good English by our driver, who it seemed from what he said, had been among the pro-democracy student protesters in Tiananmen Square.

As we waited to board our return flight to Hong Kong at Beijing Capital International Airport, we met Stuart Saunders, our UCT vice-chancellor, and his wife, Anita, arriving for a visit to China. We had no prior knowledge of their coming. The world suddenly seemed to shrink. We were not the only Capetonians or UCT faculty members in Beijing that day.

Back home, I was appointed to serve on the National Centre for Science Development's advisory panel for research in Theology, Religious Studies, Philosophy and Ancient Near Eastern Studies, and did so for several years. In July and August 1990, Nicholas Wolterstorff, then a professor of Philosophy at Yale University, came to lecture in our department. This provided a good opportunity to get to know him and his understanding of the Reformed tradition better. His book *Until Justice and Peace Embrace* was, to my mind, a classic.

In October I attended another conference in Cape Town on the role of the churches in political transition. Unlike the one in Rustenburg, this was for WCC member churches only, so we more easily achieved consensus. It was the first time since the Cottesloe Consultation in 1961 that a WCC delegation visited South Africa, hoping that the occasion would coincide with the rebirth of the country. But this was thwarted by the violence wracking the country. The changes were clearly not being embraced by all. There were also indications that some churches were withdrawing into their denominational shells and no longer providing a prophetic voice in the political arena. This would have serious consequences as the years passed.

Charles Villa-Vicencio and I addressed these issues in various publications, some of them arising out of collaborative research in RICSA. Among our research assistants was the Canadian Steve Martin, one of my best doctoral students, who began to play a leading role in managing the research programme. The largest RICSA project was on "Christianity and the Social History of South Africa", which eventually took over fifteen years to complete. It resulted in the publication of two volumes, plus a special edition of the *JTSA*.[4] Charles was responsible for the first volume, and I wrote the second, which documented the role of Christianity in South Africa from the discovery of diamonds until the Land Act of 1936.[5] I regard this as one of my most important books, as did some historians who reviewed it; but it is probably the least read.

Steve and Marian presented us with our first grandchild, Thea, on 19 October 1991 – a wonderful sign of hope for the future. Steve had also just finished his doctoral dissertation and graduated at the beginning of 1992. He was capped by Desmond Tutu, then the chancellor of the University of the Western Cape, who stopped proceedings to tell the assembly something about Steve's witness during the struggle years. We were immensely proud parents – and grandparents.

18

Saved by hope

> How tragic it would be if, at this very moment when the birth of a just society is at hand and so much blood has been spilt, we gave up hope ... To work for a better future is to say "no" to such evil; it is to say "yes" to the one in whom we believe and who requires us to "do justice and love mercy." It is to be saved by hope.
>
> (From *A Book of Hope*)[6]

In January 1992 I was elected a fellow of the University of Cape Town. This was an acknowledgement of my scholarship by my peers, and therefore a special honour. I also became a member of a think-tank convened by Alex Boraine, the director of IDASA, to draft a proposal for a Truth and Reconciliation Commission (TRC). Under IDASA's auspices, I attended several international conferences around these issues, and in May I joined other academics, trade union leaders and politicians on a study tour to Eastern Europe to learn how others were dealing with their transitions to democracy. On the way to Berlin, we spent a night in Bad Godesberg and, to my delight, the Bethges joined us for dinner and discussion at the Friedrich Naumann Foundation.

In Berlin we talked with Joachim Gauck, a Lutheran pastor and currently the president of Germany, who was responsible for overseeing the investigation of the STASI files. These extensive and controversial files were used by the dreaded security police in the former German Democratic Republic to exercise control. The information in them, often fabricated, had led to imprisonment and murder. As a result, there had been an outburst of anger against the STASI after the changes, so the management of the process was highly sensitive. The consequences of unearthing the past could seriously damage reputations and hinder reconciliation. We were familiar with the arguments, but felt that, while it was essential to get at the truth, it should be for the sake of nation building, not just in order to punish perpetrators.

We travelled by bus to Prague, one of the most beautiful cities I have ever visited. I remember more about the city itself – the bridges over the Vltava River, the Gothic architecture and Hussite history – than I do about the meetings we had. But I do recall that some of us felt that the trade unions had sold themselves out to the politicians. We attended a symphony concert, and I still have the fine wine glasses I bought for a song. Early on the Sunday morning I accompanied Jasper Walsh – a member of Parliament from Cape Town – on foot to Mass in St. Vitus Cathedral, miles from the hotel where we were staying. Being neither a Catholic nor a Czech, I felt a little out of place in the crowded side chapel. But it was a special moment for us in that historic, sacred space.

Another memorable occasion was a meeting in Budapest with leaders of the Hungarian Roma or Gypsies – the largest minority group, but also the poorest and least educated. In Europe, Gypsies are generally regarded with considerable suspicion by the majority of the population, and are often persecuted. The question they now faced was their status in the "new Hungary", and how they could be integrated into society without losing their identity.

On arrival back in Johannesburg, I flew directly to Port Elizabeth and then went by car to St. Paul's Anglican College in Grahamstown. It was the week of Pentecost and Prayer for Christian Unity and I was scheduled to preach each evening in various churches. At the seminary I heard the terrible news that David Bosch had died in a car accident in the eastern Transvaal (now Mpumalanga). I could scarcely believe it. We desperately needed people like him to take us forward into the new dispensation. But sadly and cruelly he died because apartheid regulations still governed the ambulance services in that part of the country. Only a "black" ambulance was available to take him to hospital, but this was still forbidden by law despite the changes. By the time a "white" one arrived, he had bled to death. Apartheid was not only evil and a heresy, it was also crazy.

Although negotiations were continuing apace between the government and the ANC, there was much violence in the country, spearheaded by right-wing whites and the Zulu-based Inkatha Freedom Party (IFP), with the connivance of elements within the police. This threatened to derail the transition process. Then, on 17 June 1992, the massacre at Boipatong, an impoverished township east of Johannesburg, sent shock waves through the country. Armed members of the IFP attacked ANC supporters, and a frenzy of violence and counter violence was unleashed. Negotiations ground to a halt.

It was around that time that Jaap Durand and Abraham (Braam) Viljoen, the twin brother of General Constand Viljoen, came to see me at our home in Cape Town. Braam, an old friend and theologian at UNISA, told me his brother was being pressured to lead a military coup and take over the government. I had vaguely heard rumours about this; now I discovered it was for real. Braam asked me if I would get some conservative English-speaking church leaders, whom General Viljoen respected, to convince him that a coup would be morally wrong and politically disastrous. I made a few phone calls, but I have no idea whether those I spoke to did what I requested. Fortunately there were several other far more influential figures, including a high-ranking general, who changed Viljoen's mind at the last minute. Those were frightening times.

A day or two after the Boipatong massacre, publisher David Philip phoned to ask whether I would contribute an article to a book in which South Africans would explore the meaning of hope in the present time. I agreed and was honoured to be listed with others I admired – among them Nadine Gordimer, Beyers Naudé and Njabulo Ndebele. I based my contribution on the Old Testament prophet Hosea. In a time of great national despair, he proclaimed that the Valley of Achor, a symbol of defeat in the past, would become a door of hope (Hosea 2:15). It was, I wrote, too early to speak of Boipatong as a door of hope, but it could become one if it shocked us into action.

This was the situation in August when I went to New York for the Sixth International Bonhoeffer Congress, where I spoke about Christian witness after the changes in South Africa and Bonhoeffer's theology as a resource for national reconstruction. I also had an audacious plan up my sleeve: inviting the society to hold its next congress in Cape Town in 1996; so, at an appropriate moment, I issued the invitation. There was some discussion about whether South Africa would make a peaceful transition to democracy, but in the end, with Eberhard Bethge's support, the decision was made in favour of Cape Town. The next task was the hard one: organising such an event, and to do so without any certainty about how the politics would work out.

After the congress the Bethges, Bishop Schönherr from East Berlin (who, incidentally, was a victim of the STASI investigation), his interpreter Barbara Green, and I went with the Rasmussens to participate in a workshop on Bonhoeffer's theology at Ghost Ranch in New Mexico. This spectacular location was familiar to us as a movie set and the home of the artist Georgia O'Keeffe. During a hike in the nearby hills, Schönherr (then in his late seventies) and I got lost. He did not know much English and my German was not adequate for the predicament, but we lived to tell the tale. We celebrated Eberhard's birthday one evening, and listened to him singing Schubert's "Lieder" as he used to do to Bonhoeffer's accompaniment; only now Renate played the piano.

My mother celebrated her ninetieth birthday in December 1990. She still regularly went to church with us. Irrespective of the sermon topic, she would invariably say under her breath, but loud enough for all to hear, "Why does he always preach about death!"

That was seldom a sermon topic, but for some inexplicable reason she had it in for Douglas Bax, even when he preached that God is love. Sadly she had a bad fall during Christmas 1992. We were away at Vermaaklikheid, and Esther cared for her at Groote Schuur hospital until we returned later in the day. A few weeks later she passed away in a frail-care centre. Although her death was expected and a relief for her, I was deeply saddened. Jeanelle, Isobel and I often sat with her during her final hours, but none of us were there in the early hours of the morning when she died in her sleep. Rozelle, who had come to spend several weeks with her, as Isobel and I were due to go to the UK on sabbatical, arrived an hour too late from Atlanta to say her farewells. After the funeral, held in the Rondebosch Church, the two of us ruminated on the fact that we were next in line. Little did we anticipate that the next death in the family would be that of Steve. Fortunately we seldom know what lies ahead.

My thoughts now turned to Oxford where I had been invited to be the Karl Jaspers lecturer. Jaspers, a psychiatrist and philosopher, had been an opponent of the Third Reich and later helped shape Germany's new democracy. The lectureship was in the gift of Ripon College in Cuddesdon, a rural village five miles southeast of Oxford. But I had access to the university as a visiting fellow of Christ Church, one of Oxford University's oldest colleges, where Peter Hinchliff, a former professor at Rhodes University and a good friend, was professor of Church History.

I gave the Karl Jaspers Lecture on 11 February 1993, in a crowded university examination lecture hall, on "Guilt, Amnesty and National Reconstruction: Karl Jaspers' *Die Schuldfrage* and the South African Debate". *Die Schuldfrage* was written at the time of the Nuremburg trials. In it Jaspers discussed who was responsible for Nazi war crimes – a question we were now asking in regard to apartheid. There were those who pulled the trigger and those who commanded them; there were the ideologists who had created the monster in the first place; but there were also the beneficiaries, which included all of us white folk in South Africa. We had better housing, education, health care, and many other privileges denied the victims of apartheid.

While in Oxford we again visited the Bethges in Villiprott who, as always, went the extra mile as hosts. We visited the splendid baroque palace in Brühl and, by contrast, the small Catholic Church of St. Martin in the village of Kirchsahr. The church houses a grotesque medieval statue of Mary holding a sword in her right hand and Jesus, nestling in her left, holding the severed head of a Turk by his hair. The thought of Christians beheading Muslims, encouraged by the Madonna and Child, filled us with the same horror we feel today about the actions of radical Jihadists. We also visited Aachen and its massive basilica, with the imperial throne where Charlemagne reigned as emperor of the Holy Roman Empire. Unfortunately Eberhard had a nasty fall on the cobbled streets. When we discussed the forthcoming Bonhoeffer Congress, he and Renate were no longer sure that they could make the long journey to Cape Town.

The second half of my sabbatical was spent in Edinburgh. I was a visiting fellow at New College, the Theological Faculty at the university. We were hosted by Duncan Forrester and his wife, Margaret, whom we had come to know over the years. On the way there we drove up the east coast of England visiting Lincoln, York and Durham. Once settled in, we made several trips around Scotland, including to the ancient University of St. Andrews where we were taken aback by the lack of knowledge among graduate students about British colonial history in Africa. We grew to love Edinburgh: its architecture and castle, people, parks, cultural attractions, and walking up Arthur's Seat behind our apartment on the Meadows, within easy distance of the Mound. But our settling in was shockingly disturbed on Easter Saturday by the news that Chris Hani, the charismatic general secretary of the Communist Party in South Africa, had been assassinated. This was a serious setback and threatened to derail the negotiations yet again.

The major outcome of my sabbatical was *Christianity and Democracy* published by Cambridge University Press in 1995, and later, for reasons I have never fathomed, translated into Japanese and published in Tokyo. Much of my writing and lecturing at that time was about the Church's responsibility in democratic transition and transformation. At a conference on democracy in Africa, held at Leeds University that September, I referred to Ali Mazrui's contention that democratisation in Africa is its second liberation struggle – one proving to be as difficult as ridding the continent of colonial domination. I gasp at the quixotic boldness I must have had to countenance such a broad topic, but at least Desmond Tutu, who responded, expressed his appreciation.

Jeanelle graduated as a medical doctor at UCT in December 1993, and we proudly joined her when she took the Hippocratic Oath. She had already obtained a Bachelor of Arts degree, so she had been a student for eight years. But in the middle of her medical studies she had taken a year out in 1990, first in New York, and then at Holden Village in Washington State where we had been in 1983. Upon her return that Christmas, she told us that she was a lesbian. We had suspected this for some time, but it was still difficult for us to accept all the implications, even though we were supportive of her coming out. We soon saw that this made an enormous difference to her sense of personal wellbeing, demonstrating so clearly that being gay is not primarily a choice, but an acknowledgement of who you are. Jeanelle later went to study further in England, returned home to work on a research project on medical doctors during the apartheid years,[7] and in 1999 went back to the United Kingdom to work in public health for the National Health Service in the Midlands.

As president of the Theological Society in South Africa, I had been talking for several years with Bernard Lategan at Stellenbosch University about the need for a South African Academy of Religion that would link the various societies for the study of Religion, Bible, Church History and Theology. In due course these ten societies gave the go-ahead, and I became the chair of the planning committee. The academy's first congress took place at the University of South Africa in Pretoria in January 1994. This attracted a good number of participants, and its success was enhanced by the performance of the Soweto String Quartet at the conference dinner. Unfortunately the academy did not fulfil its promise at that time. In any case, all eyes were now focused on the forthcoming first post-apartheid general election.

In anticipation, I was invited to a meeting of social scientists to reflect on the election's viability, given the violence that was still gripping the country. We met for two days to evaluate the available information. As the meeting drew to a close, we were convinced that it could not be free and fair, and should be postponed. But then I impulsively took off my social science cap.

"Speaking theologically," I said, "we have to take the risk of hope. Hope is a refusal to accept the prevailing notion that change is not possible."

There was silence, but then agreement that the risk had to be taken. I doubt whether our deliberations had any influence on the unfolding events, but I have no doubt that the indefatigable hope that Nelson Mandela embodied, and the hard work involved in turning that hope into action, saved the country from sliding into confusion and chaos.

19

Proudly South African

Few South Africans who witnessed the inauguration of Nelson Mandela as president on 10 May at the Union Buildings in Pretoria were unmoved by the unfolding liturgy ... "For the first time in my life," Steve told me, "I really felt I belonged somewhere and was proud of the fact."

(From "Waving the Flag" in *The Christian Century*)[8]

It was one of the most exciting days of my life. Simply standing next to Steve – with baby David, our new grandchild, in his arms – in the long line of black and white South Africans – who had come to cast their vote at the polling station near our home, was a wonderful experience. Too much blood had been spilt to bring us to this moment, but the news media were astounded by the lack of violence on the day. Some commentators still speak of 27 April as a "bloody miracle". I voted for the ANC, which won by an overwhelming majority. But irrespective of who we voted for, we were all proudly South African.

During the first session of the new Parliament, virtually all apartheid legislation was consigned to the dustbin of history. The legacy of apartheid, however, did not automatically disappear. The hard work of building a just and inclusive democracy had only begun. The final clause on the "Promotion of National Unity and Reconciliation" of the Interim Constitution, approved late in 1993, pointed the way ahead:

> ... a legacy of hatred, fear, guilt and revenge ... can now be addressed on the basis that there is a need for understanding but not revenge, a need for reparation but not for retaliation, a need for ubuntu but not for victimisation.

The final paragraph spoke of the need for amnesty for those who had been engaged in political crimes as a necessary precondition for reconciliation and reconstruction.

So the way was prepared for the first cabinet meeting to agree to the establishment of the TRC as a catalyst towards nation building. Its mandate included providing a record of gross human rights violations committed by both the upholders of apartheid and the liberation movements, and to identify the victims and their fate; to recommend possible measures of reparation; to process applications for amnesty and indemnity; and to make recommendations regarding measures necessary to prevent future gross human rights violations. This was "not another Nuremberg", but a space "where the deeper processes of forgiveness, confession, repentance, reparation and reconciliation can take place".[9]

The seventeen commissioners, led by Desmond Tutu (who had recently retired as archbishop) and Alex Boraine as deputy, were appointed by President Mandela after a lengthy process of hearings. They were reasonably representative of the broad political, ethnic and cultural spectrum in South Africa. But it was almost two years before the TRC could actually begin its task, so I will postpone discussing its work and my own involvement.

One of my doctoral students, who registered at UCT after the changes, was Isabel Phiri, a Malawian who had studied and then taught at the University of Malawi in Zomba. She was the first of several of my graduate students from other parts of Africa. Her research on the role of women in the Church in Malawi was groundbreaking, and when it was completed she returned to Zomba full of enthusiasm for her task as a lecturer at the university. Soon after, I was appointed an external examiner in the Department of Religion of the same university, and Isobel and I went to Malawi in July 1994. In between my examining, we spent an exhilarating weekend on Zomba Plateau and a few days on the shore of beautiful Lake Malawi. Unfortunately, shortly after we left, Isabel was forced to resign because of opposition to her feminist critique of Malawi's patriarchal society. She returned to South Africa to teach at UCT and then became a professor at the University of KwaZulu-Natal's School of Theology in Pietermaritzburg.

Upon our return from Malawi, Isobel and I rented a car in Johannesburg and drove to Kuruman in the Northern Cape to visit Steve and Marian who, together with Thea and David, had moved there after the election. Steve had become director of the Moffat Mission, a historic station founded by Robert Moffat of the LMS in the early nineteenth century. David Livingstone, who married Robert Moffat's daughter Mary, lived there prior to his explorations into central Africa. The apartheid authorities had decimated the mission in the 1960s when they moved the indigenous Tswana population miles away to a barren township. But even though there was no longer a local worshipping congregation, the mission continued as a conference centre and tourist site. The grand old stone and thatched church, built by Moffat, was still used for daily prayers and the occasional service.

A few months later we visited Kuruman again, taking Jeanelle with us to be with the family for Christmas. This required a long car drive of nine hundred kilometres from Cape Town up the West Coast, famous for its wild flowers and wines. Going further north, we ascended the majestic Van Reenen's Pass, and then travelled on the plateau through the desert landscape with its isolated towns, until we reached the banks of the Orange River with its vineyards and lush farmlands. We grew to love that journey, and over the next few years, sometimes with Anton and Esther, we visited the mission several times. We enjoyed learning about its history, being with Steve, Marian and our grandchildren (now including Kate), and exploring the surrounding area.

During his tenure at the mission, Steve built a new conference and educational centre, as well as a library, all designed by our friend Julian Cooke. He also developed a museum that told the story of how Moffat had translated the Bible into Setswana, and housed the press on which he had printed it. Steve was in his element. On occasions he took visitors on a "pilgrim walk", which ended in the cemetery where the remains of missionaries and their children, and now also his mentor Joe Wing, lay. Invariably he wore his white clerical robe and sang Taizé songs along the path, accompanied by his guitar. And there, within the sacred burial ground, he told the story of past days and led those gathered in prayer.

On one of our visits, Anton reintroduced me to woodturning. I had already decided, encouraged by Isobel, that the time had come for me to get back into woodworking to escape the daily round of university responsibilities. But my workshop was a shambles, my tools blunt, and my skills all but forgotten. I resolved to get some new tools, but never imagined that I was embarking on an adventure that would become such a part of my life in the years ahead. Around the same time, Isobel was developing her skills as a painter, so there was mutual encouragement.

The fears expressed at the Bonhoeffer Congress in New York that South Africa might not be safe enough to host the next one in 1996 became the fears of many during the intervening years. But we were committed and I had an excellent team to help prepare for the event. We were fortunate to obtain a great venue: the UCT Business School campus adjacent to the Waterfront. This was housed in an imposing prison, built during the nineteenth century to incarcerate felons guilty of illicit diamond buying. Close by were hotels to accommodate the two hundred participants who would come from six continents.

It was mid-January and midsummer. Table Mountain towered over the city and the water in the yacht basin nearby glistened as two large buses pulled up to the entrance to the Business School and delegates, who had been met at the airport, disembarked. How good it was to see familiar faces from distant places in Cape Town at last. Sadly, Eberhard and Renate Bethge were not among them – the first time they had missed an International Bonhoeffer Congress.

The opening Sunday service was held in St. George's Cathedral. In his welcome, Beyers Naudé reflected on the theme of the congress: "Is Bonhoeffer still of any use?" If Bonhoeffer was present, Naudé said, he would ask us whether our witness to Christ was still of any use.

If we had anticipated that there would be unanimity among the speakers in response to the theme, Chung Hyun Kyung, a Korean feminist theologian, dispelled that illusion the next morning in her opening address, "A Letter to Bonhoeffer". Her words immediately caused a stir: "Dietrich Bonhoeffer. What's your response to my non-stop talking? 'Shut up and meditate more?' I am waiting for your response."[10]

Among the other speakers was Konrad Raiser, the general secretary of the WCC, who reminded us that the "inspiration which the South African movement of Christian resistance against apartheid received from Dietrich Bonhoeffer" made it "very appropriate that we should assemble for this congress commemorating Bonhoeffer's ninetieth birthday in the new South Africa".[11]

On Robben Island we listened to Naudé again outside Mandela's cell, where the new president had taken his exercise and planted a garden. I went and sat in a shady corner next to Njongonkulu Ndungane, who soon after became Tutu's successor as Anglican archbishop of Cape Town. He was reflecting back on his own years of imprisonment on the island. Ndungane had long been a friend and was also a colleague of Steve's when he was the bishop of Kimberley and Kuruman. On the ferry back to the Waterfront harbour, delegates sat quietly, reflecting on what they had experienced.

One evening we went in two large buses to visit Gugulethu, a sprawling township on the outskirts of the city. We began at the Presbyterian Church where Spiwo Xapile, a former student of mine, was the minister. His church was a centre for ministry to HIV/AIDS victims, and a hive of activity in the community. From there we went to the hostels. People were returning home from work, the smoke from the cooking fires filled the air as children played noisily in the alleyways. Spiwo had negotiated our visit, but even so we were invading their living space. The delegates, despite having been asked to stay together near the buses, streamed into the darkening and narrow alleys lined with shacks. Eventually I had to rescue a few who had become embroiled in an argument with some angry residents who asked what right the delegates had to come to tell them how to solve their problems. The scene was turning ugly, so I burst into our national anthem, "Nkosi Sikelel' iAfrika", which got everybody singing, while I quickly shepherded the delegates back into the bus.

The congress banquet, held in the gracious, wood-panelled dining hall of Smuts Hall on the UCT main campus, was in stark contrast. We were welcomed outside by the vibrant playing of marimbas, and after dinner we listened to Beyers Naudé and Desmond Tutu share their experiences of the struggle. What a memorable occasion that was, especially for delegates from afar.

The congress concluded on the campus of the University of the Western Cape, where Russel Botman, a professor of Theology, told us that experience made us suspicious of easy answers and pursuing solutions that serve our own interests alone. We had to do more than parrot Bonhoeffer's words and ideas with the coming generation in mind.[12] Botman later became a professor at Stellenbosch, and then its first black rector. He tragically died aged sixty, leaving a fine legacy, at the time I was writing these memoirs.

By all accounts the congress was a great success. It also provided Isobel and me an opportunity to welcome many friends who had shown us hospitality over the years into our home. Nan Oosthuizen, my secretary and administrator of the *JTSA*, did much to make the congress a success, but decided to retire after it was over. She had worked with me for over ten years. Her place was taken by Lyn Holness, who had recently become one of my PhD students.

Academic life continued with a vengeance in February as the first semester of a new academic year started. Isobel and I were also planning a new adventure. It had all began at the Founding Congress of the Academy of Religion in Pretoria two years before, when I met the Polish ambassador to South Africa, Stanislaw Ciennich. I told him in passing that Isobel's maternal grandmother had been born in Poland and came to South Africa as a young girl. Soon after the congress, we received an invitation from the Polish Embassy to visit Poland and for me to give some university lectures.

We went in May 1996, seven years after the end of communist rule, beginning our visit in Warsaw. The old city centre, which had been seriously damaged during the Second World War, was now beautifully restored, in stark contrast to the Jewish ghetto, which remained much as it was when the Nazis flattened it. The more modern parts of the city were dominated by Soviet-style buildings, such as the Grand Hotel where we stayed for the week. Our companions at breakfast each day were a few hundred heavily muscled men and women who had gathered from around eastern Europe for the World Weightlifting Championship.

The day after our arrival, we went to a Lutheran seminary where there was an ecumenical theological discussion underway between Protestants and Catholics. Catholicism dominates Polish culture, but there was a time soon after the Reformation when Protestants presented such a threat to the Catholic Church that the pope had to send in the Jesuits to sort things out. Fresh in our own memory was the fact that the first Polish pope, John Paul II, had played a key role in the overthrow of communism, alongside Lech Wałęsa, the leader of the trade union movement Solidarity.

My lecture at the university on the religious situation in South Africa was necessarily elementary, but I was impressed by the students' questions, which led to an interesting discussion on modern religious movements. Our itinerary was full, but we had time to wander through the National Museum and art gallery, as well as beautiful Łazienki Park. On the Sunday we went on a bus tour to several famous country estates and churches, including one in Brochów where Frédéric Chopin was baptised. Later we listened to a Chopin piano concert on the grounds of the manor house in

Żelazowa Wola where he grew up. We had lunch with the South African ambassador, met with the under-secretary of state for foreign affairs at the Presidential Palace, and were treated to dinner at the Fukier Restaurant in the old city on our final evening in the city.

We left Warsaw on Ascension Day and caught an express train to Krakow in the south, travelling for the most part through attractive countryside. We were welcomed by Professor Halina Grzymała-Moszczyńska of Jagielloński University, where I repeated my lecture on the religious situation in South Africa. Halina guided us throughout our stay in this wonderful old city with its amazing square – probably the largest in medieval Europe – on the banks of the Vistula River. Soon after our arrival we went to St. Stanislaw's Church, a fourteenth-century Gothic cathedral in the square, to attend the Ascension Day Mass.

We went on two day tours while in Krakow. The first was to the quaint old farming village of Zakopane in the tranquil Tatra Mountains. The second was to Auschwitz-Birkenau, the biggest of the Nazi concentration camps. We had previously visited Buchenwald, but nothing really prepares you for the horrors on the other side of the forbidding iron gates with its inscription "*Arbeit macht frei*". We remained silent for much of the tour.

Another reason why we went to Poland was to visit Nakło (formerly Nakel), where Isobel's great-great-grandfather, a Prussian general named Otto Brandenburg, married Ottilie Block in 1840. Their granddaughter, Alma Lux, who became Isobel's grandmother, was also born in East Prussia, in Bromberg (now Bydgoszcz), not too far from Breslau (now Wrocław) where Bonhoeffer was born. My hope was also to go on to Finkenwalde near Stettin, where Bonhoeffer had directed the Confessing Church seminary prior to the Second World War. But Finkenwalde was now in Germany, and we could not take a rental car from the one country to the other.

We set off in the direction of Nakło on roads that were often under construction, with signs that were unpronounceable. Along the way through Silesia, we came to Jasna Góra, the famous monastery of the Black Madonna, in Częstochowa. The city was packed with pilgrims, and there were busloads of them inside the fortress monastery, which dated from 1382. We attended the daily service of healing in the crammed chapel with many people in wheelchairs. At an appropriate moment the icon of the Black Madonna was displayed, and precisely then there was a loud clap of thunder. All the lights went out – except those lighting up the Madonna. Whether or not this was stage-managed, the thunderstorm raging outside was real. It was awesome, even for non-Roman Catholics.

The next night we stayed in Gniezno, the cradle of Poland, a somewhat dismal industrial town, despite its historic past and imposing old cathedral. A few days later we arrived at Nakło and were fortunate to meet a Catholic priest, Piotr Jakubowski, who could speak English. He took us under his wing, starting with coffee in his apartment, where we told him about Isobel's family connection with the city. He doubted whether we would be able to find any records, because everything that had a German and Protestant association had been expunged, and all records had been moved to Bydgoszcz after the Second World War. But we did visit the grounds where the German cemetery had been, as well as the Catholic Church which had once been the German Lutheran Church.

Our visit to Poland helped us understand the remarkable role it has played in the history of Europe. We also learnt that Poland was one of the first countries in the world to have a liberal democratic constitution. And my thoughts constantly turned to the role of the Catholic Church in the building of a democratic future and what we might learn from it.[13]

On 8 May 1996 the new South African Constitution was approved by Parliament. The Constitution does not describe reality on the ground, but I believe it points us in the direction that Christian faith supports. This does not make it "Christian" in any narrow sense, for it embraces people of all faiths and none. But it is my Christian responsibility to defend its commitment to inclusive justice and human rights.

On the same day the Constitution was approved, Deputy President Thabo Mbeki made his celebrated "I am an African" speech. I was entranced by its cadences capturing the mood of a nation celebrating its rebirth in search of an inclusive identity. His journey had been very different to mine, but his words resonated with my soul. I, too, am an African, but one grafted onto European and English stock in South African soil. I, too, am a cultural hybrid, though my ancestry is different from those whose genealogy is African or Asian. I am a *South* African.

20

Restoring justice

> Reconciliation is an event, an action … a process and celebration, before it becomes a doctrine or theory.
>
> (From *Reconciliation: Restoring Justice*)[14]

In November 1996, Isobel and I went to a WCC Conference at Tantur, a Catholic ecumenical centre outside Jerusalem. Larry Rasmussen was also a participant, but as he had to attend a pre-conference meeting, his wife, Nyla, Isobel and I hired a car to do some touring. This was soon after the Oslo Peace Accord, so it was possible to go to places and do things that would now be much more difficult. From Tel Aviv we drove north to Netanya and Caesarea, and east to the famous archaeological site at Tel Megiddo. We then went further north to the border of Lebanon. We lost our way trying to find Safed, a town famous for its Hasidic connections. Some Arab shepherds told us to go back the way we had come. We did so but suddenly found ourselves at the entrance to an Israeli army outpost where we were asked, "What the hell are you doing here?" We mumbled an apology and fled. We found Safed, but it was not as romantic as I remembered from my visit in 1969.

That night we stayed on a guarded kibbutz near the Lebanese

border. The next day we visited the Hula Nature Reserve and observed huge flocks of birds migrating through Hula on their way from Siberia to where we live. Turning south to Galilee, we visited sites associated with the life of Jesus, spending a night each in Nazareth and Tiberias. I had not previously been to the church in Cana where Jesus turned water into wine. There we met some Russian Orthodox pilgrims who were uncertain about our Christian credentials. But the Greek priest made us feel welcome and over tea gave a fine exposition of Jesus' first sign. He also gave us a bottle of wine, repeating the miracle as it were, because we had arrived with only water bottles.

We continued our journey down the east side of the Sea of Galilee, passing the Golan Heights, spending another night on a Kibbutz, and finally going through the Jordan Valley to Jericho. A Palestinian in Tiberias advised me to place a keffiyeh on the dashboard just in case we encountered some angry young Palestinians. I did so, but wondered how Israeli soldiers might have responded if they had stopped us. We arrived safely in Jericho, checked out the famous archaeological site, and then took an alternative route to east Jerusalem along a single track road littered with warnings that the area was mined. There were only military vehicles in the area, and we felt closely observed. Arriving in Jerusalem through the streets of Palestinian suburbs was quite different from entering on the main highway. We lost our direction several times, but eventually made it to Tantur, situated just off the main road from Jerusalem to Bethlehem.

One morning Isobel and Nyla walked to Bethlehem and back along this road, going through a checkpoint manned by the Israeli military. You can't easily do that now. I felt angry and uncomfortable as I witnessed the way in which arrogant young Israeli soldiers treated Palestinians old enough to be their grandparents. This reminded me too much of apartheid, and I decided not to return until justice and peace came to Jerusalem. That probably means waiting a very long time, because peace cannot be achieved without justice, and my sense is that those in power – even though not all Israelis – have little interest in a just peace.

The whole conference went down to Bethlehem as well for discussions with the Greek Orthodox patriarch at the Church of the Nativity. We also shared one evening at Tantur in a gathering of Jewish and Muslim leaders to discuss their hopes for the future. I don't think anyone present anticipated the first *intifada* (uprising) which was looming on the horizon. A visit to the Armenian Quarter in Jerusalem and the Cathedral of St. James, under the expert guidance of the dean, were memorable. The Armenians first came to Palestine as soldiers in the Roman army at the time of Jesus, and some were numbered among the first Christians.

The fact that we had attended a conference sponsored by the WCC and spent time with Palestinians was known to those in authority when we eventually tried to leave from the airport in Tel Aviv. The process took an inordinately long time with many questions, mirroring those asked when we had arrived. When we finally got to the counter, we were informed that we had lost our seat on the flight to Rome. Fortunately we were able to find a taxi whose driver, contrary to regulations which forbade him from picking up people at the Departures entrance, made an exception for us at that late hour and took us to a hotel. It turned out to be the same taxi driver who had met us on our arrival some two weeks previously.

At Tantur we became friends with an American Capuchin friar, Bill Henn, who taught at a Catholic seminary outside Rome. As I understand it, the brown habit of the Capuchins, a Franciscan Order, is the origin of the word cappuccino – one of my favourite drinks, and a fine reminder of Bill's conviviality. He met us when we arrived in Rome and took us to a small hotel near the Piazza Navona – an ideal location. Early one morning we went to the Vatican Museum and, once inside, directly to the Sistine Chapel. Arriving ahead of the hordes of tourists, we virtually had that amazing space to ourselves.

The next morning Bill drove us to the Frascati hills. After a hilarious journey in his small car, which included riding down a steep flight of steps when we got hopelessly lost, we had lunch at a monastery high on the hills. We saw the papal summer residence at Castel Gandolfo, and visited the nearby famous Villa d'Este Gardens in Tivoli, as well as the magical Lake Nemi mentioned in the opening paragraph of James George Frazer's classic study *The Golden Bough*. "No one who has seen that calm water, lapped in a green hollow of the Alban hills," Frazer wrote, "can ever forget it."[15] I can vouch for that.

Early in February 1997, Isobel and I once again packed our bags. I was co-leader of an ecumenical group invited to Egypt by the patriarch of Alexandria, the Coptic Pope Shenouda III. The visit was organised by George Malek, a Copt by birth, who would later become a UCCSA minister. It was an ambitious undertaking, involving thirty-four South Africans of different denominations, backgrounds and professions.

"Copt" means Egyptian, but now refers specifically to those Orthodox Christians who trace their roots back to the church founded in Alexandria by Saint Mark in 64 AD. The church suffered intense persecution in the third century at the hands of the Roman Emperor, so martyrdom is deeply etched into its story, as are the beginnings of Christian monasticism under Saint Anthony in the fourth century. After the Council of Chalcedon in the year 451, the Copts, together with other churches (Syrian, Armenian and Ethiopian) that did not accept its Christological dogma, separated from Eastern Orthodoxy. It was only after the Arab invasion in the seventh century that Islam replaced Christianity as the dominant religion in Egypt and Arabian culture became entrenched. Today Copts constitute about 10 per cent of the population, but they are under constant pressure and sometimes violent threat.

From the moment we arrived in Cairo we were overwhelmed by Coptic hospitality. Although we visited the pyramids at Giza and many other cultural and historic sites, we were ecumenical pilgrims. So our visit started with a week at the monastery of Bishoi in the Western Desert, where we had several meetings with Pope Shenouda. He was an impressive, large-hearted but no-nonsense man with decided views, as we soon discovered. A few years later he visited us in Cape Town, spoke at a lunchtime meeting at UCT and then at a dinner at the Rondebosch United Church. He was accompanied by Bishops Markos and Paulus, who have played an important ecumenical role in Africa.

We also visited other monasteries in the vicinity of Bishoi, attending an early morning Eucharist in one of them. While their fortress-like walls reminded us that the Copts are continually under threat, it was in Alexandria that we sensed the hostility towards them as we joined our hosts on a walk near the harbour. It was there, too, in the Cathedral of St. Mark, that we were guests among a congregation of two thousand who had gathered for Sunday evening worship and Pope Shenouda's Bible exposition. This is how it was in the early centuries of the Church, when Alexandria was a major centre of Christianity and the patriarch gave weekly guidance to his flock, surrounded by his clergy. We experienced the same a few days later in Cairo, in the more modern cathedral, with several thousand other worshippers.

In Cairo we were most impressed by the social work undertaken by the Copts, especially among the poor and the garbage collectors who live in their own "city" in the Mokattam Hills. We spent most of a day there visiting the Church of the Virgin Mary and St. Samaan, a huge structure built in a cave on the mountainside. We then visited a modern hospital close by. When asked why there were so few patients in the hospital, we were told by a doctor that people living on a garbage dump soon become immune to disease. We were also delighted to visit an icon-painting school near the cathedral where young people were learning this ancient craft. I came away with a delightful icon of the holy family fleeing on a donkey into Egypt.

The Coptic Church is not only the oldest in Africa, but it has had to learn how to co-exist and relate to Islam since the seventh century. This has made it a church that holds on tightly to its traditions and identity, while expanding its mission in sub-Saharan Africa and other parts of the world. I concluded an article after the visit with these words: "On looking back from some future vantage point, I would be surprised if Coptic Orthodoxy had not played an increasingly significant role in the shaping of the ecumenical African church of the new millennium."[16] My only fear now is that the very unsettled situation across the Middle East today will have an adverse effect on the church's life. But it has been through equally bad times in the past.

Soon after the TRC had been established, I was approached to serve in the research section, but declined. I was glad when Charles Villa-Vicencio was appointed director of research, even though that ended almost seventeen years of us working together. I did, however, lead a day-long "retreat" for the commissioners prior to the commencement of the hearings. We met at the Lord Milner Hotel in Somerset West on 18 September 1996 – the same place where returning ANC leaders gathered prior to the negotiations in 1990. Over lunch that day I noticed Alex Boraine in deep conversation with a high-ranking police official. I would have loved to have been a fly on the wall for that discussion. The security forces were recognising the need to participate in the TRC for their own sake, if nothing else.

Although I was not formally involved in the TRC, I was engaged in writing and speaking about the issues, giving special attention to reconciliation understood as a theological issue as well as a political process, and to the problem of guilt and forgiveness. All of this came into sharp focus when, in June 1997, I went to the Evangelischer Kirchentag held in Leipzig, at the invitation of its general secretary, Margot Käßmann. The Kirchentag started after the Second World War as an attempt to bring together Christians from around Germany to keep alive the spirit of the Confessing Church struggle. Over the years, these biannual events attract thousands of participants, the vast majority being lay and relatively young people, and comprise many lectures, forums, much music and drama, and lively discussion. The Kirchentag in Leipzig was no exception. This was my first Kirchentag, the first to be held in the former GDR, and the first time I had been back there since 1984.

Reflecting on the work of the TRC, I gave a lecture entitled "Healing the Past for the Sake of the Future" in which I spoke about the power of truth, forgiveness and hope in the search for justice and reconciliation in South Africa. But most memorable was a discussion one evening, before a packed audience and many television viewers around Germany, on the topic "Is reconciliation possible?". There were six of us on the podium, the others all civic and political leaders in the new Germany. The proceedings were moderated by Professor Ernst Benda, president of the Constitutional Court. Each of us had to introduce ourselves in an opening statement of ten minutes and indicate our position on the subject.

Reflecting on our South African experience, I said that reconciliation does not mean ignoring racial, ethnic and economic realities, but overcoming their power to divide and destroy. It means enabling people to accept one another as human beings and to work for the common good. But any attempt to achieve reconciliation without working for justice is bound to fail; it might even result in a worse situation than before. I also said that reconciliation requires acknowledging guilt and making reparations, and that vengeance embroils everyone in a never-ending cycle of violence and retribution. As the discussion proceeded, with questions and interjections from the audience becoming more heated, I found myself in the middle of a very tense situation. Former East Germans were angry about what was happening to them in the new dispensation. I thought to myself, if people – all Germans speaking the same language – can't resolve their problems, God help the rest of us. But then I reflected further: Despite the fact that Africa is regarded by many as a continent of failed states, Europe has been the scene of the most devastating wars in the past century. Human nature is universal.

Jeanelle and Isobel joined me in Leipzig, and we went by train to Prague and Vienna, spending a few days in each city. Afterwards we rented a car and drove along the Danube on our way to Frankfurt. When hiring the car, we were convinced that it was diesel powered, but were assured it was not. We thought no more about this until we were about forty kilometres from the airport when it was necessary to fill the tank. We had no sooner rejoined the autobahn than the car shuddered to a halt. We were now running out of time for Jeanelle to catch her flight to London. In addition it was raining, and cars and trucks flashed past us at speed. Eventually a young man in a small car stopped. We transferred all our luggage, and he got us to the terminal in time. I immediately informed the car hire company, complained about the wrong information I had been given, and told them where we had left the car.

Six weeks later we were having lunch in Cape Town, when the telephone rang. The German speaker checked on my identity and then asked in a despairing tone of voice, "*Herr de Gruchy, wo ist unser auto?*" Maybe the car is still standing on the side of the autobahn.

Towards the end of the TRC, it was decided that special hearings should be held for certain major role players of the apartheid era who had avoided scrutiny. Organised business, the media, the legal profession, and other sectors were invited to make submissions, both in writing and at hearings specially convened for them. The faith communities, comprising all religious traditions, were invited to do the same. RICSA was asked to advise on the setting up of these hearings, and then to attend the three-day session in East London in order to write a report. This was held in November 1997.

I asked Steve Martin, the coordinator of RICSA, and Jim Cochrane, who had recently joined our department and RICSA, to share in the task. We attended the hearings and listened to all the presentations made by the representative bodies of virtually all the faith communities. These included the Zion Christian Church (ZCC), the largest of the African initiated churches in the country and, with at least eight million members, the largest of all the churches. Even its bishop, B.E. Lekganyane, attended, though he passively sat through the presentation of his church's statement, and refused to be drawn into the discussion that followed. Not even Archbishop Tutu, who chaired the hearings, was able to get him to speak or answer questions. This was ZCC protocol and, while frustrating for the rest of us, it enhanced Lekganyane's status in the eyes of his followers. After all, prime ministers and presidents attend his Easter service in Limpopo each year; he does not need to go to them. But he did come to the TRC.

In many ways the Faith Community Hearings were symbolic of the endpoint of the involvement of religious communities either in giving support to apartheid or to the struggle against it. They were also unique in that they were inclusive of all faith communities who were willing to participate. Each accepted the need to take responsibility for their past and to indicate their commitment to the present and future. The extent to which they committed themselves to this task can be judged from the report.[17] But what they have subsequently done about it remains a subject for scrutiny.

Critics of the TRC have complained that it was too Christian, and that its mode of operation sometimes resembled a pastoral counselling chamber presided over by a father confessor rather than a court of law chaired by a judge. But unlike the Nuremberg trials, the TRC was not established by foreign powers for the sake of punishing war criminals. It was an instrument constituted by South Africans for the sake of dealing with the past in a way which would bring healing and reconciliation. The TRC itself could not bring these about; it could only be a catalyst for this to happen. In the end, the failings of the TRC are really the failings of South Africans, of the new government, and of white South Africans who were the major beneficiaries of apartheid. The truth is, there can be no reconciliation without the restoration of justice.

21

An aesthetic turn

> Art has the potential to change our consciousness and perception through its ability to evoke imagination and wonder.
>
> (From *Christianity, Art and Transformation*)[18]

Sometime before leaving UCT, Charles Villa-Vicencio burst into my office wanting to know what theological issues I was going to write about now that the struggle was over.

My ill-prepared response was immediate and took both of us by surprise: "I would like to explore theological aesthetics!"

Several years passed while I mulled over the topic and found a focus for the project in conversation with Julian Cooke. One day, as we drove past the dismal townships on the outskirts of Cape Town, I asked him why he spent so much time trying to upgrade the appalling apartheid-created hostels into decent housing. Not that the task was unimportant, but I wanted to know why a creative architect was doing what could be done well enough by others.

His reply opened my eyes: "Apartheid was not only unjust, but ugly."

Transformation required a radically new approach to the built environment, one which affirms the dignity of those who were the victims of injustice. It required a recovery of beauty. If aesthetics literally means seeing things differently, then this was an aesthetic moment for me.

The more I thought about this, the more I became interested in the role of art and architecture in social transformation, and therefore about the need to rethink the relationship between the Christian faith and beauty in the pursuit of social justice. These thoughts were evolving just in time for my next sabbatical, which we spent in England, from January to June 1998, first in Cambridge and then in Durham.

The week before we left for London, Bill and Sylvia Everett arrived to stay in our house in Rosebank and, as it happened, to become close friends from then on. Bill taught ethics at Andover Newton Theological School in Boston, and Sylvia was an accomplished artist. Bill had planned his sabbatical anticipating that he and I would be able to spend time together. That was not to be. But the two of us had enough time to discover that we were woodworking buddies and shared the same zany humour, and Sylvia and Isobel found they shared a common interest in art. The foundations were laid for an ongoing and creative relationship between us.

At Cambridge I was a visiting fellow at Selwyn College and associated with the Faculty of Theology, where Professors David Ford and Nicholas Lash welcomed me. We stayed in a cottage on the grounds of Martin and Pamela Cressey's home in Girton. Martin had been principal of Westminster College when I had given the Reid Lectures there in 1986, and Pamela was a doctor who was increasingly involved in helping refugees.

Cambridge in the middle of winter was not my ideal place. The days were short and the nights long. Cambridgeshire is also flat. When Isobel and I went in search of the Gog Magog Hills, the highest point in the shire, we drove right past without realising that we had done so. One afternoon, soon after settling in, I attended a seminar on Philosophical Theology and then decided to walk back to Girton, despite the distance and the cold. It was soon dark, and the darker it got the more depressed I became, not least because the discussion had been far too abstruse for my liking. That having been said, it was good to be in Cambridge with its many attractions, intellectual stimulation and conversation partners.

Early in March we went to Birmingham University, where I gave a lecture on the "Legacy and Metamorphosis of British Christianity in SA". I repeated it shortly after at the University of Wales in Aberystwyth. In the *Church Struggle* I had written collectively about those settler churches whose British antecedents and use of English as their language of communication distinguished them from the Afrikaans-speaking churches. But by the middle of the twentieth century the majority of their membership was black; they were multilingual and first-language English speakers were in the minority. Moreover, their leadership was increasingly African or "coloured". My question was whether there remained a legacy to cherish and maintain in the new South Africa. There was, I argued, but only if the white membership came to terms with the new reality in ways that contributed to transformation.

At the end of March we went to Dublin as guests of Sister Geraldine Smyth, the Dominican director of the Irish School of Ecumenics. I gave a public lecture at Trinity College, entitled "Seeing Things Differently: Recovering Ecumenical Vision in a Post-Ecumenical Age". We toured the city, drank some Guinness, and hired a car to explore the enchanting west coast. Geraldine then took us to Belfast, enabling us to see the countryside and places of historical significance along the way. In Belfast we stayed with Catholics who, in the service of reconciliation, lived in a Protestant neighbourhood. Living next to the high wall that separated the neighbourhoods was as disturbing as the graffiti on the walls. I gave a seminar to an ecumenical group on the process of reconciliation in South Africa, and at the Seventy-fifth Anniversary of the Irish Council of Churches, held in Dromantine, Newry, I repeated my lecture on "Seeing Things Differently".

On one of our sightseeing trips from Cambridge we drove to Chichester, where Bonhoeffer's friend George Bell had been bishop at that time. Bell was largely responsible for the renewal of interest in the arts in the life of the Church of England, and his legacy was much in evidence when we visited Chichester Cathedral. On the way to Chichester we visited Arundel and the village of Climping, where my paternal grandmother, Mary Irish, was born. We visited the parish church and confirmed that her father's name was omitted in the baptismal register.

Other trips took us to the Norfolk coast where we watched birders observing a rare specimen not seen in Britain for many years. Used to more exotic bird life, we were unimpressed by the small, sparrow-like "little brown job" and, its rarity apart, could not understand what all the excitement was about. In Norfolk we also went to the pilgrimage town of Walsingham, with its Marian shrine beloved by Anglo-Catholics, and to the cathedral city of Peterborough. Another outing took us to John Constable country along the River Stour at Dedham to see the landscape which he had made so memorable through his paintings.

After Cambridge we took our time travelling north to Durham. We stopped for a few days in the cathedral city of Ripon so that I could do a woodturning course with master-turner Allan Batty. As I was still a beginner, I was helped in getting the basics right, and I resolved that when we returned to Cape Town I would enlarge my workshop, buy a bigger lathe with a swinging headstock to turn large bowls, and join a woodturning club. We also visited the ruins of the famous Cistercian Fountains Abbey, and the site in Whitby on the coast where that decisive church synod was held in 664, which swung British Christianity away from its Celtic roots towards Rome.

Once settled in Durham, we went hiking on several occasions in the Yorkshire Dales and visited a church where John Wesley once preached and services are still held. Isobel attended a week of art instruction in Kettlewell, a beautiful town featured in the movie *Calendar Girls*. We also visited Jarrow and the church associated with the Venerable Bede, the late seventh-century historian of British Christianity and the British Isles. Those were the days when my Viking ancestors were pillaging the east coast of Britain, burning churches and slaughtering Christians.

I was the Richardson Fellow in the Faculty of Theology at Durham. The lectureship was in honour of Alan Richardson, a distinguished professor a generation previously. My visit was arranged by Professor Ann Loades, and I was fortunate to have the use of her office near the majestic Norman Durham Cathedral, now a World Heritage site. Each morning I walked through its precincts on my way to Ann's office, usually stopping to admire some aspect of the building or its works of art, and sometimes to offer a prayer. Built in the eleventh century, the cathedral is associated with Saint Cuthbert, the seventh-century bishop of Lindesfarne, whose tomb has attracted pilgrims through the centuries. The cathedral achieved more recent fame as one of the sites for the *Harry Potter* movies.

I gave the Richardson Lecture on 14 May, reworking "The Legacy and Metamorphosis of British Christianity in South Africa". I remember wearing a colourful Mandela shirt for the occasion. I suspect it was somewhat out of place, but I was making a statement about the metamorphosis I was lecturing about. We were delighted to meet Alan Richardson's widow, who also entertained us at lunch. Her husband's book *Christian Apologetics* was the first serious theological book I bought and read while a student.

At the end of May we travelled to Edinburgh, where I gave the first Maitland Memorial Lecture at New College, reworking my Irish lecture on "Recovering Ecumenical Vision" for the occasion. Soon after we set off again, this time to the island of Iona, alongside the Scottish west coast. Anton and Esther had come from Cape Town to join us, and we met them in the coastal town of Oban. We took the ferry to Iona, where Saint Columba had established a monastery in 563. From there missionaries evangelised Scotland and northern England. The monastery adopted the Benedictine Rule in the thirteenth century and survived until the Reformation. Then, in 1938, George MacLeod, a Church of Scotland minister, established the Iona Community for the purpose of renewing church life through the integration of spiritual formation and social and political action. I had much earlier read his book *We Shall Rebuild*, so I had some prior knowledge of his vision. But actually being on Iona, worshipping in the Abbey church and exploring the island, was unforgettable.

After returning to Durham for a brief farewell, we continued our journey, travelling down the east coast to revisit Lindesfarne. Turning west we headed for the Lake District where we explored Wordsworth country before going on to Wales. There we stayed for a week in a small cottage in the remote hamlet of Zoar, a good base camp for visiting Harlech, Portmeirion, Snowdon and Caernarfon. Then we returned to Cambridge to say goodbye to the Cresseys and to start the long trek back to Cape Town. *Christianity, Art and Transformation*, the major outcome of my sabbatical, was published by Cambridge University Press in 2000, and it won the

AN AESTHETIC TURN

UCT Meritorious Publication Award three years later. I was told that it offered fresh insight into the relationship between theological aesthetics and social transformation.

While in Durham, I had received an invitation to give a week-long teaching mission on Christianity in the modern world at the Manning Road Methodist Church in Durban that August. So soon after our return from England, I travelled to Durban and found myself in the church vestry on the first evening. I had prepared several addresses on the most pressing issues facing Christians and the Church, and was readying myself to give the first. But as I was about to go into the church sanctuary, I suddenly felt compelled to do something quite unplanned.

I began by speaking about a young woman I knew well, who had struggled for years with her identity. She eventually came to accept that she was a lesbian and was helped to come out by Christian friends. I spoke about how she had experienced the Church as both a help and hindrance in the process, being accepted by some and rejected by others. And then I confessed that I was talking about Jeanelle. I moved on to speak about other issues, but not before making the point that Jesus' ministry was not one of exclusion, but one of embrace, and that the Church's ministry could be none other. After the service, more people came and talked to me about their gay relatives and friends than about anything else. There was a great desire to break through the silence in the Church and find direction in dealing with what, for most, was an unsettling situation in their families. I vowed that I would not miss opportunities to deal with the issue of homosexuality when it was appropriate, and to share the story of Jeanelle, which she told in her own words in a book edited by her brother Steve.[19]

In December I went as a consultant to the Eighth Assembly of the WCC, held in Harare, Zimbabwe. Apart from meeting many friends and making new ones, a highlight was a trip to Great Zimbabwe, one of the most important archaeological sites in Africa, dating back to the eleventh century. I had not been back to Zimbabwe since my visit in 1980 when I was chair of the UCCSA. Robert Mugabe was still in power (as he remains), but when he came to speak at the assembly, he was loudly booed by Zimbabweans in the vast audience. From what I could see, not much had changed in the country and there were signs of decline.

"Would South Africa go the same way as Zimbabwe?" I was asked several times.

"Anything is possible," I replied, "but nothing is inevitable."

The two situations could not be simplistically compared. But this did not mean the way ahead was plain sailing, or that the churches knew how to exercise their prophetic responsibility in the new dispensation.

22

Critical solidarity

> Critical solidarity means taking sides with all who remain oppressed in a new democratic society, and participating with them in their never-ending struggle for justice, human dignity, and liberation.
>
> (From *Christianity and Democracy*)[20]

The Department of Religious Studies at UCT was established in the Faculty of Arts and then relocated to the new Faculty of Social Science and Humanities in 1980. Between 1984 and 1986 I was deputy dean, then acting dean from 1986 to 1987, and again deputy dean from 1988 to 1989. In the late 1990s a mega Faculty of Humanities was established, which incorporated the Faculties of Arts, Social Science and Humanities, together with the Schools of Education, Music, Fine Arts and Drama. It was the largest faculty in the university. In addition, the National Education Department introduced outcomes-based education throughout the educational system. Much time was now spent creating courses that would meet this requirement within the stipulated timelines. And we had to do so under the leadership of a new dean, Wilmot James, who had the unenviable task of managing the changes. Anger and frustration among academics was palpable.

I had been on sabbatical in the UK during the initial frenzy, but soon after my return early in 1999 I was persuaded to become deputy dean of Humanities with responsibility for graduate studies and research. I accepted on condition that I could develop a graduate school as the hub for both graduate studies and research units. The draft proposals were accepted by the university senate, and it was also agreed that the school would be housed in the building previously occupied by the Faculty of Law. So it was that I became the director of the Graduate School in Humanities in 1999, with Lyn Holness as my personal assistant, and in 2000 we moved into our new building. Apart from my new responsibilities, I was also teaching and supervising graduate dissertations. My students now came from across the globe, as well as from South Africa. As several of them were interested in Bonhoeffer's theology, I had already established the Bonhoeffer Circle, which continued to meet regularly.

Jim Cochrane, who had already joined the Department of Religious Studies, took over the editorship of the *JTSA* and leadership of RICSA. In the latter capacity he organised an ambitious project on the role of religion in public life, which we named ME 99 (ME being the acronym for Multi-Event). This brought together academics as well as political and church leaders for a week-long event in February 1999. Among them were my friends Bill Everett, Ann Loades, Graham Ward and Jean Bethke Elshtain, a political scientist from the University of Chicago and a well-respected Bonhoeffer scholar. Also on the list of speakers were Methodist Bishop Mvume Dandala, Frank Chikane, Mercy Amba Oduyoye (the well-known feminist theologian from Ghana), Naledi Pandor (the minister of education), and Deputy President Thabo Mbeki. Mbeki addressed a special evening session on the Church in the new South Africa.

During the years of struggle, the Church had to pronounce a

categorical "no" to apartheid; the agenda of ME 99 was to discern how it could now say "yes" to building a new nation. An early tangible outcome was an invitation to RICSA to organise a workshop in Parliament on corruption in public life. A team of us spent two days at the House with a group of members of Parliament to facilitate discussion. In the concluding session Thabo Mbeki spoke strongly about the need to rid public life of the scourge of corruption. But as corruption continues to plague public life, it seems the exercise was not very successful.

In March that year I turned sixty, an event marked with appropriate celebrations. I did not feel older; for most people who have been privileged with good health, sixty is a transition to a new phase of life. I determined to set fresh goals for my work in the Graduate School and my research. Working closely with colleagues, who were mostly secular humanists but shared many of my Christian values, I began to reformulate my understanding of Christian faith in terms of Christian humanism, something that I discerned in Bonhoeffer's own theological journey. An opportunity to develop this theme into some lectures came when Professor Anna Marie Aagaard invited me to be a visiting professor at Aarhus University in Denmark in April 1999.

In Aarhus I was introduced to the fascinating blend of Lutheran Christianity and Danish culture represented in the work of the nineteenth-century theologian N.F.S. Grundtvig. Grundtvig was the father of the folk high school system which has played an important role in the shaping of Denmark's education and cultural life. He reminded me of the Dutch theologian and politician Abraham Kuyper, who had a similar influence in Afrikaner circles in South Africa. I once again came to appreciate the importance of working out a creative relationship between Christian faith and culture – an important theme in Christian humanism through the centuries. But I also had to keep in mind the opposition of Grundtvig's most famous contemporary Danish opponent, the philosopher and iconoclast Søren Kierkegaard.

From Kierkegaard, whom I had first heard about as a student at UCT and who had greatly influenced the young Barth, my theological generation had learnt to say "no" to Christendom, as well as to Nazism and apartheid. But when Barth began to affirm the humanist imperative in the gospel, a way was opened up for us to say "yes" to secular culture – but only if and when it expressed the humanitarian values of Christian faith.

I later had a chance to visit the Kierkegaard Research Institute in Copenhagen and speak to its director. There was not much love for Grundtvig in evidence. Mindful that I was in a different Danish space, I went down the street to the University of Copenhagen, where I lunched with the Faculty of Theology before giving a lecture in which I compared Bonhoeffer's humanist turn *to* the aesthetic with Kierkegaard's turn *from* the aesthetic. I was treading where angels feared to go in lecturing on Kierkegaard in his hometown and among experts.

Isobel and I returned to Europe in June to attend the Kirchentag in Stuttgart. We first visited the Bethges, knowing that Eberhard was in poor health. It was the last time we would see our old friend and mentor. He managed to walk to a nearby restaurant for Sunday lunch with us and other family members. We also went together to revisit the famous Catholic monastery at Maria Laach, where we reminisced over coffee. Back home, we continued the conversation in his study, which was lined with what had remained of Bonhoeffer's library. His days of reading and writing were now past, and his memory was slipping. But he had more than accomplished what he had set out to do in handing Bonhoeffer's legacy on to the next generation.

At the Kirchentag my main assignment was to present one of the daily Bible studies. The passage given to me was Isaiah 65:17-25 in which the prophet proclaims God's promise of "new heavens and a new earth" and the coming of a just peace on earth. The prophet had already said "no" to the corrupt politics of his day, but now he was saying "yes" to a new vision of justice and peace. This remains the essence of prophetic theology: not the attempt to predict the future, but to challenge the politics of the present. To say "no" when we must, but also to know when and how to say "yes".

Following the Kirchentag, Isobel and I set off for a holiday in Spain, which began with a visit to Málaga and a trip down the coast to Gibraltar – that rugged yet quaint outpost of the British Empire. Together with Elsie and Ron, who joined us later in Málaga, we drove to the small mountain village of Cortes de la Frontera. There we were the guests of the parents of Juan Garces, one of my former students. The town was a convenient launching pad from which to visit other beautiful places in Andalucía. We ended in Granada with its exquisite Alhambra, bringing back to mind that creative chapter in the history of culture when scholars of the three Abrahamic faiths engaged with one another, before the Spanish Inquisition brought their efforts to a disastrous end.

Our good friends Bill and Sylvia Everett heard that I was once again headed to the States in October, so they invited me to participate in a symposium at Andover Newton Theological School on Christianity and the Arts. From there I went on to Penn State University – a university with its own airport built, so it seemed, in the middle of nowhere. The reason was a conference on Bonhoeffer's Dilemma: The Ethics of Violence, at which I compared Bonhoeffer's involvement in the plot on Hitler's life with Nelson Mandela's decision to embark on the armed struggle in 1961. The comparison still makes interesting reading. After Penn State, and a shaky flight in a thunderstorm, I returned to Boston early in November to attend the AAR, where I lectured on "Bonhoeffer and the Recovery of Aesthetic Existence". I hastened home soon after, with Christmas and a new millennium rapidly approaching.

23

A new millennium

This second millennium of the Christian era is a significant moment for people around the globe to take stock of the world, to reflect on its past failures, and to express hope for the future. But it is naive to think that wars will cease and utopia arrive, or that tragedy will not strike without warning.

(Adapted from a sermon preached at Rondebosch United Church, 2 January 2000)

On the evening of 18 March 2000 we had guests to celebrate my sixty-first birthday. During dinner I received a telephone call from Sabine Bethge to tell me that her father had died that day in Villiprott. He had celebrated his ninetieth birthday in style just a few months previously. I had missed that party, but Clifford Green and I from the English-speaking section of the Bonhoeffer Society were able to attend his funeral on Saturday 25 March in Bad Godesberg. Later, in *Daring, Trusting Spirit* – my biography of Bethge – I described the funeral and recounted the tributes paid to this great-hearted and humble *mensch*. I also described how the large congregation walked through the streets of Bad Godesberg to Burgfriedhof where he was laid to rest. As Wolfgang Huber (then the bishop of

Berlin-Brandenburg) said at the reception afterwards, he had lived a fulfilled, accomplished, masterly and well-rounded life.

After the funeral I went on to Cambridge for a workshop on "The Role of Religion in the New Millennium", arranged by the Council for World Mission, successor to the LMS. It was a stimulating event, but little did we know that religion would soon once again become so notorious. The next month, back in South Africa, I gave a paper on my theological journey to the Annual Congress of the Theological Society, which I called "From Fundamentalism to the Discovery of Beauty". For the first time, I weaved my own story into a theological paper, preparing the way for *Being Human*.

The new millennium brought with it some family changes. In July 2000, together with the Cookes, we travelled to Kuruman for the opening of the new library and conference centre designed by Julian. This coincided with Steve's farewell as director of the Moffat Mission. He had accepted a position at the School of Theology and Religion at the University of KwaZulu-Natal in Pietermaritzburg. The farewell was attended by the premier of the Northern Cape, Manne Dipico, as well as the Anglican bishop of Kimberley and Kuruman, Itumeleng Moseki, both of whom spoke well about what Steve and Marian had achieved. It had been a remarkable decade for them, but Thea had developed diabetes and needed more specialised care, and schooling had become a problem for all the children. It was time to move on. Like me, almost thirty years before, Steve was about to become an academic. I could understand that.

We left for home the day after the farewell celebrations, but went on a circuitous route. We spent a few days at the Augrabies Falls; visited Pella, a remote town on the edge of the Kalahari Desert, with its amazing Catholic cathedral; passed through the town of Pofadder (named after a venomous snake); and explored a nature reserve outside Springbok, the last town of any size before leaving South Africa on the road to Namibia.

Earlier in 2000 I had received a letter from the president of the Evangelical Church of the Union in Berlin, informing me that I had been awarded the Karl Barth Prize for my work on Bonhoeffer and the Barmen Declaration in relation to the church struggle against apartheid. The Church of the Union, to which Bonhoeffer and Bethge belonged, was a union of the Lutheran and Reformed Churches in Prussia in the early nineteenth century. The award ceremony was scheduled to coincide with the next Congress of the International Bonhoeffer Society in Berlin in August.

The ceremony was held on the preceding Sunday evening in the Dom, the massive Protestant cathedral that dominates the skyline beyond the Berlin Opera as you travel up the Unter den Linden and across the river Spree. Isobel was there, as were Lyn Holness and several of my graduate students in the Bonhoeffer Circle who were attending the congress. Never in my wildest dreams could I have imagined that my interest in Bonhoeffer would lead to such an honour. But I did reflect on the irony that, whereas Bonhoeffer had been virtually banished from Berlin and ended his life in ignominy at the hands of the Gestapo, I was being feted in Berlin simply for writing about him.

The theme of the congress was "The Future of Christianity in a Pluralistic World", a topic I addressed in my lecture. Pluralism was not just a challenge facing us in South Africa; it had become a major issue throughout Europe. In his *Ethics*, Bonhoeffer had anticipated that the day would come when Muslim leaders would find it necessary to stand against the tide of secularism in post-Christian Europe. It was not only religious fundamentalism and radicalism that posed a danger to global society, as secularists insisted, but secularism, too, was problematic in its promotion of selfish individualism, and its lack of moral values.

One of the participants at the congress was the film director Martin Doblmeier, who was working on a movie on Bonhoeffer. I gladly agreed to an interview before full lights and cameras at the hotel where we were staying. When the movie was finally premiered, I became something of a minor movie star, but I wished that on that day I had not been wearing a bright blue shirt. People seem to remember that more than what I said. After the congress, Isobel, Lyn and I travelled down to Bavaria to visit Flossenbürg concentration camp, where Bonhoeffer had been executed after a mockery of a trial. We stood by the unmarked mass grave where his body had been dumped and tried to imagine that awful day.

In September I travelled back to Europe, but this time to a conference on "Theology through the Arts" held at the University of Cambridge. I guess the fact that I had linked theological aesthetics to the struggle for justice in *Christianity, Art and Transformation* had led to my invitation. While in Cambridge, I also participated in a conference at the Centre for Advanced Religious and Theological Studies (CARTS), where I gave a lecture on "The Rhetoric and Reality of Reconciliation". Preceding me was the distinguished Jewish philosopher George Steiner, the author of *Real Presences*. His lecture was, for me, the highlight. After mine, an editor from SCM Press in London asked me to consider writing a book on reconciliation, to which I agreed.

My somewhat hectic travel and lecturing schedule continued into the new year. In January 2001 I was at the University of Virginia, where I spoke on the "Rhetoric of Reconciliation", making the observation that it was important to distinguish between theological and secular understandings of reconciliation, yet find ways to relate them to each other. I went on to Union Theological Seminary in Richmond, Virginia, to give one of the Sprunt Lectures on "Holy Beauty: A Reformed Perspective on Aesthetics within a World of Unjust Ugliness". And finally I travelled to Duke University in Durham, North Carolina, to lecture, once again, on reconciliation. There I renewed contact with Ebrahim Moosa, who had been a lecturer in Islamic Studies at UCT. Sadly, he and his family had come under attack from a radical Muslim group in Cape Town and decided to leave the country.

In the meantime, I was planning another overseas ecumenical tour with George Malek, this time to Rome with a delegation of church leaders and theologians. The visit took place between 19 and 25 August. We were welcomed warmly by the Vatican Secretariat for Promoting Christian Unity, which arranged an excellent programme. Apart from visits to the main basilicas, we were also guests of the Sant'Egidio community in Trastevere, sharing in their evening worship followed by a reception. This remarkable lay Catholic community, comprising largely professional people, had helped resolve the conflict between the FRELIMO government in Mozambique and RENAMO – a post-independence ethnic movement that staged a long war against the post-colonial Marxist state. Towards the end of our stay, we had a private discussion on ecumenical relations with Cardinal Walter Kasper, head of the Secretariat for Promoting Christian Unity.

To crown it all, we attended Pope John Paul II's weekly public audience. The synod hall was packed for the occasion, with people from many different countries present. There was great excitement when His Holiness entered amid much clapping, singing and the waving of national flags. Showing signs of his advancing Parkinson's disease, he welcomed us in many different languages and gave us

South Africans, seated together near him, a special word of welcome. After his address, which was a simple biblical homily on the lectionary reading for the day, we were each invited to go forward to meet him personally and receive his blessing.

When our visit to Rome was over, I caught a flight to the British Midlands to meet Isobel. She went with me to Edinburgh for the retirement academic colloquium on Public Theology in honour of Duncan Forrester, at the University of Edinburgh. The colloquium began at New College. I was only scheduled to speak later after we had relocated to a conference centre, Carberry Tower, an hour's drive away in the countryside. But on arrival in Edinburgh I was informed that the speaker for the opening public lecture that evening was ill, and I was asked to give my lecture in his place. I agreed, unaware that the audience would include many people from the university, church and city who had come especially for the occasion. I was a little overawed. My lecture on "The Contribution of Theology to Public Life in South Africa" has been widely referred to since then.

The colloquium was a fitting celebration of a fine human being and one of the leading voices in public theology in the second half of the twentieth century. It was there that I first met Timothy Gorringe, professor of Theology at the University of Exeter and now a good friend. Tim's theological insight and creativity is undoubtedly amongst the finest I have come across. Max Stackhouse from Princeton, another good friend over the years, also gave one of the papers. Afterwards, the discussion became heated between Max and myself over United States policy in Iraq. I was perhaps more vocal than is wise and ventured to say that I feared something awful would soon take place in vengeful retribution for the bombing of Baghdad. The next day we returned to Cape Town.

A few days later, on 11 September, I had a faculty executive meeting. When I returned to my office, Lyn Holness's face was ashen. She pointed to her computer screen. There had been an attack on the twin towers of the World Trade Center in New York. We could only gape. Could this possibly be true? I did not know that my good friend Alex Boraine was right then fleeing for his life from the scene. In one hour the world had suddenly changed, and the promise of the new millennium had been reduced to ashes. A new era of religious terror had also erupted.

24

A time for endings

> It is a time for endings,
> a time for closing the door
> on a worthwhile activity,
> a time for saying goodbye ...
> Doors close but not for good.
> New doors will open ...
>
> (Isobel de Gruchy)[21]

An invitation to give the Hulsean Lectures in the Faculty of Divinity at Cambridge University took Isobel and me back to England in May 2002. The six lectures, entitled "Reconciliation and Christian Tradition", were given over two weeks and published that same year as *Reconciliation: Restoring Justice*[22]. During the past decade I had often lectured on or written about reconciliation; now I had the opportunity to bring all my thoughts together in a coherent way between the covers of a book.

We spent several weeks in the UK and, among other things, paid a return visit to Durham as requested by SCM Press. I had been invited to preach in the cathedral through which I had walked each day during my sabbatical in 1998, never dreaming that I would one day be honoured in this way. Professor David Brown, a canon theologian of the cathedral, hosted us during our stay in his extensive medieval apartment, which housed a remarkable library and collection of stuffed animals. This was also an opportunity to renew contact with Ann Loades.

Isobel and I then flew to Chicago, where I received an honorary doctorate (DLitt) from my alma mater, Chicago Theological Seminary. This was the first time Isobel and I had been back there together since 1964, so it was a nostalgic visit. We were delighted to meet the president, Susan Thistlethwaite, who told me that one reason for the doctorate was the publication of my book *Christianity, Art and Transformation*. The convocation ceremony was held in one of the large churches in Hyde Park. It was a splendid multicultural and colourful event, which began with a long procession from the seminary to the church. I gave the commencement address on "Is there life after CTS?". There had been for me, and CTS certainly played a role in shaping it.

From Chicago we flew to New York to visit our friends the Rasmussens, who were about to retire from Union Seminary. As on other occasions, we stayed with them and one evening had dinner there with our friends Alex and Jenny Boraine. Alex had established the International Center for Transitional Justice, based in New York, after the TRC had ended its work. It was remarkable how, not least through his vision and energy, the TRC had become instrumental in inspiring such initiatives around the world.

During our short stay in New York we visited the World Trade Center site to see for ourselves the terrible destruction that had occurred there on 9/11. Alex, who had been working in his office nearby that day, had described for us what happened in graphic, frightening terms. We were silent as we read the story told in thousands of messages stuck to the fences around the site. It was difficult to think that human beings, whatever the convoluted reason, could do this terrible deed. I thought long and hard about this question, seeking some meaningful answers.

During a short stay in London on our way home, we visited Westminster Abbey to see the statue of Dietrich Bonhoeffer, which had recently been unveiled above the great West End, alongside other twentieth-century martyrs. The group included Manche Masemola, the sixteen-year-old South African girl who was killed in 1928 by her parents because of her Christian faith. In the bookshop I bought Archbishop Rowan Williams' little book *Writing in the Dust: After September 11*. He had also been there that horrific day. Without being anti-American or apocalyptic, he makes the point that such an act could only have been committed by people who were insanely angry about what had been done to them, their culture and religion, and who were driven by ideology to wreak vengeance. The bombing of Baghdad and the destruction of the Twin Towers cannot be separated.

Towards the end of July, I returned to the United Kingdom to fulfil two engagements. The first was to preach again at Westminster Abbey. The date was 21 July, the day after the anniversary of the failed attempt to assassinate Hitler in 1944 – a plot in which Bonhoeffer had participated. The epistle reading that Sunday, which provided my text, was Romans 8 ending with the words "in hope we were saved" (8:24). Nothing better summed up Bonhoeffer's life and testimony. My second engagement was to give a paper at the Annual Conference of the Ecclesiastical History Society at the University of Leeds. My topic was "From Resistance to National Reconciliation: The Response and Role of the Ecumenical Church in South Africa".

I returned to the US in November to give a lecture on "Christianity, Judaism and Islam, and the Restoration of Justice in South

Africa" at the Institute for Philosophy and Religion at Boston University. Without excluding other faiths from the mix, I argued that it was critical in our time to restore mutual respect within the Abrahamic religious traditions if there was to be global peace. But the challenge to do so was enormous given the new religious and political dynamics following 9/11.

My diary reminds me that during the following February, 2003, as the new academic year began, I was busy supervising dissertations; helping establish a course in Disability Studies; handing over the editorship of the *JTSA* to Steve, who was then on the faculty of the University of KwaZulu-Natal in Pietermaritzburg; attending the launch of my book *Reconciliation: Restoring Justice* at Clarke's Bookshop in Long Street; rating applications for research grants; preaching at the induction of Robert Steiner – one of my PhD graduates – as the new minister at the Rondebosch United Church; lecturing to students at Stellenbosch on the ecumenical movement; meeting with the university librarian; giving my weekly graduate seminar; and going to Pretoria for a meeting of the National Research Foundation (NRF), which also, around that time, renewed my A-rating as a researcher. And the year had only just begun.

I was invited to revisit Uppsala University in March 2003 to give some lectures in the Faculty of Theology. I had arranged to visit Renate Bethge on my way home, in order to discuss a proposed biography of Eberhard with her. I met Vicki Barnett, who had kindly agreed to co-author the book, at Frankfurt Airport, and together we went to Villiprott. We spent a week there, most of the time in Eberhard's study working through his papers. We also had many helpful conversations with Renate. Vicki later withdrew from the project because of other commitments, but not before she had helped a great deal with the research. So I became the sole author of *Daring,*

Trusting Spirit.[23] The book was later translated into German and, from what I gather, was well received in Germany.

At the end of 2002, I had been surprised to receive a *festschrift* in honour of my looming retirement, edited by Lyn Holness and Ralf Wüstenberg, a German Bonhoeffer scholar who had done some of his post-doctoral work with me at UCT. Entitled *Theology in Dialogue: The Impact of the Arts, Humanities, & Science on Contemporary Religious Thought*, it encapsulated the kind of theology I had focused on in the post-apartheid era and had encouraged my students to pursue. I was pleased that it was published by Eerdmans, who had done my first book twenty-five years before.

My retirement colloquium was planned for 2 to 3 June. Several international and local colleagues, as well as many of my former graduate students, attended. Lyn Holness did all the administration, and the Graduate School building was the designated location.

A week prior to the event, Isobel was diagnosed with Parkinson's disease. She had suspected that this might be the case, but had kept her thoughts to herself. So when she phoned me at my office I was devastated. We decided not to mention this to anyone until after the colloquium, as Isobel did not want it to put a damper on the celebration. It was a sign that age was beginning to catch up with both of us, even though we were remarkably well in every other way. In fact, at the age of sixty-four I had never had a serious illness or spent any time in hospital, except when my tonsils were removed when I was very young.

The theme chosen for the colloquium, inspired by one of Bonhoeffer's comments in prison, was "Fragments and Connections". As Lyn would later write: "… it was vague – but deliberately so. Yet somehow we felt confident that there would be coherence, and we were not disappointed."[24]

Bill Everett spoke on the connection between our mutual interest in woodworking and spirituality, and Timothy Gorringe on the theological imperative of town planning, to which Julian Cooke responded. Graham Ward from Manchester spoke on Christian political practice, Cornel du Toit from UNISA on Christian values in a post-democratic world, and Tinyiko Maluleke from the same university spoke about reconciliation in the new South Africa. Dwight N. Hopkins, a professor at the University of Chicago, who had written a second doctorate on Black Theology and Culture under my supervision, was also among the speakers.

The closing banquet was held in the Smuts Hall dining room, where we had gathered six years previously for the Bonhoeffer Congress dinner. The event was hosted by the dean of Humanities, Robin Cohen, with whom I had worked closely over the past few years. I was glad that so many faculty colleagues from the wider university, as well as visitors from neighbouring universities, were there. My oldest friend on the UCT faculty, Martin West, then deputy vice-chancellor, shared some memories, and Hans Pfeiffer, doyen of Bonhoeffer scholars in Germany, made a speech which, if I were a more humble fellow, would have embarrassed me.

So my thirty years as a full-time academic at UCT came to an end. But that was not the only ending, for the day came shortly after when we had to leave our Rosebank home. Our close friend Carolyn Butler came to visit us as the furniture was being taken out to the removal van. We sat in the garden and she led us in a short liturgy designed to mark this transition. We recalled the wonderful times we had in this place over so many years. Images of our family life, of my parents, of visiting friends, of birthday parties and Christmas dinners, of the games we played and the dogs who were part of our lives (Kim, Karma and Tamba) flashed through my mind. It was inconceivable that this house was no longer home, or Vredenburg Avenue no longer the road on which we lived, or, perish the thought, Cape Town no longer my city. But as the house grew empty and the curtains came down, the time had come to move on. There was still a way to go.

PART FOUR

The Volmoed years

2003-2015

John and Isobel come to make this new place carved out of creation, home.
It becomes home at a time of change, expected and unexpected.
It becomes home for them, their children and grandchildren.
Into it will come the myriad of family and friends, colleagues and co-workers, friends as yet unmet who will add their own fullness and blessing.
Out of it will flow things of great beauty: artistry of paint, colour and wood, wisdom in poetry, articles, books and ministry.
God of love, bless those who dwell here, those who come into this place and the gifts that will flow of it.

(Carolyn Butler)[1]

25

Life in community

Thomas Merton once wrote of his monastery in Kentucky: "This is the center of America ... an axle around which the whole country turns." I have also thought of Koinonia Farms in Georgia, Ghost Ranch in New Mexico, and Holden Village in Washington. One afternoon ... I stumbled on such a potential center for South Africa ... Volmoed they call it.

(Martin Marty)[2]

Anton first told us about Volmoed early in 1986. At his suggestion, Isobel and I visited there shortly after with Martin and Harriet Marty from Chicago. We drove up a narrow and winding dirt road to discover a derelict farm overgrown with alien trees, the only building standing being an old farm house without electricity or piped water. But there was a raw beauty, and the first resident members of the embryonic Volmoed Community, Bernhard and Jane Turkstra, had vision, skill and energy. After his return to Chicago, Marty captured its potential in *The Christian Century*: "Volmoed they call it. 'Full of hope, but not only hope; also courage.'"

Ever since I visited the Taizé Community in France in 1964, I have been attracted to life in community. This was reinforced when

Isobel and I, sometimes with Steve, Jeanelle and Anton, visited other intentional communities, some of them mentioned by Marty in his *The Christian Century* article: Reba Place in Evanston, Koinonia Farm in Americus, Holden Village in the Cascades, and Iona in Scotland. Each is different, but all have a family resemblance. It is humbling for those of us who are now part of the Volmoed Community to be included in their number.

Isobel and I often talked about what we would do after I reached the UCT mandatory retirement age of sixty-five. She felt we should live elsewhere, possibly in Hermanus, a coastal town 120 kilometres southeast of Cape Town, but I had no desire to leave the city I loved. It was a stalemate. Then, during Easter 2001, we went with the Rondebosch Church for a weekend retreat at Volmoed as part of its centennial celebrations. We were surprised to see how it had developed since we were last there. The gardens were well-established; there were numerous guest houses and a refectory, and a sense that Volmoed was becoming what Marty had predicted.

After the Friday evening session, I walked from the meeting room to Faith Cottage where Isobel had already gone. Along the way I was surprised by a voice saying, "You will come and live here." My early interest in living in community had undoubtedly resurfaced, but could this be God's call? I rushed to tell Isobel and without any hesitation – something unusual when I come up with harebrained schemes – she said, "Yes, I think it is."

The next day we spoke to Bernhard Turkstra about the possibility of joining the community. He encouraged us to think and pray further and promised to discuss it with the board of trustees and community. A period of testing and reflection was necessary. This involved spending time at Volmoed, learning its ethos, working in the kitchen, and getting to know the community and staff. Six months later Bernhard phoned to invite us to join the community. We sold our house to raise the funds for building our new one, designed by Julian Cooke and built by the community. By May 2003 it was ready, and the next month we moved there. As we drove up the winding road that morning in June, we entered a new era in our lives.

When I first visited Hermanus as a schoolboy, it still retained much of its character as a fishing village. With its beautiful mountain scenery and beaches, its whales, restaurants and wine farms, it has since become a thriving retirement, holiday and tourist centre; the home of artists and writers, and the many people who service the town. Some of these are descendants of old fishing families or farm labourers; others are more recent migrants from the rural Eastern Cape or refugees from around Africa. For all its beauty, Hermanus faces major challenges in providing housing, employment, education and health services for its burgeoning population, which mirrors the gap between the global rich and poor. Fortunately there is a wealth of experience and commitment to tackle these problems and to make a difference in the lives of those in need. But much needs to be done, and urgently.

Volmoed is nine kilometres from Hermanus, located in the wine-farming Hemel en Aarde Valley. Its recorded history begins in 1823 when Lord Charles Somerset, governor of the Cape, invited Moravian missionaries from Genadendal to minister to the lepers living there. They gave the valley its name, "because so high are the hills, which closely embrace the valley all round, that they seem to touch the sky and you cannot see anything but heaven and earth".[3] They also gave the name Volmoed to the place where they established their mission. But then, in 1845, the lepers were moved to Robben Island in Table Bay. The property was sold, and the valley was divided into farms – one of them being Volmoed. In time it became well known for its indigenous *fynbos* and cultivated flowers.

When the present Volmoed Community bought the farm, a condition of sale was that the name be kept. How appropriate, for it not only linked the new community to that earlier mission, but it also required courage and hope to make the new vision of "bringing wholeness to broken people" a reality. Even under normal circumstances this would have been so. But South Africa was then in a State of Emergency as protest, resistance and repression gathered momentum. Many of those who first came to Volmoed had experienced this at first hand, and some were traumatised as a result. South Africa desperately needed places of hospitality where God's ministry of reconciliation and healing could be embodied and experienced.

Over the past thirty years Volmoed has developed substantially. Apart from the resident community, others come to work here each day, and there is a wider network of those who support its ministry. There is accommodation for sixty people; a well-equipped office, resource centre and conference room; and a fine chapel complex, which includes the sanctuary where the community meets every day for morning prayer. Barry Wood, the resident chaplain, provides counselling and a healing ministry. On Thursdays we celebrate the Eucharist, which attracts people from the wider community. I usually lead this service and give a brief meditation. In April 2001 Volmoed became associated with the Community of the Cross of Nails, centred at Coventry Cathedral in England – a sign of its recognition as a place of reconciliation. We are honoured to have Desmond Tutu as our patron.

When we first arrived at Volmoed we were not at all sure what we would do with our time apart from participating in the daily life of the community. Many of our friends in Cape Town also wondered about this. But as the years have passed it has proved to be an ideal place for us to live and work, and a wonderful base for a wider arrange of activities.

Isobel has honed her skills as an artist and published several books of her poetry as well as a book on Julian of Norwich. She also produced the *Volmoed Book of Morning Prayer* soon after we arrived, and a series of *fynbos* flower paintings which adorn the walls of the resource centre. I developed my skills as a wood-turner and furniture maker, and together we told the story of Volmoed's first twenty years in *The Volmoed Journey*.[4] We had many friends in Cape Town and regularly visited them, or they came to stay with us at Volmoed. But soon our circle of friends began to expand in Hermanus. We helped start Table Talk, a monthly discussion group of people interested in religion, law and art; Isobel became part of the network of artists living in the area; and I lectured on occasion at the University of the Third Age (U3A), which attracts hundreds of retired people to its extensive programmes.

Volmoed is primarily a place and a community that provides hospitality for retreats, conferences and workshops, and a large number and range of groups make use of our facilities. Amongst those with which I am regularly involved is the annual retreat for theological students from Stellenbosch; an annual theological colloquium which has emerged out of my graduate seminar and Bonhoeffer Circle at UCT; and the study abroad programme of Marquette University (Wisconsin, US), which is coordinated by the Desmond Tutu Peace Centre in Cape Town. This was initially directed by Judy Mayotte, one of the most remarkable people we know; a tireless advocate for peace and justice around the world, despite being confined to a wheelchair.

Soon after retiring, I was elected an emeritus professor and appointed as a senior scholar at UCT. This required continuing my research and publishing, supervising graduate students, and mentoring younger academics in the Humanities through the Emerging Researcher Programme. Lyn Holness became the director of the programme, and after several years of working together, we co-authored *The Emerging Researcher*,[5] which documents what we attempted to do. In addition I was also appointed an extraordinary professor in the Faculty of Theology at Stellenbosch University in 2004 and soon made to feel at home among friends, including Russel Botman, Dirkie Smit, Elna Mouton, Nico Koopman and Robert Vosloo.

Our years of "retirement" at Volmoed have involved much travel, continuing the pattern long established in our lives. We had not anticipated that this would be so. If home is where you long to return after you have travelled elsewhere, then Volmoed has become that place for us. We love its daily routine of work and prayer, walking in the surrounding mountains and on the coastal path, or meeting friends for coffee or a meal and conversation. Travel expands our horizons, but it exhausts the body; being at home renews the soul and gives stability and balance to life. And I guess it is that balance which we have sought and found amongst our busyness at Volmoed.

26

A Christian humanist

> De Gruchy ... has written a book in which he outlines a new form of Christian humanism ... No doubt many readers will be surprised to learn that he has decided to don the robes of Christian humanism for our global times. I can only cheer about this book.
>
> (William Schweiker)[6]

Some months after settling in at Volmoed, I received a phone call from Dave Woods, the vice-chancellor of Rhodes University: "Would you be willing to receive an honorary doctorate from the University?"

I was taken aback because the Faculty of Theology had long been discontinued, so I had no idea who could have nominated me for this honour. I had revisited Rhodes over the years to give lectures or to attend conferences, but this was a special homecoming, made more so because Rozelle and Dick, together with Isobel and Lyn, attended the ceremony and celebrations. And to my great pleasure, my academic host for the weekend – the first in April 2004 – was Ian MacDonald, a Philosophy professor, who had been my best man at our wedding. I received a Doctoris Legum (Doctor of Law), and the university orator said I was receiving it for my contribution to the process of transformation in South Africa. That was over the top, I thought, as I knelt before and was capped by Chancellor Jakes Gerwel – a genuine struggle hero, former director general of President Mandela's office, and previously the vice-chancellor of the University of the Western Cape.

During 2003 Steve had reminded me that the following year would mark the twenty-fifth anniversary of the publication of *The Church Struggle in South Africa*. He proposed that we should revise it and publish an anniversary edition. We did so. Steve edited it, made the language inclusive, and wrote an excellent new final chapter drawing lessons from the struggle against apartheid for the struggles now facing the Church. I was particularly moved by his opening essay in which he critically located the book within South African historiography, suggesting that it was now a classic – something echoed by Desmond Tutu in the new foreword.[7]

But there was another book gestating in my mind, awaiting its time for me to tell the story of my journey in Christian faith and understanding. Early in 2004, when I was awarded a Rockefeller Fellowship to spend July at its Institute in Bellagio, Italy, I knew that time had come. Fortuitously, the Ninth International Bonhoeffer Congress was held in Rome that June, so Isobel was able to attend it with me. My paper on Bonhoeffer as Christian Humanist was an indication of the direction my thoughts were taking and Bonhoeffer's influence in doing so. It was also at the Rome congress that I was asked to edit the new edition of Bonhoeffer's *Letters and Papers from Prison* – a task that would occupy much of my time for the next five years. Arguably Bonhoeffer's most famous volume, this new edition, volume eight of the *Dietrich Bonhoeffer Works in English*, is almost nine hundred pages in length.

After the Bonhoeffer Congress in Rome, we travelled north to Bellagio, a beautiful resort on Lake Como, where we would be in residence for the next month. The conditions were that I write a book, share the midday meal, and attend a weekly seminar with other scholars. What a privilege to do so in the company of a dozen other academics, and also to have the time to explore the towns and hills along the lake.

So it was that I began to work on *Being Human: Confessions of a Christian Humanist*, an attempt to write theology in a more personal way. I had found it increasingly difficult to identify with the dominant image of Christianity being portrayed in the social media and the countless books displayed in religious bookshops. Christian humanism, an honoured tradition critically retrieved, offered an authentic alternative. I presented an early draft of my first chapter at a Bellagio seminar and immediately discovered that there were others who identified with what I was saying. Isobel also led a seminar on *Fynbos* in the Western Cape at the request of the other participants. We returned home energised by our Bellagio experience.

Soon after we returned, we went back to Cape Town for my valedictory service as a minister in the UCCSA, held in the Rondebosch Church. The preacher was Rod Botsis, the moderator of the Presbyterian Church, who had also been the speaker the night I felt called to Volmoed. Several UCCSA church leaders also spoke about my ministry over the years. But my ministry was not over; I had simply shifted location. And just when I thought I could settle down to the rhythm of life in community, I was getting invitations to lecture or speak elsewhere. I will spare you all the details, but allow me to share some cameos from the next few years.

Close by St. George's Cathedral in Cape Town there is another, even more historic church, which stands in bold contrast. Die

Groote Kerk is the mother congregation of the DRC. During the heyday of Afrikaner nationalism, it was where prime ministers and presidents were sworn into office. I never imagined I would preach there, but I did on the first Sunday of September 2003. I suspect my colleague at UCT, Henning Snyman, who was an elder in the congregation, had something to do with it. After a warm welcome in the consistory, I was soon climbing the steep steps into the massive pulpit supported at its base by four enormous lions sculptured by Anton Anreith in 1789. Looking down from that considerable height added to the awesomeness of the occasion. It was encouraging to see the multiracial congregation below, a welcome sign of transition.

In October Isobel and I went again to the UK. I had been asked to speak at the Diocese of Devon's Clergy Conference on the relevance of the Old Testament patriarchs. I had spent a great deal of time revisiting the appropriate texts in Genesis in order to prepare something of relevance for clergy in England today, but I don't think I succeeded. Fortunately they also asked me to say something about Christian humanism, which they found more helpful. During the conference, I shared a stimulating session with Archbishop Rowan Williams. He was not only brilliant in response to difficult questions, but also profoundly pastoral in the way in which he dealt with them.

After Devon we went to Oxford, where I gave the David Nicholls Memorial Lecture at Regent College. Nicholls, before his untimely death in 1996, had been a Church of England priest and a political philosopher. My lecture on Christian humanism as an antidote to fundamentalism and secularism seemed to strike the right chord with the sizeable audience, and affirmed the direction in which I was now moving. I gave the same lecture the following March at Wesleyan University in Middletown, Connecticut, at Union Theological Seminary in New York, and at the Center of Theological Inquiry at Princeton. I was beginning to feel like a Christian humanist evangelist, and perhaps I was, for the good news of Christian faith is all about becoming more truly human in Christ.

In July 2005, I returned to Ghost Ranch in New Mexico, this time with Isobel, to participate in a programme on the Christian witness for peace. The Rasmussens were now living in Santa Fe, so we had an opportunity to explore together some of the historic and scenic parts of New Mexico. This included the old Spanish mission at Chimayo, famous for its "holy dirt" that is reputed to cure various illnesses. I had previously met a Jewish medical doctor from Texas who told me that he regularly went to Chimayo to get his supply, because it actually worked! At Ghost Ranch, Larry and I were part of a workshop on right-wing fundamentalism, together with Susan Thistlethwaite, the president of Chicago Theological Seminary. With 9/11 and the bombing of Baghdad still fresh in our minds, there was much anger aimed at the Bush administration and the way in which fundamentalist Christianity was influencing policy and manipulating the media.

I returned to the US in November to attend the AAR in Philadelphia. When going through passport control in Atlanta, I was ordered to go into a side room without any explanation. It was empty, except for two young uniformed officials, both wearing guns. When I asked them why I had been detained, I was brusquely told that they asked the questions, not me. I had a connecting flight to catch, but was kept in the room for about an hour without any discussion. Eventually I was asked some questions, the answers to which had all the time been in my documents before them, and I was told I could leave. I hastily did so, but not before telling the officers that they were behaving just like the police in apartheid South Africa. Prior to the AAR, I gave the Frederick Neumann Memorial Lecture at Princeton

Theological Seminary. There I told the president about my airport experience. Apparently I was one of several visiting academics known to him who had been harassed in this way.

In January 2006 I married Rozelle and Dick Lindwall in the Volmoed Chapel. Rozelle's previous husband, Bill, had died several years earlier, and Dick, whose wife had died from cancer, had long been a friend. This was a great family celebration. Rozelle's daughter, Othene, and granddaughters Samantha and Grace, as well as many of her friends were there. The music was provided by Steve, Marian and our three grandchildren, all accomplished musicians.

Back in the nineteen-seventies, Hans Engdahl, a Swedish Lutheran priest working in Cape Town, had registered to do his PhD with me at UCT. That proved impossible, so he eventually wrote it in Uppsala, and I was asked to be the external examiner at his *viva* or oral examination. On the way to Uppsala I stopped over to give a lecture at the University of Gothenburg at the invitation of Bishop Carl Axel Aurelius. That is why I found myself on a British Airways flight from London to Gothenburg on 8 March 2006.

The moment we landed passengers on the opposite side to me began gesticulating at something outside the aircraft I could not see. We were told to disembark speedily and were hurriedly ushered through passport control into the baggage collection hall. But our baggage never arrived. Instead after a while we were instructed to evacuate the hall and go to the domestic terminal some distance away. It was freezing cold outside, and when we got there the terminal was crowded. Bishop Aurelius's chaplain met me, and I was soon settled in at the Church of Sweden chaplaincy office. There we learnt that the plane had been held up by armed masked men who had placed a parcel under the fuselage with the threat to blow up the plane if there was any resistance. They then forced the ground crew to open the hold and escaped in a car at speed, with millions of pounds and dollars destined for European banks. We had to wait until a bomb disposal unit arrived several hours later and discovered that the parcel was harmless before we could leave the airport. I had travelled all the way from South Africa, where hijacking was endemic, only to experience this in a country that always seemed so safe.

I gave my lecture on Bonhoeffer the next day at the University of Gothenburg, after which Bishop Aurelius and I caught the train to Uppsala for Hans's *viva*.

The impressive hall was full. As the "opponent", I had to lead the "attack" by asking Hans seven critical questions. Then the three examiners had their chance until the dean finally called a halt and invited the four of us to lunch, followed by a meeting at which we decided that Hans should be awarded the degree. That evening there was a formal banquet in celebration of his achievement. I had not come prepared and found on arrival that everyone was dressed in their finery while I looked rather scruffy, having anticipated something more informal. And then I discovered that I was one of the speakers and was placed at the high table next to the bishop and the dean.

That year, 2006, was the centenary of Bonhoeffer's birthday, so there were many celebrations around the world. I was invited to lecture at several of these. In March I gave the Hugh Price Hughes Lecture on Bonhoeffer's legacy at the Hyde Park Methodist Church in London. An interesting result of my visit was the request to make a new baptismal font for the church. The bequest that funded the project stipulated that it should be made out of an African indigenous wood. I made it from kiaat. It was heavy and cost far more to freight to London than it did to make.

In May I was the guest of the Reformed Church and the University of Zurich, where I again lectured on Bonhoeffer's legacy. During my visit I was taken to some of the historic sites associated with the Anabaptists when they were persecuted by Church and State, and many forcibly drowned – a parody on their desire for "rebaptism" – in Lake Zurich. The Reformed Church, the established church in this Swiss canton, has since confessed its guilt. But that ugly blot in church history remains. At a public meeting I was one of a panel that addressed the problems of multiculturalism and immigration in Switzerland today. It soon becomes evident in such discussions that, no matter how much Europeans may have said they opposed apartheid, racism is not far below the surface.

The same is true of us white South Africans, of course, but I was pleasantly surprised shortly after when I visited Beaufort West, a farming town about 300 kilometres from Cape Town, to discover some glimmers of hope. I was invited to give a talk on Bonhoeffer to the Karookring (Karoo Circle), a monthly meeting of townspeople, farmers, teachers and ministers – the brainchild of my UCT colleague Henning Snyman. Not too many years before, such a multiracial gathering would have been inconceivable.

The next event I attended in celebration of Bonhoeffer's birthday was a conference in Melbourne, Australia, where I gave three lectures.[8] I found Melbourne a very attractive city, met some fine people, and to my delight my friend Keith Clements was also a speaker at the event. I was dismayed, however, when a few participants, who asked me my opinion on the ordination of gays, vehemently attacked me for my views. They were leaders of a group that had withdrawn from Australia's Uniting Church to form their own "confessing synod", claiming to be following Bonhoeffer's example and that of the Confessing Church in Germany and South Africa. I think they were mistaken on both counts, but I was more upset by the lack of love shown by them towards those who disagreed.

From Melbourne I went to St. Mark's Library in Canberra to lecture again on Bonhoeffer. While there, I reconnected with John Painter, who was my colleague when I first taught at UCT. Then I repeated the three Melbourne lectures at the Macquarie Christian Studies Institute in Sydney, one of the most beautiful cities in the world.

Wherever I went in Australia I met South African expats. Some were apologetic about having left the country; others had little good to say about the land of their birth. But every now and then I met those who longed to be back home and who still avidly supported touring South African sports teams. I wondered again about how it would have been if Isobel and I had left South Africa to live somewhere else. Our lives and those of our children would certainly have turned out differently. I was glad we had stayed put and, as always, equally glad when the time came to head back to the rhythm of life in community.

Being Human was published late in 2006 in London by SCM, and then in the US by Fortress Press under the title *Confessions of a Christian Humanist*. By all accounts it proved a timely contribution to the need to provide an alternative vision for being Christian today. It was also well received in scholarly circles and merited a special session at the AAR in Montreal in 2009. In a lengthy review article, William Schweiker of the University of Chicago said that the book was something to cheer about.

In March 2007 I visited the University of Pretoria to give a paper on art, culture and transformation at a conference arranged by the Faculty of Theology on "Arts and Reconciliation in Civil Society". The last time I had been on the campus it was a bastion of Afrikaner nationalism; now it was in the process of transformation. Symbolic of the changes was an evening session when Archbishop Tutu addressed

A CHRISTIAN HUMANIST

a packed lecture hall. In former times he would have been hounded from the campus precincts.

I've already told about our early visits to the FEDSEM when it was located near Fort Hare. It was then expropriated by the apartheid government and, after a brief sojourn in Umtata, relocated to a new, award-winning campus outside Pietermaritzburg. But this great ecumenical venture was controversially closed in 1993 and its buildings vandalised.[9] As a result the churches had to establish new centres of theological education, as happened at the University of KwaZulu-Natal and, for the Methodists, at Kilnerton near Pretoria.

I visited Kilnerton for the first time in June 2007 to attend the Annual Congress of the Theological Society. This brought back sad memories of the demise of FEDSEM, and I could only hope that there might be some way to recapture its vision. A few years later the Methodists moved from Kilnerton to the Seth Mokitimi Methodist Seminary in Pietermaritzburg, a splendid new high-tech campus. Steve, as head of the School of Theology at the nearby university, served on its planning committee, and his books (including some of mine) are now part of the seminary's library.

I had thought that *Being Human* would be my last book. But I had not counted on the arrival in Hermanus of Anna-Marie Bands, an iconographer trained in the Russian Orthodox tradition. Isobel attended icon writing classes with her for two years, and some residential workshops were held at Volmoed. In the process Isobel wrote (the correct description for painting them) some fine icons, including one based on Andrei Rublev's *Icon of the Holy Trinity*, which is now in the Volmoed Chapel. I, in turn, wrote *Icons as a Means of Grace*, published by Lux Verbi in 2008. This has subsequently received a new lease on life among church groups beyond my normal circle, including

Pentecostals, who have become interested in the role of tradition and art in the life of the Church.

Throughout my life I have always had good health. But suddenly, in August 2007, while giving a talk at the Hermanus Art Society, I became dizzy and could not continue. That night I collapsed, and the next day I was immediately booked in at the local Medi-Clinic where I was diagnosed with hepatitis B. This was my first experience of being hospitalised. I felt terrible and was decidedly not at home. But I was impressed by the care of the nurses and the skill of the doctors. As I began to recover over the next ten days, I thought of the many people who do not get the same medical attention, and doubted whether I would have coped so well. It was a sobering experience, a reminder of mortality, and a reason for being grateful.

At the time I fell ill, I was preparing to give a lecture at York Minster in England as part of its Ebor Lecture Series on globalisation and identity. This had to be cancelled. By November I was back on my feet and ready to travel overseas again to attend the AAR in San Diego, and to give some talks at a church in Los Angeles. On the way I stopped over in Washington DC to preach and give a lecture. Remembering my experience of being detained at the airport in Atlanta on my last visit to the States, I anticipated further trouble. But when I said that I was coming to preach that weekend at a Presbyterian Church, assuring the officer on duty that this was indeed a Christian church, and promising to pray for her daughter who had a drug problem, I went through in record time.

Vicki Barnett was my host in Washington. She was then the church liaison director at the Holocaust Memorial Museum, which I visited for the first time. I had been to the Holocaust museums in Berlin and Cape Town, each of them different, but the experience is always sobering. Anti-Semitism, like racism and xenophobia, is a crime against humanity. So too is the Zionist oppression of the Palestinians.

During my stay I also went to give the Capps Lectures at the University of Virginia in Charlottesville, at the invitation of another Bonhoeffer scholar and friend, Charles Marsh. The first lecture, which I gave in the magnificent domed university hall designed by Thomas Jefferson, was on "Christian Identity amidst Global Contradictions". The second I entitled "Christian Humanism against Fundamentalism and Secularism".

I then went on to Los Angeles where I had been invited to speak at several evening meetings at a local church. I had no prior knowledge of this church or how they even knew about me. And I only had the vaguest idea about what they wanted me to talk about. I was intrigued. A lapse in communication delayed those who were meant to meet me at the airport, so I had to wait on the sidewalk outside arrivals for an hour. Then a black van with dark windows screeched to a halt and a well-built man with a baseball cap pointing backwards jumped out and told me to get in quickly. I must admit that I hesitated for a moment. Was I being kidnapped? But I soon discovered to my relief that he and the driver were both leaders in the congregation to which I was headed.

If I had thought I was going to some mega-church like Crystal Cathedral, my expectations would soon have been dashed. The nondescript building was situated in a lower-middle-class neighbourhood where unemployment was rife. The church was fundamentalist by background, but in the process of breaking free from those constraints. I was soon impressed by the commitment of its leadership in responding to the challenges facing the community. But why had they invited *me* to speak to their congregation? The reason, I soon discovered, was because they had studied *Confessions of a Christian Humanist,* found it something to cheer about and wanted to know more.

During the four days I was there, I spoke each evening and preached at the Sunday revival service. In my sermon I said that when Jesus told Nicodemus he had to be born again, he was not talking about going to heaven when you die, but about the need to change direction if Nicodemus was to participate in the coming of God's kingdom of justice, which Christ embodied. After the service, an elder, who had resisted my coming, complained that I had not made an altar call for people to become Christian humanists. He would have been the first to respond, he declared. I came away more convinced than before that being a Christian is about becoming more truly human in solidarity with those in need. Maybe I had become a Christian humanist evangelist after all.

From Los Angeles I was taken by car through southern California to San Diego. I was glad not to miss seeing this part of the US, which was new to me. Before my commitments in San Diego, I had a free day to explore the massive harbour – home to a large part of the United States Pacific Fleet – and to visit one of the aircraft carriers open to the public during Veterans Day weekend. I had never been on anything like it and was amazed by its sheer size and fighting capacity. Then I learnt that even bigger ones were being built. I was not only overwhelmed by the experience, but also by the extent to which the arming of the nations appears to be escalating instead of scaling back. Where will it all end?

Vicki Barnett and I had arranged a three-day workshop for the translators of Bonhoeffer's *Letters and Papers* prior to the AAR. This helped us achieve a coherent translation of this large and diverse book of letters, poems, essays and cryptic notes. For once I did not present a paper at the AAR, but then the main value for me in attending has always been meeting colleagues and discussing research projects. The worst part is the long haul back to Cape Town, made less onerous only by the prospect of seeing Table Mountain and being back home.

During 2007 I became an adjunct professor in Applied Ethics at the University of Fort Hare in a new programme on Leadership in Africa. We visited the campus in March 2008, together with the Everetts. I had not been back to Fort Hare since I was a student at Rhodes. Much had changed, and I was encouraged by what I saw. I lectured on Christian humanism and its ethical implications for society. The students were bright and their questions sharp. We visited the archives of the ANC and were reminded of the role that the university had played in the education of African leadership. We stayed in the spectacular mountain village of Hogsback – where Fort Hare is developing a conference centre on property left to it in the estate of Professor Monica Wilson – and had a good visit there in the company of my UCT colleague Francis Wilson.

Late in 2007 Anton and Esther unexpectedly told us they had decided to emigrate to the United States. Anton's software development company had offered him a job in Atlanta, which he had enthusiastically accepted. We were distraught. This would mean that none of our immediate family would be anywhere near us. So the thought of them leaving for good was heartbreaking. But we acknowledged that it was important for them to experience life in another part of the world. I could not help but think that my grandparents never saw their parents again after they left England and Jersey. I also recalled how Rozelle and I had left home on the same day, leaving our parents on their own. How sad they must have felt. Anton and Esther settled in Atlanta in May 2008.

That June I received the Andrew Murray-Desmond Tutu Prize for *Being Human,* and how good it was that Tutu himself was the speaker on that occasion. The next month, Isobel and I went to Porthleven in Cornwall to celebrate her seventieth birthday, staying in the harbour house where her grandfather had been born. Steve, Jeanelle and our granddaughter Thea joined us for the celebration. From Cornwall we went to the Tenth International Bonhoeffer Congress in Prague. There we had another birthday celebration, with Jeanelle coming for the occasion and several close Bonhoeffer friends sharing in it.

No sooner were we back home than Desmond Tutu came to visit Volmoed for a few days as patron. He addressed a packed meeting in the Dutch Reformed Church in Hermanus, where he spoke on reconciliation and participated in the life of the community for a few days. Those hectic years of "retirement" are memorable, but the next year would become the one we treasure most.

27

Special moments

Who knows what experience led the Psalmist to say that "the days of our life are seventy years, or perhaps eighty, if we are strong; even then their span is only toil and trouble; they are soon gone, and we fly away" (Psalm 90:10). But as you turn 70, dad, I hope that a reflection on your life will indicate more than just toil and trouble, even though that may be what you felt at times being a father. And while there are many things that can be said on this occasion, I do hope that our shared involvement in and engagement with the South African theological world has been a special part of those years – as it has for me … And thanks for the fun and many shared special moments.

(From Steve's letter to me on my seventieth birthday)

In March 2009 I turned seventy. Many longstanding friends joined the Volmoed Community in celebrating the occasion. None of our children or grandchildren could attend the party, but Dick and Rozelle, together with her granddaughter Samantha, were there. Those absent sent wonderful letters that I cherish, especially the one that turned out to be the last Steve wrote to me. I wish I could quote it in full here, but the fragment above must suffice.

As he observed, seventy years is our allotted lifespan, and therefore a good time to take stock. Perhaps it was time to let go and settle more fully into the rhythm of life in community. After all, Steve's academic career was going well, and he was providing leadership in circles that were, in earlier times, my turf, as well as developing an increasingly distinguished niche of his own in theology and development.[10]

But then, in anticipation of the five-hundredth anniversary of the birth of John Calvin, I was commissioned by Lux Verbi to write a book about the Reformer. This was the brainchild of Luke Stubbs, an Anglican priest who, shortly after I began, died of cancer. I recall visiting him in the hospice and thinking how tragic it was that someone still in his forties should be struck down in this way.

John Calvin: Christian Humanist and Evangelical Reformer was an attempt to rescue Calvin from the frightful injustice done to him within the narrow confines of Calvinism. One positive reviewer, an Afrikaner theologian, wryly commented that the book certainly said much about De Gruchy's theology, if not always Calvin's. Maybe he had a point. But there was more than sufficient material in Calvin's legacy for me to argue my case, and I think there was some relief among Dutch Reformed Christians that there was an alternative take on Calvin to that which made him a burdensome bogeyman.

As part of the celebration of the five-hundredth anniversary of Calvin's birth in his adopted city, the University of Geneva, which he had founded, hosted an international conference during May. On the way to Switzerland Isobel and I, together with Carolyn Butler, went on a visit to Venice. We rented an apartment between the Basilica of Santa Maria della Salute and the Accademia Bridge – an ideal place from which to explore this remarkable island city. It was exactly a year since Carolyn's husband, Ron, had died. We lit candles in his memory, not thinking that soon we would be doing the same in memory of Steve.

From Venice we went by train to Ravenna, a city that adopted Christianity in the second century and became the capital of the Byzantine Empire after the Fall of Constantinople. Among its ancient churches, some dating back to the sixth century, was the octagonal Basilica of St. Vitalis with its Byzantine mosaics – the most famous outside of Istanbul. Calvin visited Ravenna on one of his early journeys after fleeing France, and I wondered how this might have influenced his thinking. With that in mind, we journeyed on to Geneva.

The Geneva conference was attended by mostly secular historians of the Reformation. I gave one of the opening lectures in which I examined the historical role of Calvinism in South Africa. This was followed a few days later by a more theological lecture on Karl Barth and Calvin in South Africa at the University of Basel, where Barth had taught. I gave it in the room in which he had often lectured, and did so with him looking down on me from a large portrait hanging nearby.

Afterwards a young man in the audience stood up to make a comment: "My grandfather would have liked your lecture very much!" The next day over lunch I had an opportunity, at the Karl Barth Archive, to talk further with Barth's grandson and his mother, Barth's daughter-in-law.

Earlier in 2009 I became a fellow of the Stellenbosch Institute for Advanced Study (STIAS), directed by nuclear physicist Hendrik Geyer. Throughout the year, cohorts of scholars from around the world come together at STIAS for several months at a time to pursue their research. To be a fellow, it is necessary to have an approved research proposal related to the wider STIAS agenda. Mine was taking my Christian humanist project further. In conversation with Bernard Lategan, who established STIAS and was a co-director, the New Humanism Project took shape.

The project involved thirty-nine fellow academics who were committed to the humanist vision embodied in the new South African Constitution. Not all the participants were Christian; some were Muslim, others atheist or agnostic; some were scientists, others lawyers, poets, philosophers and public activists; but all shared the same concern. William Schweiker also came from Chicago to participate in the first symposia held in July 2009, where the focus was on the meaning of humanism. Later, at the second symposia in February 2010, the focus shifted to the question "What does it mean to be human in South Africa today?" Given the multidisciplinary character of the project, and the range of perspectives brought to the conversation, it was not surprising that the complexity of the problem soon became evident.

My contribution to the 2009 Calvin birthday celebrations ended at a conference held at the University of Stellenbosch in September, when I gave a lecture on John Calvin, Karl Barth and Christian Humanism. During that week, which coincided with the 150th celebration of the theological seminary, Stellenbosch University gave me an honorary doctorate, along with Denise Ackermann, Bernard Lategan, Wentzel van Huyssteen and Mercy Amba Oduyoye from Ghana. Steve came from Pietermaritzburg especially for the event. I still see him walking down the street to meet us that afternoon; I still see his delight as he poured a bottle of champagne to celebrate the event with our friends the Cookes and Lyn Holness; I know he was proud of me beneath his usual banter.

Steve and I sometimes found ourselves at the same conference listening to each other's papers, as happened at the Joint Conference of Academic Societies in Religion and Theology, held at Stellenbosch soon after. After each of my lectures, he would invariably ask me a difficult question during the discussion that followed, and I would do the same in return. But sometimes he would also acknowledge our agreement.

"What do you think your father would say about that?" someone asked him at the Joint Conference.

A characteristic impish grin spread across his face as he replied, looking towards me in the back row: "If you have known the son, you will also know the father."

This was the last time I would hear him give a lecture – something he always did with great passion, humour and insight.

Late in 2009 I finished editing Bonhoeffer's *Letters and Papers from Prison*. It had been a long and demanding assignment, but I had a remarkable team of translators, and Vicki Barnett was a superb general editor. Despite the daily effort of closely reading the text and then writing the introduction, it had been a privilege to edit one of the great classics of the twentieth century. Fortunately I had finished my task before Steve died. I would not have had the emotional capacity to do so afterwards. As it was, I had tears in my eyes when I read those final pages in which the reader discovers that Bonhoeffer never received the last letters that his parents sent to him, and they in turn never heard from him again.

I saw Steve again at Christmas when the family gathered at Vermaaklikheid. I remember him fixing the pergola above the veranda; supervising the braai on several evenings; playing his guitar; fishing in the river; walking along the beach with Jeanelle; and the projects we discussed. Then the family all came to Volmoed for a few days to celebrate New Year. I remember him, together with Marian, Thea, David and Kate, renting kayaks and paddling around the coast in

Hermanus; I remember that he beat me at chess; I remember us walking up the river to our waterfall and plunging into the pool. Most of all, I remember hugging him farewell the evening before they all left to drive back to Pietermaritzburg. Isobel and I would not see him again. I often think back to those very special shared moments.

28

A road unforeseen

> None can foretell what will come to pass, if we take this road or that ... Now at this last we must take a hard road, a road unforeseen. There lies our hope, if hope it be ... The road must be trod, but it will be very hard.
>
> (J.R.R. Tolkien)[11]

Steve drowned on Sunday 21 February 2010 in the Mooi River in KwaZulu-Natal. He was forty-eight years old. During the week that followed, friends and family gathered every day at the family home in Pietermaritzburg to remember him and to share our grief. The next Saturday more than a thousand people attended the funeral in the Anglican Cathedral in Pietermaritzburg. Jeanelle came from London to be with us; David played his saxophone; Thea and Kate spoke, as did Marian and I; and Isobel read a poem she had written for the occasion. The service was a celebration of a life well lived, but also one of great sadness. I shed tears as his coffin was taken out of the cathedral on his final journey. It had been a long week.

The next Tuesday a memorial service was held at the Rondebosch Church, Steve's spiritual home. Again there was a large gathering of friends, colleagues and family present, including Anton and Esther who had just arrived from Atlanta. Elsie, his aunt, spoke about what he had meant to the wider family, and Jeanelle and Anton spoke about what their brother had meant to them. A message from Archbishop Rowan Williams was read. Methodist Bishop Mvume Dandala read another from the South African Parliament: An unopposed motion passed that day in appreciation of Steve's contribution to the life of the country. I have described the events of those days and my response to them in *Led into Mystery* and refrain from doing so again in detail. Even after five years, it is too painful and unnecessary to repeat here all that happened.

Experiencing grief is an inescapable aspect of being human, but nothing actually prepares you for the death of one of your own children, nor does the grieving end, for love cannot forget. Life does not get back to "normal", as though you can "get over" what has happened. But Isobel and I reckoned that the way forward, which Steve would have chosen for us, was to live as fully as we were able, and therefore to do those things that had always been important to us and to him. She painted and wrote numerous poems, and in due course wrote *Making All Things Well*, a book on Julian of Norwich's *Revelations of Divine Love* which had long been her companion.[12] As for me, even the week after Steve's memorial service in Cape Town I was determined to give my weekly meditation at the Volmoed Eucharist. We are fortunate to be part of a caring community, and sensed that Steve, too, was empowering and urging us on, just as he had always done through his life.

In March we went with Carolyn Butler to the Eastern Cape, where I was again scheduled to give seminars at Fort Hare. This was our first journey and my first academic commitment after Steve's death. On the way, we visited Ian and Joan Huskisson in Knysna, amongst our oldest friends, and Mike and Marijke Kirby, who had lost a son while we were still with them at St. Mungo's Church. In times like those, friends who have travelled the distance with you are among God's greatest gifts.

After Fort Hare we returned to Port Elizabeth, where I gave a series of seminars to DRC ministers of the Eastern Cape Synod as part of their continuing education programme. We returned to Cape Town by overnight train, something we had not done for years.

One of the most difficult parts of grieving is negotiating anniversaries, birthdays, and celebrations. Steve drowned on a Sunday afternoon. For months I found that the most difficult time of the week. Later it was his birthday on 16 November and the anniversary of his death on 21 February. In between there were other birthdays in the family when his absence was sorely felt. We also found it difficult to attend the celebrations of others, especially when their children made speeches. And then there were funerals. But we were determined to be present, to share in the joys and sorrows of others, and found ongoing consolation in the visits of family and friends. We were also regularly in Cape Town for me to give seminars at UCT, and I always made sure that I had coffee with Robert Steiner, the minister at the Rondebosch Church, who was a great support. Then, in June 2010, the FIFA World Cup was a God-sent distraction. David, our grandson, came from Pietermaritzburg and, along with Bernhard Turkstra and his son, Martin, we went to see Spain play Mexico at the enormous new Cape Town Stadium.

There were other timely distractions. I had to edit the papers from the New Humanist Project at STIAS and turn them into a book. Due to Steve's death, I had missed the second symposium, so I not only had to read the papers I had previously heard, but also those given in my absence. *The New Humanist Imperative in South Africa* was launched on 15 June at STIAS, with Desmond Tutu taking centre stage as the speaker.

In August I attended the annual conference of the Swedish Christian Humanist Society in Jönköping, where I gave a lecture on Confessions of a Christian Humanist. I also participated in a discussion with K.G. Hammar, the former archbishop of the Church of Sweden, who subsequently visited Volmoed.

In September I led a retreat for UCCSA ministers – the first of several that would be held at Volmoed over the next few years. Soon after, I went to give a lecture at the Annual Congress of the Theological Society of South Africa, held at the University of the Free State. And then, at the end of September, Isobel and I went to Pietermaritzburg to be with the family and to attend the annual board meeting of the *JTSA*. At that meeting Professor Gerald West and Janet Trisk, an Anglican priest and scholar, were appointed the new editors.

When Steve died, Rozelle and her husband, Dick, gave a cash gift to Volmoed to be used in memory of Steve. We were overjoyed when they were present on 6 October to participate in the dedication of Steve's Place: a wooden gazebo built on a promontory overlooking the Onrus River as it flows through Volmoed. The whole community and many friends came for that milestone in the process of grieving. We always go there on Steve's birthday and the anniversary of his death to share a glass of wine and some snacks. We imagine him walking up the river bank as he often did to swim in the waterfall pool with his children. Many others now go there for quiet meditation.

There were two fiftieth anniversaries to celebrate in January 2011: our wedding and my ordination. I celebrated the latter by preaching at Union Congregational Church in Kloof Street. I had not been back there since it had severed its connection with the UCCSA, but we received a warm welcome and enjoyed a reception in our honour. Then we celebrated our golden wedding anniversary with a party at Volmoed worthy of the occasion. Many of our close friends and extended family were there. Jeanelle and her partner, Heidi, came from London, and Thea came from Pietermaritzburg. This was our first wedding anniversary without Steve, for he had been born ten months after our marriage. I found it difficult to celebrate without tears. Isobel expressed her thoughts in poetry:

> We have grown up together, you and I,
> Acquaintances, friends and then lovers,
> Teenagers, eager to spread our wings,
> Testing the waters and tested by death;
> Catapulted into instant adulthood.
>
> We have grown together, you and I,
> Shouldering responsibility, ill-prepared,
> Buoyed by shared values, shared faith,
> Dreaming, exploring, risking,
> encouraging each other, flying high.
>
> We have grown apart at times, you and I,
> Going down different roads, absorbed,
> excited, leaving the other behind,
> but halting, turning, finding one another again,
> each growing as we struggled to mend the rifts.
>
> We have grown each other, you and I,
> Each with our own interests, talents,
> Urging the other to participate, to learn,
> sometimes dragging the other along,
> Kicking and screaming, but enabling them

To grow – petals unfolding like a flower
touched by the sun's kiss.

We have grown old together, you and I,
By God's grace and love, support,
Encouragement each for the other,
By the gift of children, grandchildren, friends,

And we have been tested again by death,
But, because of all that has gone before
We have been able to walk on – together.

Before Steve died we had talked together with him, Marian, Jeanelle and Anton about celebrating our golden anniversary as a family in some exotic place. Should we now go ahead in Steve's absence? Once again I could hear him say, "Go for it, Mom and Dad!" So we started making plans, and in April Jeanelle, Thea, Kate, David, Isobel and I spent a week in Mauritius. It was a time of special bonding.

Before his death, Steve and I had also talked about jointly writing a book on basic Christian theology. We talked about it again the Christmas before his death, during a long walk at Vermaaklikheid. Sadly, this was not to be. But in June 2011 I presented a paper at the Congress of the Theological Society of South Africa, on "Revisiting *Doing Theology in Context*", in which I mentioned some of the ideas we had shared.

In the middle of October, Isobel and I went to London to spend time with Jeanelle and Heidi, and then we went to the US to visit with Rozelle and Dick at their holiday apartment in Panama City on the Gulf of Mexico. From there we went to Atlanta to be with Anton and Esther. Together with them, we visited the Everetts in

Waynesville, North Carolina, and the Rasmussens in Santa Fe, New Mexico. We then travelled to New York for a conference at Union Seminary, to celebrate the completion of *Dietrich Bonhoeffer Works in English*. The project had taken fifteen years. Our travels sound frenetic in retrospect, but somehow we coped well.

But we grieved that Steve was no longer around to share in these events, and even more that the promise of his own life-long dreams, which he had aplenty, would never come to fruition. He would have turned fifty that November. It was difficult to grasp that he would have reached that milestone, and even more difficult to accept that he did not. He had achieved so much in the course of his life, which was now being acknowledged and celebrated in memorial lectures, publications and other ways. We could only hope that he was able to enjoy the satisfaction, but where, as Isobel poignantly asked:

> Where have you gone?
> Gone to some place
> where we will meet you again?
> Or have you gone to some huge Waiting Room,
> with a multitude of others,
> milling around,
> impatient with inactivity,
> thinking that if this is heaven you want out?

By then I was beginning to own my grief in writing *Led into Mystery*. More than fifty years before, I had first studied Theology and tried to answer the questions of my congregation in Sea View, untested by much experience of life or death. I had come a long way since then. My theological understanding had developed and grown in different ways, not least through our time in Chicago and during the church struggle. I had become a professor of Theology, helping students to think theologically in responding to the challenges of our time. Later, as that phase came to an end, I had discerned that I had become a Christian humanist and described that development in *Being Human*, and I had talked with Steve about writing a book with him that would help people understand the Christian faith better in today's world. But now the key questions of faith, the reality of doubt, the meaning of God, the inevitability of death, and the challenge of hope confronted me in a way they never had before. I was discovering that theology is a journey through life and death, embraced by the One in whom we live, move and have our being. It is being led into and by the mystery we name God.

Led into Mystery was undoubtedly the most difficult book I had ever written; it was also the only book I wished I never had to write. But it became a source of blessing and strength as I found myself entering into dialogue with Steve in a way that I had not anticipated, and subsequently with others who walked the same path. Silent as Steve had become, I could still hear him speaking. I was glad we had finally written the book we had talked about, even though now seeped with unanticipated sadness.

29

Completing the circle

> What matters ... is whether one still sees, in this fragment of life that we have, what the whole was intended and designed to be ...
>
> (Dietrich Bonhoeffer)[13]

Some on Volmoed have nicknamed me the "sage on the hill"; I think in jest, but it brings me back to the question with which I began: Who am I, as the years of autumn pass rapidly into winter. There is good reason for me, now well beyond seventy, to reflect even more on the fragments of life, as Bonhoeffer counsels, in order to discern the intention of the whole.

Family and friends continue to tell me to slow down. There is no need for them to do so. I can feel the slowing in my muscles and bones despite visits to the gym. But even as I pause to take stock and contemplate the meaning of life and death, I am blessed in my measured busyness, which I far prefer to boredom. "Old age," Joan Erikson tells us, "demands that one garner and lean on all previous experience, maintaining awareness and creativity with a new grace."[14]

Isobel and I are not only blessed with a caring family, but also with wonderful friends of many years, and new ones who have entered our lives these past few years. Not all their names have been mentioned in the story I have told, nor can I list those who have now become part of it. But I must mention Edwin Arrison, an Anglican priest whose energy and vision is making a remarkable contribution to both the Church and society in South Africa today. Edwin was a student activist and younger colleague of Steve's, and it was he who instituted the memorial lectures in honour of Steve in Cape Town. He is now a trustee at Volmoed, and a leader in the Kairos South Africa group and at the Centre for Christian Spirituality. He also keeps me well informed.

In April 2012 Lyn Holness, Edwin and I went to an ecumenical conference in Assisi. I had not been there for many years, and it was a first for Edwin and Lyn. The conference had many highlights, but simply being in the old hilltop town again, walking through its winding streets and looking out over the Umbrian landscape far below, was worth the visit. We went to share our concerns and insights about the Church's witness in South Africa, but we received much more than we gave. For who can resist the challenge of Saint Francis's life and his call to be instruments of God's peace?

A few days after our return to Cape Town, Desmond Tutu gave the first of the Steve de Gruchy Memorial Lectures, which he entitled "God is God's own worst enemy". Why does God allow people in the prime of life, who have so much yet to give, to die? He did not answer the question, but he probed deep beneath the surface in a way that helped me in my journey into mystery. In 2013 Denise Ackermann gave the lecture; in 2014 it was given by Mitri Raheb, a Palestinian Lutheran theologian from Bethlehem; and in 2015 by Roderick Hewitt, a Jamaican theologian and friend of Steve's. Annual memorial lectureships are also held at the University of

KwaZulu-Natal in Pietermaritzburg, keeping alive Steve's legacy. We are deeply indebted to all who make these possible and participate.

Isobel's *Making All Things Well* was finally published by Canterbury Press in the UK in 2012. Desmond Tutu, a member of the Order of Julian, commended it highly in his foreword. He also told Isobel that she was a better theologian than me! I usually respect his judgement. I am delighted that her work has gained such recognition and that her book was later also published by the Catholic Paulist Press in the United States.

In May I received the 2012 Andrew Murray-Desmond Tutu Prize for *John Calvin: Christian Humanist & Evangelical Reformer*. The book was subsequently published in a new edition by Wipf and Stock, and is in the process of being translated into Portuguese.

The following month, Isobel and I spent some time with Jeanelle and Heidi in London. I went on to Berlin to visit Wolfgang and Kara Huber, and while there gave a lecture on Bonhoeffer at the Humboldt University, where Bonhoeffer had been a student and part-time lecturer. From there, Wolfgang and I went to Sweden at the beginning of July to attend the Eleventh International Bonhoeffer Congress, held in the resort town of Sigtuna. It was there that Bonhoeffer met Bishop Bell for secret discussions on the German Resistance during the Second World War.

In October Thea turned twenty-one. We celebrated this milestone in her life in Pietermaritzburg. She had also just completed her bachelor's degree in Philosophy at the University of KwaZulu-Natal before going to the University of the Witwatersrand in Johannesburg to do graduate work. In 2015 she received her master's degree with first class honours. How proud Steve must be!

At the end of 2012 and over New Year, we hosted a family reunion at Volmoed for the Dunstans, Isobel's side of the family. This was largely Isobel's doing, and it was an enormous success. Over thirty family members came from around the world for the occasion, as did Anton and Esther, and Jeanelle and Heidi.

In January 2013 Bill and Sylvia Everett came to visit for the month. Once more Bill and I worked on projects in my workshop and dreamt about writing a book together on the way in which woodworking had influenced our lives. That same month our grandson, David, started his studies at the University of Cape Town, following in the footsteps of Steve and myself. It has been good to have him close by.

Reinette Swartz, who grew up on a farm in the Hemel en Aarde Valley, came to work at Volmoed shortly after we had arrived, and also helped Isobel on a part-time basis. At the beginning of 2013 she asked to work for us more permanently. This helped a great deal, as running our home had become more demanding with so many visitors and guests coming to stay. At the same time, Serghay van den Bergh, who grew up at Karwyderskraal, a nearby Moravian mission-farm, began to spend some of his free time working with me in my workshop.

During 2013 my contract as a senior scholar at UCT and my appointment as extraordinary professor at Stellenbosch were renewed for the forthcoming years. My NRF accreditation as an A-rated scientist was also renewed for another five-year term. So there were seminars to give, articles to publish, students to supervise and emerging researchers to mentor.

Led into Mystery was finally published in May 2013. It was launched at a conference on "The Soul" held at Oxford, at which Graham Ward graciously spoke. At the conference I had the pleasure of responding to Marilynne Robinson, the American author, and met Iain McGilchrist, the Scottish neuropsychologist and author of *The*

Master and his Emissary, which has rightly received much acclaim. After the conference Isobel, Jeanelle, Heidi and I had a holiday in Sicily exploring the region around Syracuse.

Upon our return home, there were further launches of *Led into Mystery*, and Isobel and I received several invitations to speak about *Making All Things Well* and *Led into Mystery*. During Easter we spoke at the Randpark Ridge United Church in Johannesburg, when I also took the opportunity to visit the Apartheid Museum and the Constitutional Court accompanied by Craig Morrison, the minister of the church and a long-time friend of the family. On another occasion we went to the Anglican Benedictine monastery Mariya uMama weThemba outside Grahamstown to lead the monks in a series of seminars.

In the meantime, the Swedish Christian Humanist Society decided to translate my *Being Human: Confessions of a Christian Humanist* into Swedish. This led to an invitation to the Gothenburg International Book Fair in 2013. At the fair I was interviewed by Archbishop K.G. Hammar in a televised discussion before a large group, and again later at a public meeting. After the fair I went with Lisa Tegby, dean of the Lutheran Church in Umeå, to visit her congregation. I also led a seminar at Umeå University for graduate students in Religion, at the invitation of another friend, Professor Karin Spörre. Denise and Laurie Ackermann were there that week, so Denise participated with me in the seminar. Umeå University is, so I was told, the second furthest north in the world.

In November Isobel and I returned to Atlanta to visit Anton and Esther and to attend our brother-in-law Dick's eighty-fifth birthday celebration. While there, we went north to Stockbridge to visit our friend Joyce Hovey. We renewed contact with the Stockbridge Church, visited the Hancock Shaker Village, and enjoyed the first snow of winter. Then we headed back south to Washington DC to stay with Judy Mayotte, who had set up the Marquette University's study abroad programme. I spoke about *Led into Mystery* at the National Cathedral on the Sunday morning.

From there, we went to Baltimore for the AAR Congress. I was honoured to be part of a session, hosted by several academic societies, on *Led into Mystery*. There was a large attendance and much discussion during question time, some of which has continued via email. It was good to see our friends Wentzel and Esther van Huyssteen in the audience, and to welcome them back in South Africa more recently. They had also tragically lost a son since we last met. We are members of a club that no parents want to join.

Anton and Esther fetched us by car to go to Charlottesville, where I gave a lecture at the University of Virginia on "Theology as Journey into Mystery". We also visited Monticello, the famous house built by Thomas Jefferson. We travelled back through Shenandoah National Park and Waynesville where we visited the Everetts. Bill, Anton and I spoke at length about the book that Bill and I were writing on woodworking and spirituality. Entitled *Sawdust and Soul*, it was published late in 2014.[15] But the best moment on our trip happened in the car when Anton and Esther told us that they had decided to return permanently to South Africa. What a joyful moment that was for us! And how delighted we also were when our youngest grandchild, Kate, came to give a piano recital in Hermanus just before Christmas, after our return from the US.

At the end of February 2014, Isobel and I made another trip to Pietermaritzburg where I gave Steve's Memorial Lecture which I called "Poo Protests and Olive Theology". This reflected some of the major themes in the last lecture I heard Steve give the year in which he brought together his ecological concerns and those of justice and peace. The lecture related these concerns to current events in South African political life. It was, as always, a pleasure to renew contact with Steve's former colleagues at the University of KwaZulu-Natal.

Early in May I went to Canada to receive an honorary doctorate from Knox College, one of the theological colleges affiliated to the University of Toronto. During the week I gave my lecture on "Theology as Journey into Mystery", and at the convocation I spoke about "Stewards of God's Mysteries in an Age of Disenchantment". I also gave some talks and preached at the St. Andrew's Presbyterian Church in downtown Toronto, where Bob Faris, one of my former doctoral students, was the associate minister. Soon after my return from Canada, on 22 May, I received the Andrew Murray-Desmond Tutu Prize for the third time for *Led into Mystery*.

On 18 March 2014 I turned seventy-five, and much of the rest of the year turned into a rolling celebration, beginning with a party at Volmoed. As part of the celebration, we went with David, Kate, Jeanelle and Heidi for two week's holiday in London and Jersey Island. Unfortunately the other family members could not join us. Going to Jersey, our ancestral home, was something that Steve, Jeanelle, Anton and I had talked about for a long time, so I was keeping a promise to Steve. After a hectic week in London, we headed off by air for Jersey and stayed in an apartment in St. Brelade's Bay. I must leave it to the reader to imagine the fun we had together and the great times we shared exploring the De Gruchy connections, especially Trinity Parish where my grandfather was born.

That is where the circle of my life began. Along the way there were many significant moments and forks in the road where I made choices that determined the next step. Not least was my decision, now so many years ago, to "become a Christian", for without that choice it would all have been different. I have come a long way since then but faith in Christ – however compromised in practice or inadequate in conception – has been central to the rest. Without that I would not have become a theologian, studied at Rhodes, married Isobel, taught at UCT, participated in the church struggle for justice and reconciliation, travelled the world, been enriched by so many friendships, ended up at Volmoed, or had any awareness of the gracious mystery into which I have been led and sustained throughout.

From 31 August to 2 September, my annual theological colloquium was held at Volmoed. There were more than forty participants from UCT, Stellenbosch, UWC, Pietermaritzburg and Bloemfontein, including graduate students, former doctoral students and faculty members. Clifford Green, Keith Clements and Larry Rasmussen helped us focus on Bonhoeffer's legacy in relation to ethics, ecumenism and ecology, and Graham Ward came from Oxford to be the main respondent.

We then moved to Stellenbosch where the Faculty of Theology had arranged a Seventy-fifth Birthday International Conference on "Theology at the Edge". Dean Nico Koopman, conference chair Robert Vosloo, and their staff had gone the extra mile to make it a success. The programme was structured around my major books. With that in mind, I had written *A Theological Odyssey: My Life in Writing*, which was launched on the first day of the conference.

Wolfgang Huber and Nico Koopman lectured on Bonhoeffer; Graham Ward, along with Frank Burch Brown, whose work on Christianity and the arts has been seminal, lectured on Theological Aesthetics; Denise Ackermann and Jim Cochrane spoke on Christian humanism; Iain McGilchrist and Wentzel van Huyssteen on science and theology; and Allan Boesak, along with Serene Jones, president of Union Theological Seminary, spoke about the church struggle today, especially with regard to poverty and injustice.[16] The focus was on what these themes might mean for coming generations in church and theology. A splendid banquet added to the festivities. During the week we also launched the Bonhoeffer Research Unit and decided to invite the International Bonhoeffer Society to hold its congress at Stellenbosch in 2020.

One outcome of the conference was the establishment of AHA (Authentic, Hopeful Action), a nationwide programme to encourage local initiatives in responding to the challenge of poverty. I was unaware of this encouraging development until some weeks later when the planning committee invited me to be the patron of AHA. I was honoured, but suddenly felt my age.

On 27 September David and I went to the Newlands Rugby Stadium to watch South Africa beat the Australian Wallabies. I had not been back there since I was a student and young academic, and here I was with my grandson, now a UCT student. On 7 January 2015 Isobel and I celebrated our fifty-fourth wedding anniversary. Later that month Anton and Esther returned from Atlanta to live in Hermanus, and my son rejoined me in my workshop. On 27 March Jeanelle celebrated her fiftieth birthday with a party at Volmoed worthy of such an occasion. So many parts of Isobel's and my life were coming to fulfilment. We could not possibly ask for more. Yet, on each occasion someone was missing. Our gratitude was tinged with sadness as we gathered at Steve's Place for the fifth anniversary of his death, just as I was putting the final touches to this autobiography. Yes, we have all come a long way and there may still be a way to go, but

> As we journey on
> we tend to journey back.
> Life is not a straight line from start to finish,

I HAVE COME A LONG WAY

like a race, eyes fixed on the tape.
It is more like a circle,
a snake trying to swallow its tail;
the longer the snake,
the easier to touch
the beginning.
Not just Shakespeare's second childhood:
no hair, no teeth,
being led by the hand,
but the mind stretching back,
searching its dark recesses,
remembering, remembering,
sometimes reliving,
hopefully restoring.
The further on we travel
the clearer the view;
the more we see.
Does God grant us this
so that we can grab our tail
and gobble up the regrets,
and the bits that hurt,
and end life complete,
whole, a full circle?

And if life is cut short,
suddenly, without warning,
will God supply what's missing,
to make the circle complete?[17]

Notes

Prologue

1. Alan Paton, *Journey Continued* (Cape Town: David Philip, 1988), p. 2.
2. Isobel de Gruchy, "Struggle Tapestry" (March 2004). Unless otherwise indicated, all of Isobel de Gruchy's poems in this book are from her collection *Between Heaven and Earth* (Eugene, OR: Wipf and Stock, 2015) and are used with the permission of Wipf and Stock Publishers.
3. C.G. Jung, *Memories, Dreams, Reflections* (New York: Vintage Books, 1965), p. 5.
4. Dante, "Purgatory", translated by Anthony Esolen (New York: Modern Library, 2003), p. 283, canto 26, line 75.

Part 1

1. Marcel Proust, "In Search of Lost Time", *Remembrance of Things Past Volume 5: The Prisoner* (1922-1927).
2. Walter J. Le Quesne and Guy M. Dixon, *The de Gruchys of Jersey* (St. Helier, Jersey: Channel Islands History Society, 1991), adapted. p. 5.
3. Z.A. de Beer and Mary J. de Beer, *The de Gruchys of South Africa* (Rondebosch, Cape Town: self-published 1996), p. 12.
4. Richard Rive, *'Buckingham Palace', District Six* (Cape Town: David Phillip, 1986), p. 1.
5. Vivian Bickford-Smith, Elizabeth van Heyningen and Nigel Worden, *Cape Town in the Twentieth Century: An Illustrated Social History* (Cape Town: David Phillip, 1999), p. 156.
6. John W. de Gruchy, *A Theological Odyssey* (Stellenbosch: SUN, 2014), p. 2.
7. Isobel de Gruchy, "Greeting", *Offerings: Words and images* (Hermanus: self-published, 2000), p. 34.
8. Georges Bernanos, *The Diary of a Country Priest* (London: Fontana-Collins, 1977), p. 11.
9. Christoph Engels, *1 000 Sacred Places: The World's Most Extraordinary Spiritual Sites* (Potsdam, Germany: Tandem Verlag, 2010), p. 6, adapted.
10. Dietrich Bonhoeffer, "Protestantism without Reformation", *Theological Education Underground*, vol. 15, *Dietrich Bonhoeffer Works*, ed. Victoria Barnett, 2012, p. 439.
11. Beyers Naudé, "Die Tyd vir 'n 'Belydende Kerk' is daar," *Pro Veritate* (15 July 1965), no. 4, p. 3.
12. See Steve de Gruchy & Desmond van der Water, *Spirit Undaunted: The Life and Legacy of Joseph Wing* (Pietermaritzburg: Cluster Publications, 2005).

13 John W. de Gruchy, "Becoming the Ecumenical Church", in Barney N. Pityana and Charles Villa-Vicencio (eds.), *Being the Church in South Africa Today* (Johannesburg: SACC, 1995), p. 12.
14 John W. de Gruchy, *The Dynamic Structure of the Church: A Comparative Analysis of the Ecclesiologies of Karl Barth and Dietrich Bonhoeffer*, doctoral dissertation (Pretoria: UNISA, 1972).
15 See Philippe Denis, *Journal of Theology for Southern Africa* no. 146 (July 2013), pp. 6-22.

Part 2

1 B.B. Keet, "The Bell has Already Tolled" in *Delayed Action!* (Pretoria: NG Kerkboekhandel, 1961), pp. 5, 10.
2 Simone Weil, *Waiting for God* (London: Fontana-Collins, 1950), p. 76.
3 *Reformed World* vol. 33, no.1 (March 1974); and *Ned. Ger. Teologiese Tydskrif* vol. 15, no. 2 (March 1974).
4 Dietrich Bonhoeffer, "Letter to Reinhold Niebuhr" in *Theological Education Underground* (1939), p. 210.
5 John W. de Gruchy, "Preface" in *The Church Struggle in South Africa*, second edition (London: Collins, 1986), p. xviii.
6 Bernard Lord Manning, *Why not abandon the Church?* (London: Independent Press, 1958), p. 37.
7 David Bosch, "Nothing but a Heresy", *Apartheid is a Heresy*, edited by John W. de Gruchy and Charles Villa-Vicencio (Cape Town: David Philip, 1983), p. 36.
8 Eberhard Bethge, "Foreword" in John W. de Gruchy, *Bonhoeffer in South Africa* (Grand Rapids: Eerdmans, 1984), p. vii.
9 *Kairos Document*, second revised edition (Johannesburg: ICT, 1986) p. 1.
10 *Online Etymology Dictionary*, © 2010 Douglas Harper. http://www.etymonline.com
11 After 1994 IDASA changed its name to the Institute for Democracy in South Africa.
12 John W. de Gruchy, "Racism, Reconciliation and Resistance" in *On Reading Karl Barth in South Africa*, edited by Charles Villa-Vicencio (Grand Rapids: Eerdmans, 1988), p. 155.
13 Charles Marsh, *Strange Glory: A Life of Dietrich Bonhoeffer* (New York: Alfred A. Knopf, 2014), p. 26.
14 In a speech to the Free Ethiopian Church of Southern Africa (Potchefstroom, 14 December 1992).

Part 3

1 Gretchen Sleicher, "A Gratitude Song" from the website *Songs for the Great Turning*. Used with the kind permission of the composer. www.songsforthegreatturning.net
2 Konrad Raiser, "Foreword", *Being the Church in South Africa Today*, edited by Barney N. Pityana and Charles Villa-Vicencio (Johannesburg: SACC, 1995), p. xii.

NOTES

3   Charlotte Bauer, "Believing in the right to believe or not" in *Weekend Mail* (12-18 October 1990), p. 11.
4   The third volume was published as a special edition of the *JTSA* prepared by Jim Cochrane and Bastienne Klein, "From Dark Days to Liberation: Perspectives on the Social History of Christianity" in *Journal of Theology for Southern Africa* special edition, no. 118 (March 2004).
5   John W. de Gruchy, *Christianity and the Modernisation of South Africa: 1867-1939: A documentary history* (Pretoria: UNISA, 2009).
6   John W. de Gruchy, "Boipatong: A door of hope" in *A Book of Hope* (Cape Town: David Philip, 1992), p. 63.
7   Laurel Baldwin-Ragaven, Jeanelle de Gruchy and Leslie London, *An Ambulance of the Wrong Colour: Health professionals, human rights and ethics in South Africa* (Cape Town: UCT Press, 1999).
8   John W. de Gruchy, "Waving the Flag" in *The Christian Century* (15-22 June 1994), p. 596.
9   *The Truth will set you Free*, SACC brochure (1995), p. 24.
10 Chung Hyun Kyung, "Dear Dietrich Bonhoeffer" in John W. de Gruchy, *Bonhoeffer for a New Day: Theology in a Time of Transition* (Grand Rapids: Eerdmans, 1997), p. 19.
11 Konrad Raiser, "Bonhoeffer and the Ecumenical Movement" in de Gruchy, *Bonhoeffer for a New Day*, p. 320.
12 H. Russel Botman, "Is Bonhoeffer still of any use in South Africa?" in de Gruchy, *Bonhoeffer for a New Day*, p. 372.
13 John W. de Gruchy, "The Catholic Church and Democracy in Poland" in *Journal of Theology for Southern Africa* no. 96 (November 1996), pp. 34-43.
14 John W. de Gruchy, *Reconciliation: Restoring Justice* (London: SCM, 2002), p. 75.
15 J.G. Frazer, *The Golden Bough: A Study in Magic and Religion* (London: MacMillan, 1967, first published in 1922).
16 John W. de Gruchy, "From Cairo to the Cape: The significance of Coptic Orthodoxy for African Christianity" in *Journal of Theology for Southern Africa* no. 99 (November 1997), pp. 24-39.
17 *Facing the Truth: South African faith communities and the Truth & Reconciliation Commission*, edited by James Cochrane, John de Gruchy and Stephen Martin (Cape Town: David Philip, 1999).
18 John W. de Gruchy, *Christianity, Art and Transformation*, (Cambridge: Cambridge University Press, 2001), p. 200.
19 Jeanelle de Gruchy, "The Story of my Beginning" in *Aliens in the Household of God: Homosexuality and Christian Faith in South Africa*, edited by Paul Germond and Steve de Gruchy (Cape Town: David Philip, 1997), pp. 17-21.
20 John W. de Gruchy, *Christianity and Democracy*, (Cambridge: Cambridge University Press, 1995), p. 223.
21 Isobel de Gruchy, "Endings" in *Something New: Words and Images* (self-published, December 1999), p. 9.

22 John W. de Gruchy, *Reconciliation: Restoring Justice* (London: SCM; Minneapolis: Fortress, 2002).
23 John W. de Gruchy, *Daring, Trusting Spirit: Bonhoeffer's Friend Eberhard Bethge* (London: SCM; Minneapolis: Fortress, 2005).
24 Editorial, *Journal of Theology for Southern Africa* no. 123 (November 2005); some of the papers were also published in this edition of the *JTSA*.

Part 4

1   Carolyn Butler, "House Blessing" (Volmoed, July 2003), final stanza.
2   Martin E. Marty, "Hope and Courage in Volmoed" in *The Christian Century*, (10-17 September 1986).
3   For references and quotations, see Bernhard Krüger, *The Pear Tree Blossoms: The History of the Moravian Church in South Africa 1737-1869* (Genadendal, 1966), pp. 146-156.
4   John W. and Isobel de Gruchy, *The Volmoed Journey* (Hermanus: Volmoed, 2006).
5   John W. de Gruchy and Lyn Holness, *The Emerging Researcher* (Cape Town: Juta/UCT Press, 2007).
6   William Schweiker, *Dust that Breathes: Christian faith and the New Humanisms* (Oxford: Wiley-Blackwell, 2010), p. 207.
7   John W. de Gruchy and Steve de Gruchy, *The Church Struggle in South Africa*, third edition (London: SCM; Minneapolis: Fortress, 2004), p. ix.
8   *Bonhoeffer Down Under*, edited by Gordon Preece with Ian Packer (Adelaide: ATF Theology, 2012), pp. 3-56.
9   Denis Philippe, "FEDSEM ten years later: The unwritten history of an ecumenical seminary" in *Journal of Theology for Southern Africa* no. 117 (November 2003), pp. 68-79.
10 See *Keeping Body and Soul Together: Reflections by Steve de Gruchy on Theology and Development,* edited by Beverley Haddad (Pietermaritzburg: Cluster Publications, 2015).
11 J.R.R. Tolkien, *The Lord of the Rings* (London: George Allen & Unwin, 1966), p. 284.
12 Isobel de Gruchy, *Making All Things Well* (London: SCM, 2012; New York: Paulist Press, 2014).
13 Dietrich Bonhoeffer, *Letters and Papers from Prison*, (Minneapolis: Fortress Press, 2010), p. 306.
14 Joan M. Erikson, *The Life Cycle Completed: Erik H. Erikson* (New York: W.W. Norton & Company, 1997), p. 9.
15 John de Gruchy and William Everett, *Sawdust and Soul: A Conversation about Woodworking and Spirituality* (Eugene, OR: Wipf and Stock, 2014).
16 Most of the lectures are published in English in *Ned. Ger. Teologiese Tydskrif* vol. 55, supplementary issue 1 (December 2014).
17 Isobel de Gruchy, "Full Circle".

Acrocnyms and abbreviations

AACC All Africa Conference of Churches
AAR American Academy of Religion
AE African Enterprise
AIC African Independent/Indigenous Churches
AME African Methodist Episcopal Church
ANC African National Congress
BBC British Broadcasting Corporation
BCC Bantu Congregational Church
BD Bachelor of Divinity
CI Christian Institute
CO Conscientious Objector
COSATU Congress of South African Trade Unions
CTS Chicago Theological Seminary
CUC Church Unity Commission
CUSA Congregational Union of South Africa
DBWE *Dietrich Bonhoeffer Works in English*
DRC Dutch Reformed Church
FEDSEM Federal Theological Seminary
IBS International Bonhoeffer Society
IDASA Institute for Democracy in South Africa
JTSA *Journal of Theology for Southern Africa*
LMS London Missionary Society
MCC Marylebone Cricket Club, i.e. the English national team
ME 99 Multi-Event 1999
MTh Master of Theology
NRF National Research Foundation
PAC Pan Africanist Congress
PACSA Pietermaritzburg Agency for Communal Social Action
PCR Programme to Combat Racism (WCC)
PCSA Presbyterian Church of Southern Africa
PhD Doctor of Philosophy
RICSA Research Institute on Christianity in South Africa
SABC South African Broadcasting Corporation
SACC South African Council of Churches
SACLA South African Christian Leadership Assembly
SACP South African Communist Party
SACS South African College School
SCA Student Christian Association
STIAS Stellenbosch Institute for Advanced Study
SUCA Student Union for Christian Action
SWAPO South West Africa People's Organisation
TRC Truth and Reconciliation Commission
U3A University of the Third Age
UCC United Church of Christ (US)
UCCSA United Congregational Church of Southern Africa
UCT University of Cape Town
UDF United Democratic Front
UNISA University of South Africa
US United States
UWC University of the Western Cape
WCC World Council of Churches

Index of subjects and places

Aachen 185
Aarhus 219
Aberystwyth 211
Aesop's Fables 30
aesthetics 209-210, 215, 220, 226, 227
African Enterprise (AE) 90-91, 118
African National Congress (ANC) 39, 54, 66-67, 71-72, 83, 131, 153, 162, 163, 181, 257
Afrikaanse Weerstandsbeweging (AWB) 117-118
Afrikaner Broederbond 34, 65, 99
  Nationalism 34-35, 65, 117, 247, 257
Alexandria 202-203
Alhambra cinema, Cape Town 24
Alhambra, Granada, Spain 221
All Blacks 33
Alsace 156
American Academy of Religion (AAR) 112, 113, 222, 248, 252, 256, 278
American Board of Commissioners of Foreign Missions 70
Amsterdam 155
Anabaptists 136, 251
Andover Newton Theological School, 210, 221
Andrew Murray-Desmond Tutu Prize 257, 275, 279
Anglican Church 7, 42, 43, 68, 69, 72, 73, 86, 115, 122-123, 167, 181, 193, 224, 274, 277
  Students' Federation 142
  Synods 122
Aotearoa 172

Apartheid 11-12, 13-14, 34, 45, 46, 53-54, 65-66, 71-72
  reform of 8, 16
  ugliness of 34-35, 39, 49
Apartheid is a Heresy 127
Armenian Christians 201, 202-203
art 111, 195, 209-210, 213, 226, 242, 252, 253-254
Arundel 23, 212
'As we journey on' (De Gruchy, I.) 281-282
Assisi 128, 274
Athens
  Greece 160
  Ohio 58
Augrabies Falls 224
Auschwitz 196
Australia 251-252
Bachelor of Divinity 41
Bad Godesberg 179, 223
baptism 23, 26, 85, 212, 250, 251
Barmen Declaration 136, 137, 225
Battle of Blood River 117
  Waterloo 22
Beaufort West 251
Beijing 175, 176
Being African 198
Being Human: Confessions of a Christian Humanist 15, 224, 246, 252, 253, 255, 257, 272, 277
Belfast 211-212
Belhar Confession 127
Bellagio 245, 246
Berlin 82, 131, 134-135, 146-147, 159, 163. 180, 183, 224, 225, 254, 275
Bethany Theological Seminary 157
Bethel College, Kansas 101, 105, 109, 111, 148

Bethlehem 200-201, 274
Bhagavad-Gita 95, 101
Bible 35, 37, 45, 53, 69, 147, 148, 191, 203
Birmingham University 211
Birthdays 24, 82, 133-134, 146, 151, 183, 193, 223, 250-251, 262, 275, 280
  Anton 72
  Isobel 257-258
  Jeanelle 281
  John 15, 20, 49, 117, 159, 219, 223, 259-260, 279
  Stephen 267, 268, 271
Black Consciousness Movement 107
Black Madonna 197
Blombos Caves 158
Blyde River Canyon 157
Boipatong 181-182
Bonhoeffer 8, 45, 58-60, 61, 66, 77, 82, 87-88, 97-98, 101, 129-130, 132, 134-136, 143, 145, 152
  Celebrations 8, 106-107, 146, 151
  Circle 218, 225, 242, movie 226
  Society (International Bonhoeffer Society - IBS) 104, 105-106, 118, 131
Bonhoeffer and South Africa 113, 132
Bonhoeffer Congresses
  Amsterdam 155
  Cape Town 8, 192
  Düsseldorf 87-88
  East Berlin (Hirschlu) 131
  Geneva 105
  New York 182, 192
  Oxford 118, 172
  Prague 258
  Rome 245
  Sigtuna 275

INDEX OF SUBJECTS AND PLACES

Bonhoeffer's legacy 106, 220, 250
Interpreting 280
Boston 61, 210, 222, 232-233
British Broadcasting Corporation (BBC) 87, 147, 155
Broadway Presbyterian Church 161
Broadway Scholar 161
Buchenwald 135-136
Budapest 180-181
Bulawayo 152-153
Cadets 35
Cairo 203-204
Calvin College 112, 114
Calvin conferences
 Geneva 260
 Stellenbosch 262
Cambridge 81, 149, 172, 224
Cambridge University 185, 210-211, 214-215, 226, 230
Cana 200
Canada 87, 128, 130-131, 279
Canal du Midi 155-156
Canberra 251-252
Cape of Good Hope 22
Cape Town 8, 11, 18, 23, 24, 25, 27, 29, 32, 35, 36, 37, 39, 41, 46, 48, 50, 57, 58, 69, 82, 83, 84, 86, 88, 89, 91, 96, 97, 115, 119, 127, 129, 132, 141, 142, 143, 148, 150, 151, 153, 158, 163, 164, 170, 171, 175, 177, 179, 180, 181, 182, 185, 191, 192, 193, 203, 207, 209, 212, 214, 227, 228, 236, 239, 242, 246, 251, 254, 256, 266, 267, 274,
Cape Town Eisteddfod 29
Capps Lectures 254-255
Capuchin 201-202
Carcassonne 156
Cathars 156
Cathedral of St. James 201
Cathedral of St. John the Divine 161

Center for Theological Inquiry, Princeton 129, 247
Centre for Science Development 176-177
Charlottesville 255, 278
Chicago 56-64, 65
Chicago Theological Seminary (CTS) 55, 57, 133, 231, 248
Chimayo Mission 248
China 23, 174-176
 Cultural Revolution 175
 Great Wall 176
 Tiananmen Square 176
China Christian Council 174
Christian Apologetics (Richardson) 214
Christian Defence League 106
Christian fundamentalism 224, 225, 247, 248, 255
Christian humanism 219, 244-258
Christian Institute (CI) 66, 68-69, 71-73, 75-76, 78-79, 81, 90-91, 99, 103, 111
Christian Studies 8, 124, 145-146, 151, 252
Christianity and Culture 142, 172
Christianity and Social History 177,
Christianity and Democracy 185, 217
Christianity, Art and Transformation 98, 209, 214-215, 226, 231
Church
 and State 123, 251
 struggle 14, 58, 66, 67, 73, 77, 84, 100, 107, 111, 130, 136, 205, 225, 272, 280
 union 73, 86, 121
Church Dogmatics (Barth) 154
Church of England 212, 247

Church of Sweden 82, 249, 268
Church Unity Commission (CUC) 73, 76, 85-86, 90, 121-122
Civil Rights Movement 59
Climping, Sussex 23, 212
Cluny Abbey 156
Columbia Law School 149, 162
Community of the Cross of Nails 241
Confessing Church 65-67, 136, 196, 205, 251
Congregational Churches
 Gleemoor 155
 Grahamstown 42-43
 Groutville 54, 71
 New Forest 54-55
 Randpark Ridge United 277
 Rondebosch 96, 114, 117, 203
 Sea View 51-54, 71, 74
 St. Mungo's United 77, 121
 Stockbridge 60-62, 110, 277
 Union, Cape Town 29-30, 37, 268
Congregational Union of South Africa (CUSA) 40-41, 73 see also UCCSA
Congregationalism 29-30, 45, 48, 49, 61, 68, 70-71, 72, 122, 129
Congress of South African Trade Unions (COSATU) 138
Conscientious Objection (CO) 121, 142
conscription 105, 107
Constable country 212
Constitution of South Africa 162, 198, 262
Constitutional Court 162, 205, 277
conversion 36, 37
Coptic Orthodox Church 202-204

Cathedrals 203
Iconography 204
monasteries 203
social work 203-204
Cornwall 8, 11, 57, 257
corporal punishment 33
Cortes de la Frontera 221
Cottesloe Consultation 66, 75, 77, 83, 166, 177
Cotton Patch New Testament (Jordan) 63
Council of Chalcedon 202-203
Coventry Cathedral 241
Creation and Fall (Bonhoeffer) 162
critical solidarity 217
Crossroads 128, 139
Crusades 20
Cry Justice! 147
Cry, the Beloved Country (Paton) 111
Czech Republic 180
Częstochowa 197
Daring, Trusting Spirit 223, 233-234
David Nicholls Memorial Lecture 247
dean of Faculty 132
Denmark 219-220
Denver 110
Desmond Tutu Peace Centre 242
detention at Atlanta airport 248-249
Devon Clergy Conference 247
Die Schuldfrage (Jaspers) 184
Dietrich Bonhoeffer Works 245, 271
District Six 39
Doctor of Theology 68, 77, 88, 91, 231, 244, 249, 262, 279,
Dogmatologiese Werkgemeenskap 88, 98
Doll's House 31
Dublin 211

Duke of Norfolk 23, 24
Dunedin 172-173
Durban 16, 51-55, 66-68, 70, 72, 90, 107-108, 138, 215
Durham 185, 212-214, 227, 230-231
Durham Cathedral 213
Durham University 213
East Berlin 131, 135, 163, 183
East Germany 131, 134-136, 163, 206
Eastern Cape 30, 240, 266-267
Ebor Lectures 254
Edinburgh 185, 214, 228
Eerdmans publishers 111-112, 114, 115, 131-132, 149, 166, 234
Egypt 202-204
Eisenach 136
Emerging Researcher Programme 243
English-speaking churches 40-41, 52, 98, 109, 143-144, 182, 211
Ephesus 160
Erfurt 135
Erie, Pennsylvania 112
Ettal monastery 134
Evangelical Church of the Union 225
Faith and Order 69, 81-82, 97-98
Fall of Jerusalem 20
fellow of the University of Cape Town 179
fellow of the Stellenbosch Institute for Advanced Study 261-262
FIFA World Cup 267
Florence 128
Florida 75
Flossenbürg concentration camp 226
Forgiveness 189, 205
Fountains Abbey 213
France 8, 20-22, 63, 156, 238, 261

Frascati hills 202
Free Mandela campaign 142
French Revolution 22
Fuller Theological Seminary 153
Fundamentalism 225, 247, 248,
Galilee 80, 200
general election 187, 188
Geneva 63, 72, 77, 83, 106-107, 261
Gibraltar 221
Giza pyramids 203
Ghost Ranch 183, 238, 248,
Gniezno 197
golden wedding 268
Gothenburg 249, 250
    Book Fair 277
Graduate School in Humanities 218
Grahamstown 41-43, 47-49, 76, 85, 167, 181, 277
Granada 221
Grand Parade 39, 163, 164
Grand Rapids 111
Great Zimbabwe 216
Greece 150
Green Point lighthouse 31
Groote Kerk 246
Groote Schuur Hospital 165, 183
Gugulethu 193
guilt 184, 205, 206, 251,
Harare 120, 215
Heidelberg 156
Hemel en Aarde Valley 150, 240, 276
hepatitis B 254
Hermanus 150, 239, 240, 242, 253, 258, 264, 278, 281
    Art Society 254
hijacking 250
hiking 131, 145, 157, 213
Hinduism 55
Hirschluh 135
Hoff Lectures 157
Hogsback 257
Holden Village 131, 238, 239

INDEX OF SUBJECTS AND PLACES

Holocaust Memorial Museum, Washington DC 254
home 18, 29, 31, 63, 67, 74, 108, 111, 114, 159, 166, 181, 188, 235, 236, 243, 258, 276
homosexuality 215
Honest to God (Robinson) 58
Hong Kong 173, 174, 176
honorary doctorates
  Chicago Theological Seminary 231
  Knox College 279
  Rhodes University 244
  Stellenbosch University 262
hope 97, 139, 170, 178, 179-187, 205, 223, 251
Hosea 182
Hugh Price Hughes Lecture 250
Hula Nature Reserve 200
Hulsean Lectures 230
Human Rights Commission 167
Humboldt University 275
Hungarian Roma 180
iconography 253
Icons as a Means of Grace 253
identity 11, 12, 60, 109, 149, 173, 181, 198, 204, 207, 215, 254, 255,
Iliff School of Theology 110
Immorality Act 124
inaugural lecture 151
Inkatha Freedom Party 181
Institute for Contextual Theology 129
Institutes (Calvin) 129
Iona Community 214
Iraq War 228
Ireland 211
Irish Council of Churches 212
Irish School of Ecumenics 211

Islam 203, 204, 232
Israel 80, 199, 200, 201
Istanbul 261
Jagielloński University 196
Jarrow 213
Jericho 200
Jersey Island 8, 11
  Trinity Parish 21, 24, 26, 279
Jerusalem 20, 80, 199, 200, 201
Johannesburg 7, 41, 44, 49, 50, 63, 66, 69, 72-76, 89, 91, 112, 129, 134, 147, 181, 277
John Calvin: Christian Humanist & Evangelical Reformer 260, 275
Jönköping 268
Jordan Valley 200
Journal of Theology for Southern Africa (JTSA) 89, 177, 194, 218, 233
Kairos Document 138, 140, 143, 144, 149, 151, 166
Kairos SA 274
Karl Barth Prize 225
Karl Barth Symposium 151
Karl Jaspers Lecture 184
Kaypro computer 130
Kerkbode 99
Kettlewell 213
Killeen Lecture 157
Kirchentag
  Leipzig 205
  Stuttgart 220, 221
Koinonia Farm 62, 238, 239
Krakow 196
Kruger National Park 157
Ku Klux Klan 62
Kuruman 190, 191, 193, 224
Lake District, England 214
Lake Como 246
Lake Nemi 202
Las Palmas 56
Leadership in Africa 211, 257
Lebanon 199
Led into Mystery 9, 15, 266, 271, 272, 276-279

Leeds University 185
Leipzig 135, 206
Let My People Go (Luthuli) 54
Letters and Papers from Prison (Bonhoeffer) - 162, 245, 263
Liberal Party 53
Liberating Reformed Theology 166
Lincoln 185
Livingstone House 43, 44, 46
London 56, 63, 68, 82, 91, 96, 104, 147, 232, 250, 270, 275, 279
London Missionary Society 30, 70, 72, 73
Los Angeles 254-256
Lutheran Christianity 219,
Maitland Memorial Lecture 214
Making All Things Well (De Gruchy, I.) 266, 275, 277
Malawi 190
Maori 172, 173
Maria Laach monastery 220
Mariya uMama weThemba 277
Marquette University 242, 278
marriage proposal 47
  relationship 47
Marseillan 156
Master of Theology 57
Mauritius 270
ME 99 218, 219
Megiddo 199
Melbourne 251
Menno Simons Lectures 109, 111
Mennonites 59, 87, 101, 104
  Biblical Seminary 103, 113
  Bluffton College 103
Methodist Church 25, 36, 42-45, 68, 69, 73, 82, 85, 122, 124,
  Buitenkant Street 139
  Greenmarket Square 23, 29

291

Hyde Park, London 250
Manning Road 215
Parktown 50
Port Elizabeth 25
Walmer 25
Methodists 29, 46, 253
Milford Sound 172
military coup 181
Minneapolis 131
Mixed Marriages Act 124
Moffat Mission 190, 224
Monrovia 18, 78
Monticello 278
Mooi River 265
Muslims 157, 184, 225
My love for you (De Gruchy, I.) 48
Nakło 196-197
Namibia 73, 225
  Border War 105, 119, 121, 122
Nanjing 174, 175
  Seminary 175
Natal Congress 53
National Party 34
National Research Foundation 233
Naught for Your Comfort (Huddleston) 147
Nazareth 200
New College, Edinburgh 185, 214, 228
New England 61
New Humanist Project 267
New Mexico 183, 238, 248, 271
New York 57, 60, 63, 107, 131, 151, 160, 161, 165, 167, 182, 186, 192, 229, 231, 247, 271
New Zealand 23, 33, 56, 171, 173
Norfolk 212
Normandy 20-22
North Park Seminary 162
ordination 50, 53
Oxford 118, 172, 184, 247, 276
Oxford University 55, 184
pacifism 105

PACSA 166
Palestine 201
Panama City 270
Paris 63
Parkinson's disease 227, 234
Parliament 97, 124, 132, 148, 163, 188, 198, 219, 266
Pasadena 154
Patmos 160
Pella 244
Penn State University 221
Peterborough 212
PhD 55, 60
Philadelphia 248
Philosophy 38, 94, 176
Piazza Navona 202
Pietermaritzburg 53, 69, 81, 122, 138, 166, 190, 224, 233, 264, 265, 267, 268, 269, 275, 278, 280
Pluralism 155, 225
Poetry 8, 9, 14, 242, 269
Poland 194-197
Pollsmoor march 142
Port Elizabeth 25, 41, 47, 76, 121, 181, 267
Porthleven 257
Powell Lecture 142
Prague 180, 206, 258
prayer to end unjust rule 140
preaching 54, 103, 233, 268
Presbyterian Church 42, 43, 68, 73, 121, 161, 173, 193, 246, 254, 279,
Pretoria 26, 27, 77, 88, 117, 118, 119, 125, 142, 143, 194, 233, 253,
Princeton Center of Theological Inquiry 129
Princeton Theological Seminary 129, 161, 165, 248
Princeton University 129
professor 8, 145, 146, 151, 243, 256, 272, 276,
Progressive Party 97, 148
Protestant 104, 176, 195, 197, 212
Queen Mary 57

racial classification 34
Ravenna 261
Real Presences (Steiner) 226
Reba Place Fellowship 59
reconciliation 75, 143, 151, 166, 179, 180, 189, 205-208, 212, 226, 227, 230, 232, 235, 241, 258, 280
Reformed
  Theology 46
  Tradition 129, 162, 165, 177
Reformed Church, Switzerland 250, 251
Rengsdorf 82, 97, 106
resistance against tyranny 157
Resistance and Hope 134
retirement colloquium 234
Rhode Island 61
Rhodes University 41, 42, 44, 120, 184, 244
Richardson Lecture 213
RICSA 125, 177, 207, 218, 219
Ripon 212
Ripon College, Cuddesdon 184
Riverside Church, New York 161
Robben Island 142, 193, 240
Rockefeller Fellowship 245
Roman Catholic Church 90
Romantische Straße 134
Rome 21, 64, 66, 128, 201, 202, 213, 227, 245
Rooi Els 36
Rotorua 173
royal visit 25
Rustenburg Conference 166-167, 177
Sabbaticals 11, 109, 110, 114, 128-131, 149, 150, 160, 161, 165, 167, 173, 183, 185, 210, 214, 218
Safed 199
Salamanca 97, 98
Samos 160
Sanctorum Communio (Bonhoeffer) 59, 60

INDEX OF SUBJECTS AND PLACES

San Diego 254, 256
San Francisco 101, 102, 112
Sant'Egidio community 227
Santa Fe 248
Sawdust and Soul 15, 278
schools
  SACS 24, 33, 35, 93, 162
  St. George's 32, 33
  Tamboerskloof 30
Scripture Union 36, 37
Seamen's Home 24
Sea Scouts 34, 36
Seattle 111, 136, 137
Seeking the Common Ground (Wickeri) 174
Selwyn College
Seth Mokitimi Methodist Seminary 253
Seventy-fifth Birthday International Conference 280
Shanghai 175
Sharpeville massacre 49, 65, 105
Shenandoah National Park,
Singapore 278
Sistine Chapel 202
social transformation 60, 70, 210, 215
social transition 247
soul 14, 47, 198, 243
South African Academy of Religion 186
South African Broadcasting Corporation 87, 105, 142, 170
South African Christian Leadership Assembly 118
South African Communist Party 163, 170
South African Council of Churches 7, 16, 30, 45, 72, 73, 75-91, 105, 125, 129, 140, 167, 174
South African Defence Force 119
South African television 87, 105, 170

South West Africa People's Organisation 39
Southampton 23, 56, 58
Southern Cross 56
Soweto uprising 107, 111, 121, 139, 140
Spain 35, 97, 98, 221, 267
sport 31, 33, 43, 130, 173, 252
Springboks 33
Sprunt Lectures 227
St. Brelade's Bay 279
St. George's Cathedral 32, 96, 122, 123, 150, 164, 192, 246
St. Helier 23
St. Norbert College 157
St. Paul's College 43, 167
St. Peter's Basilica 64
St. Vitalis 261
St. Vitus Cathedral 180
Stanford University 101, 113
  Memorial Church 102
  Department of Religion 102, 149
STASI files 180
States of Emergency 138, 139, 143, 145, 156, 241
Stellenbosch 83, 98-100, 121, 129, 140, 144, 281
  gespreksgroep 99
  University 15, 66, 83, 99, 194, 242, 262, 280
  Theological Faculty 46, 243, 276
  Institute for Advanced Study 261
  death 8, 14, 15, 149, 184, 263, 265-273,
  Memorial Lectures 274, 278
Steve memorial service 265, 266
  writings 134, 143, 259, 275
Steve's Place 268, 281
Stockbridge, Massachusetts 60, 61, 62
Student Christian Association 37, 39

Student Union for Christian Action 128
Sturgeon Bay, Wisconsin 112
Stuttgart 220
Swedish Christian Humanist Society 268, 277
Sydney 252
Systematic Theology (Tillich) 49
Table Bay 18, 240
Table Mountain 18, 28, 34, 57, 151, 192
Table Talk 242
Taizé Community 63, 156, 191, 238
Tantur Ecumenical Institute 199, 200, 201
Tel Aviv 199, 201
The Analogical Imagination (Tracy) 149
The Church Struggle in South Africa 100, 109, 114, 211
  anniversary edition 245
The Christian Century 188, 238, 239
The Cost of Discipleship (Bonhoeffer) 45
The Da Vinci Code (Brown) 21
The Divine Imperative (Brunner) 45
The New Humanist Imperative in South Africa 267
The Long Search (Smart) 155
The Master and his Emissary (McGilchrist) 277
The Nature of Prejudice (Allport) 60
The Politics of Jesus (Yoder) 105, 111, 115
The Road to Damascus 166
the struggle 13, 14, 68, 72, 74, 85, 97, 103, 105, 108, 122, 129, 141, 143,

164, 178, 194, 208, 209, 226, 245
The Wizard of Oz 31
Theological Society of South Africa 153, 268, 270
Theology 44, 57, 69, 76, 79, 88, 89, 96, 125, 130, 146, 151, 176, 186, 271, 272
Theology and Ministry in Context and Crisis 149
Theology in Dialogue (Holness & Wüstenberg) 234
Theology of Hope (Moltmann) 97
Three-Self Patriotic Movement 174
Tiberias 200
tourist 155, 176, 190
tricameral parliament 124
Truth and Reconciliation Commission 179, 189, 204, 205, 207, 208, 231
Faith Community Hearings 208
Tübingen 97, 106, 172
twentieth-century martyrs 232
UCT-Stellenbosch fellowship group 140
Umeå University 277
Union Theological Seminary, New York 57, 62, 102, 118, 151, 160, 247, 280
Richmond, Virginia 227
United Congregational Church of Southern Africa 72, 73, 84, 103, 106, 107, 112, 119, 120-124, 127, 128, 152, 153, 202, 216, 246, 268
Assemblies 107, 123, 124, 127, 152, 216
United Democratic Front 128, 129, 138, 139, 142, 163
United Methodist Board of Missions 174

United States 25, 26, 60, 67, 69, 75, 87, 101, 102, 109, 110, 128, 133, 136, 148, 153, 157, 228, 232, 242, 248, 252, 256, 257, 270, 275
1963 to 1964 56-64
University of Aarhus 219
University of Basel 261
University of Cape Town 8, 16, 32, 33, 38, 39, 40, 41, 46, 80, 89, 94, 96, 98, 99, 105, 125, 128, 132, 133, 149, 150, 151, 155, 167, 175, 176, 179, 186, 190, 194, 203, 209, 220, 227, 234, 235, 239, 242, 243, 247, 252, 267, 276, 280
Faculties 217
Religious Studies 89, 94, 217
University of Chicago 55, 70, 149, 150, 218, 235, 252
University of Copenhagen 220
University of Edinburgh 228
University of Fort Hare 42, 43, 46, 68, 257, 266, 267
University of Gothenburg 249, 250
University of Heidelberg 156
University of KwaZulu-Natal 224, 233, 253, 275, 279
University of Lancaster 155
University of Malawi 190
University of Natal 55, 69
University of Otago 172
University of Port Elizabeth 166
University of Pretoria 88, 125, 252
University of St. Andrews 185
University of Santa Barbara 154
University of South Africa 77, 117, 119, 125, 141, 142, 167, 181, 186, 235

University of the Third Age 242
University of Virginia 226, 255, 278
University of Wales 211
University of Warsaw 195
University of the Western Cape 98, 155, 178, 194, 245, 280
University of the Free State 268
University of the Witwatersrand 75, 149, 275
University of Zurich 250
Until Justice and Peace Embrace (Wolterstorff) 177
US-South Africa Leadership Programme 141
Van Riebeeck Festival 36
Vancouver 128, 130, 131
Varsity Trekkers 42
Vatican 202, 227
Secretariat for Promoting Christian Unity 227
Venice 102, 260, 261
Vermaaklikheid 158, 164, 183, 263, 270
Victoria Falls 120, 153
Vienna 206
Vikings 20, 213
Villiprott 136, 184, 223, 233
Volmoed 237-282
colloquium 280
Community 8, 238, 239, 241, 259
Eucharist 266
morning prayer 241
Waiting for Godot (Beckett) 96
Walsingham 212
Warfield Lectures 161, 165
Warsaw 195, 196
Washington Cathedral 278
Washington DC 61, 62, 104, 110, 254, 278
Waynesville 271, 278
We have grown together (De Gruchy, I.) 269

INDEX OF SUBJECTS AND PLACES

We Shall Rebuild (MacLeod) 214
weddings
  Anton & Esther 165
  Harold & Mabel 26
  John & Isobel 50
  Rozelle 41, 110, 249
  Steve & Marian 155
Weimar 135
Wesley Theological Seminary 104
Wesleyan University 149, 247
Westminster Abbey 147, 232
Westminster College 81, 149, 150, 210
Wanganui 173

Where have you gone? (De Gruchy, I.) 271
Whitby 213
Whither South Africa? (Keet) 46
Willys car 31, 32
Windhoek 41
Wittenberg 135
Wolf Cubs 32
Woodturning 191, 212, 213, 242
Wordsworth country 214
World Council of Churches 7, 55, 63, 65, 66, 72, 77, 79, 81, 83-85, 90, 95, 97, 106, 128, 130, 167, 171, 177, 193, 199, 201, 215
  Cape Town conference

Programme to Combat Racism 7, 83, 84, 106, 121
  scholarship 55
World Trade Center, New York 229, 231
Writing in the Dust (Williams) 232
xenophobia 254
Yale University 130, 177
York 185, 254
Yorkshire Dales 213
Youth for Christ 37
Zimbabwe 73, 120, 122, 152, 215, 216
Zion Christian Church 207
Zionism 254
Zoar 214
Zurich 45, 250

Index of names

Aagaard, Anna Marie 219
Ackermann, Denise 119, 262, 274, 277, 280
  Laurie 119, 162, 277
Adam, Heribert 145
Allport, Gordon 60
Aquinas, Thomas 157
Arrison, Edwin 274
Aurelius, Carl Axel 249, 250
Bach, J.S. 135
Bainton, Roland 58
Bands, Anna-Marie 253
Barnett, Victoria 162, 233, 254, 256, 263
Barth, Karl 45, 58, 77, 151, 154, 156, 220, 261, 262
Batty, Allan 212
Bauer, Charlotte 171
Bax, Douglas 79, 117, 127, 139, 162, 183
Bell, George 212
Benda, Ernst 205
Bergfalk, Bob 67
Berglund, Axel-Ivar 91
Bethge, Eberhard 58, 82, 87, 88, 97, 98, 106, 132, 137, 155, 161, 182, 183, 184, 185, 192, 220, 223, 233
  Renate 82, 110, 183, 184, 185, 192, 223, 233
  Sabine 223
Beyerhaus, Peter 106
Biko, Steve 107, 111, 167
Bizos, George 162
Blake, Eugene Carson 83
Block, Ottilie 196
Boesak, Allan 127, 128, 129, 141, 142, 280
Bonhoeffer, Dietrich 8, 15, 45, 58, 59, 60, 61, 66, 77, 82, 88, 97, 98, 101, 104, 106, 107, 108, 118, 129, 132, 134, 135, 136, 142, 143, 145, 146, 150, 152, 156, 161, 173, 182, 183, 192, 193, 194, 196, 212, 218, 219, 220, 221, 222, 225, 226, 232, 234, 245, 250, 251, 252, 255, 256, 258, 263, 273, 275, 280
Booth, George 67
  June 67
Boraine, Alex 69, 72, 82, 83, 97, 132, 145, 148, 179, 189, 204, 229, 231
  Jenny 69, 114, 231
Borman, John 44, 46
Bosch, David 88, 90, 118, 127, 181
Boshoff, Carel 100
Botha, P.W. 124, 127, 138, 160, 167
Botman, Russel 194, 243
Botsis, Rod 246
Brandenburg, Otto 196
Bromiley, Geoffrey 154
Brown, Basil 30, 40, 50
Brown, Frank Burch 280
Brown, Peter 53
Brown, Robert McAfee 102, 113
Burton, Geoff 145
Buthelezi, Manas 91
Butler, Carolyn 153, 235, 237, 260, 266
  Ron 153, 260
Burnett, Bill 72, 73, 75, 76, 77, 83, 85, 97, 115, 119, 122
Burtness, Jim 131, 135
  Dolores 131, 135
Calvin, John 49, 63, 129, 157, 260-262
Cameron, Edwin 162
Carolus, Cheryl 163
Carr, Burgess 78, 130
Cassidy, Michael 90, 118
Chaskalson, Arthur 162
Chidester, David 124, 154

Chikane, Frank 167, 129, 143, 218
Chopin, Frédéric 195
Chung, Hyun Kyung 192
Ciennich, Stanislaw 194
Clynick, Des 77
Cochrane, Jim 103, 207, 218, 280
Cohen, Robin 235
Cone, James 79, 141, 161
Cooke, Judy 158, 164, 224, 262
  Julian 158, 164, 191, 209, 224, 235, 240, 262
Coulson, Gail 173
Cressey, Martin 81, 149, 210, 214
  Pamela 210, 214
Crow, Paul 100
Cumpsty, John 89, 94
Dandala, Mvumi 218, 266
Dante, Alighieri 16
Davidson, Duncan 67, 68
  Naomi 67
Davis, Jo 57
de Barentin, Jean 21
de Grouchy, Emmanuel 22
  Guillaume 20
  Nicolas 20
  Sophie 22
de Gruchy, Frederic Abram 22, 23, 24, 29
  Anton 72, 109, 113, 128, 129, 130, 150, 165, 191, 214, 238, 239, 257, 265, 270, 276, 277, 278, 279, 281
  Caroline (née de Quetteville) 22
  David 188, 190, 263, 265, 267, 270, 276, 279, 281
  Esther (née Marais) 165, 191, 214, 257, 265, 270, 276, 277, 278, 281

INDEX OF NAMES

Harold 24-26
Isobel (née Dunstan)
8, 9, 11, 14, 17, 18, 41, 44,
46-50, 52, 53, 56, 57, 59,
60, 63, 66, 69, 70, 72, 74,
75, 76, 77, 81, 82, 88, 89,
111, 112, 113, 114, 118,
128, 129, 130, 134, 149,
150, 151, 152, 153, 155,
156, 157, 160, 163, 164,
166, 171, 183, 190, 191,
192, 194, 196, 197, 199,
200, 202, 206, 210, 213,
220, 221, 225, 226, 228,
230, 231, 234, 237, 238,
239, 242, 244, 245, 246,
247, 248, 252, 253, 257,
260, 264, 265, 266, 268,
269, 270, 271, 273, 275,
276, 277, 278, 280, 281
Jean 20, 21, 22
Jeanelle 67, 68, 72, 109,
113, 128, 129, 130, 131,
150, 153, 183, 186, 191,
206, 215, 239, 257, 258,
263, 265, 266, 269, 270,
275, 276, 277, 279, 281
Kate 191, 263, 265, 270,
278, 279
Mabel (née Hurd) 25, 26
Mary (née Irish) 23, 24,
29, 212
Robin 21
Rozelle (Lindwall) 26,
29, 30, 31, 36, 41, 110,
183, 244, 249, 257, 259,
268, 290
Steve 8, 9, 14, 15, 56, 63,
66, 68, 72, 73, 103, 109,
110, 113, 117, 123, 128,
133, 134, 139, 140, 142,
143, 148, 149, 150, 151,
153, 155, 159, 163, 178,
184, 188, 190, 191, 193,
215, 224, 233, 239, 245,
249, 253, 257, 259, 260,
261, 262, 263, 265-272,
275, 276

Thea 178, 190, 224, 257,
263, 265, 269, 270, 275
de Klerk, F.W. 160, 163
Degenaar, Johan 99
Dempers, Ramon 41
Denver, John 110
Dewey, John 57
Diamond, Neil 110
Dinan, Rodney 36, 37
Dipico, Manne 224
Doblmeier, Martin 226
Dowey, Ed 129
du Plessis, Justice 90
du Toit, Cornel 235
Dube, John 70
Dunstan, Geoffrey 96, 117
Dunstan, Alan 74, 112
 Arthur 48
 Lilian 48, 49, 53
Durand, Jaap 98, 100, 117,
 132, 181
 Randu 100
Edwards, Jonathan 61
Eerdmans, Bill 112, 115, 131
Eglin, Colin 97
Elias, James 41, 46
Elshtain, Jean Bethke 218
Engdahl, Hans 249, 250
Engels, Christopher 56
Erikson, Erik 61
 Joan 273
Esterhuyse, Willie 140, 141
Everett, Bill 15, 210, 218,
 221, 235, 270, 276, 278
 Sylvia 210, 221, 270, 276,
 278
Faris, Bob 279
Faulkner, Ronald 87
French, Daniel Chester 61
Forbes, Ashley 156
Ford, David 210
Forrester, Duncan 125, 185,
 228
 Margaret 185
Forsyth, P.T. 45
Frazer, James 202
Gaffney, Heidi 269, 270,
 275, 276, 277, 279
Garces, Juan 221

Gauck, Joachim 180
George VI, King 32
Gericke, J.S. 83
Gerwel, Jakes 245
Geyer, Hendrik 261
Goba, Bonganjalo 141
Godsey, John 104, 155
 Emilie 155, 156
Gordimer, Nadine 182
Gorringe, Timothy 228, 235
Graham, Billy 37, 90
Green, Clifford 104, 162,
 223, 280
Grouchy (see de Grouchy)
Grundtvig, N.F.S. 219, 220
Grzymała-Moszczyńska,
 Halina 196
Gu, Xui 174
Gumede, Archie 53
Guthrie, Arlo 110
Gutiérrez, Gustavo 79, 172
Gysi, Klaus 135
Hammar, K.G. 268, 277
Hammerton-Kelly, Robert
 57, 101, 102
Hani, Chris 185
Hardy, Dan 118, 172
Hendricks, Alan 127, 128
Henn, Bill 201, 202
Heunis, Chris 128
Hewson, Leslie 45, 76
Hewitt, Roderick 274
Heyns, Johan 88, 155
Hildebrandt, Franz 136
Holness, Lyn 194, 218, 225,
 229, 234, 243, 262, 274
Hopkins, Dwight 235
Huber, Kara 156, 166, 275
 Wolfgang 156, 166, 223,
 275, 280
Huddleston, Trevor 147
Hurd, Herbert 25, 26, 29, 37
 Lily 25, 26, 37
Hurley, Denis 54, 69, 129
Jackson, Jesse 133
James, Wilmot 217
Jaspers, Karl 184
Johanson, Brian 77, 79
John Paul II, Pope 195, 227

Jones, Serene 280
Jonker, Willie 99, 144, 166, 167
Jordan, Clarence 63
Juhnke, Jim and Anna 111
Julian of Norwich 242
Jung, Carl 14
Kasper, Walter 227
Käßmann, Margot 205
Kaye, Danny 59
Keet, B.B. 46, 93, 99, 105
Kelly, Geoff 104
Kennedy, John F. 59
Kierkegaard, Søren 220
King, Ted 96
Kirby, Mike and Marijke 77, 266
Klaaren, Gene 149
  Jonathan 149
Koopman, Nico 243, 280
Kotze, Theo 69
Kruse, Martin 146
Kuske, Martin 135
Kuyper, Abraham 219
Langa, Pius 162
Lash, Nicholas 210
Lategan, Bernard 98, 186, 262
Leatt, James 96
Legg, Ron 87
Lekganyane, B.E. 207
Lindwall, Dick 244, 249, 259, 268, 277
  Rozelle (see De Gruchy)
Littell, Franklin 58, 136
Livingstone, David 43, 153, 190
Loades, Ann 213, 218, 231
Lombard, Johannes 77
Loveday, Marian 148, 150, 153, 155, 159, 178, 190, 191, 224, 249, 263, 265, 270,
Lukens, Michael 157
Luther, Martin 97, 135, 136
Luthuli, Albert 54, 71
Lux, Alma 196
MacDonald, Ian 50, 244
MacLeod, George 214

Maker, Alan 121
Malek, George 202, 227
Maluleke, Tinyiko 235
Mandela, Nelson 8, 16, 42, 66, 86, 142, 158, 159, 164, 165, 175, 187, 188, 189, 193, 221, 245
Mandela, Winnie 175,
Manning, Bernard Lord 116
Manuel, Trevor 163
Margaret, Princess 32
Marsh, Charles 152, 255
Martin, Steve 177, 207
Marty, Martin 150, 238, 239
  Harriet 150, 238
Masemola, Manche 232
Maxwell, William D. 49, 76
Mayotte, Judy 242, 278
Mazrui, Ali 185
Mbeki, Thabo 162, 167, 198, 218, 219
Mbiti, John 79
McBride, Clive 11
McCord, James 129
McGilchrist, Iain 276, 280
Míguez Bonino, José 82
Moffat, Mary 190
Moffat, Robert 190, 191
Mofokeng, Takatso 141
Moltmann, Jürgen 97, 172
Mosala, Itumelung 124
Moseki, Itumeleng 224
Moore, Basil 76, 79
Moosa, Ebrahim 125, 227
Mouton, Elna 243
Mouw, Richard 114
Mugabe, Robert 120, 216
Munson, Grace 249
  Othene 249
  Samantha 249, 259
Nash, Margaret 105
Naudé, Beyers 65-68, 71, 72, 73, 75, 85, 87, 88, 108, 111, 140, 142, 182, 192, 193, 194
Ndebele, Njabulo 182
Ndungane, Njongonkulu 193
Nelson, Burton 104

Niebuhr, Reinhold 62, 107, 155
  Ursula 62
  Christopher 62
Nolan, Albert 143
O'Brien, Connor Cruise 133
Oduyoye, Mercy Amba 218, 262
Olski, Don 113
  Katherine 113
Oosthuizen, Nan 125, 194
Painter, John 95, 252
Pandor, Naledi 218
Paton, Alan 11, 53, 111, 114,
Patta, Debora 128, 134, 142
Peachey, Paul 62
Pfeiffer, Hans 235
Philip, David 182
  John 30
Phiri, Isabel 190
Pityana, Barney 167
Pobee, John 79
Potgieter, F.J.M. 99
Presley, Elvis 110
Proust, Marcel 19
Putnam, Bill 110
Pyle, Jean 50
Radhakrishna, Sarvepalli 55
Raheb, Mitri 274
Raiser, Konrad 193
Ramsey, Michael 79
Rasmussen, Larry 104, 110, 155, 161, 199, 248, 271, 280
  Nyla 155, 161, 199
Ratzinger, Joseph (Pope Benedict XVI) 81
Rees, John 85, 90
Richardson, Alan 213
Ricœur, Paul 58
Rive, Richard 28, 32
Robinson, John 58
Rockwell, Norman 61
Rooks, Alfred 55
Rousseau, Pierre 126
Russell, David 122
Russell, Philip 69, 123
Sachs, Albie 162
Saunders, Stuart 132, 176

INDEX OF NAMES

Savage, Michael 95, 130, 145, 164
Schmemann, Alexander 58
Schomer, Howard 133
Schönherr, Albert 135, 183
Schweiker, William 244, 252, 262
Selby-Taylor, Robert 8, 86, 96, 97
Setiloane, Gabriel 80, 124
Shay, Charissa 153
 Danielle 153
 Don 153
 Emily 153
 Suellen 153
Shenouda III, Pope 202, 203
Shriver, Don 118, 160, 161, 163
Simon, Paul 110
Simons, Menno 109, 111
Slabbert, Van Zyl 133, 148
Slovo, Joe 170, 171
Smart, Ninian 155
Smit, Dirkie 243
Smith, Nico 99
Smuts, Jan 34
Smyth, Geraldine 211
Snyder, Ross 59, 60, 68, 69, 103, 113
 Martha 69, 113
Snyman, Henning 247, 251
Sölle, Dorothee 137
Soskice, Janet 172
Spörre, Karin 277
Stackhouse, Max 228
Steel, Elsie 75, 160, 161, 221
 Ron 75, 153, 160, 166, 221
Steiner, George 226
Steiner, Robert 233, 267
Stofile, Makhenkesi 130, 173
Storey, Peter 45

Stubbs, Luke 260
Suttner, Raymond 162
Suzman, Helen 132
Swartz, Harry 97
Swartz, Reinette 276
Tayob, Abdulkader 125
Tegby, Lisa 277
Terre'Blanche, Eugène 117
Thistlethwaite, Susan 231, 248
Tillich, Paul 58, 60
Ting, H.K. 174, 175
Tödt, Heinz Eduard 155, 156
Tolbert, Jr., William R. 78
Tolkien, J.R.R. 265
Tracy, David 149
Treurnicht, Andries 99
Trisk, Janet 268
Turkstra, Bernhard 18, 238, 239, 267
 Martin 267
 Jane 18, 238
Tutu, Desmond Mpilo (Emeritus Archbishop of Cape Town) 7, 17, 68, 86, 91, 118, 122, 123, 127, 131, 149, 163, 167, 171, 178, 186, 189, 193, 194, 207, 241, 245, 252, 257, 258, 267, 274, 275
van den Bergh, Serghay 276
van der Kemp, Johannes 30
van Jaarsveld, F.A. 117
van Huyssteen, Wentzel 262, 278, 280
 Esther 278
van Wedemeyer, Maria 107
van Zyl, Danie 71
Versfeld, Martin 38
Verwoerd, Hendrik 49, 100

Viljoen, Abraham (Braam) 181, 182
 Constand 181, 182
Villa-Vicencio, Charles 124, 125, 127, 141, 142, 177, 204, 209
Vischer, Lukas 81
Visser 't Hooft, W.A. 77, 79
von Weizsäcker, C. F. 107
Vorster, B.J. 7, 75, 84
 Koot 83
Vosloo, Robert 243, 280
Walesa, Lech 195
Walsh, Jasper 180
Wanamaker, Chuck 95
Ward, Graham 218, 235, 276, 280
Wentzel, Alan 77
 June 77
Wesley, John 26, 36, 213
West, Charles 129
West, Cornel 141
West, Gerald 268
West, Martin 95, 235
Whiteford, Robin 94
Wickeri, Philip 174
Williams, Esther 31
Williams, Rowan 149, 232, 247, 266
Williamson, Justice 157
Wilson, Francis 95, 257
 Monica 95, 257
Wing, Joe 73, 120, 123, 191
Wolterstorff, Nicholas 112, 177
Woods, Dave 244
Wüstenberg, Ralf 234
Xapile, Spiwo 193
Yoder, John Howard 105, 113, 131
Young, Ernlé 102

www.ingramcontent.com/pod-product-compliance
Lightning Source LLC
Chambersburg PA
CBHW021650230426
43668CB00008B/582